DIVINE
POETRY AND DRAMA IN
SIXTEENTH-CENTURY
ENGLAND

DIVINE
POETRY AND DRAMA
IN
SIXTEENTH-CENTURY
ENGLAND

BY

LILY B. CAMPBELL

CAMBRIDGE
AT THE UNIVERSITY PRESS

UNIVERSITY OF CALIFORNIA PRESS
BERKELEY AND LOS ANGELES
1961

PUBLISHED BY

THE SYNDICS OF THE CAMBRIDGE UNIVERSITY PRESS

Bentley House, 200 Euston Road, London, N.W. 1

AND

UNIVERSITY OF CALIFORNIA PRESS

Berkeley and Los Angeles
California

First printed 1959
Reprinted 1961

First printed in Great Britain at the University Press, Cambridge
Reprinted by offset-litho by Thoben Offset, Nijmegen, Holland

CONTENTS

v

CONTENTS

PART II

DIVINE DRAMA IN SIXTEENTH-CENTURY ENGLAND

vi

PREFACE

THE story of the freeing of the Bible from the confines set by the authorities of the church which dominated the religious life of western Europe and England has often been told, but it has generally been told in terms of the political and theological conflicts which attended its liberation. The secondary story of the use of the Bible to combat the influence of the new paganism and the new secularism which accompanied the rediscovery of ancient works of literature and art has, however, received scant attention. It is to a very small part of that story that this book is dedicated. I have, indeed, limited my study to those attempts made in England in the sixteenth century to make the Bible a part of English literature, to make its poetry English poetry, to tell its stories in English poetry and English drama. I have omitted consideration of continental backgrounds except as they were directly influential.

Miss Marianne Moore has said that acknowledgements are in danger of incriminating rather than honouring those to whom they are addressed, but, though I recognize the truth of her words, I cannot refrain from saying my *thank you's*. A Guggenheim fellowship started my writing the book for which I had long been accumulating evidence. Dr Henry Allen Moe and Dr Louis Wright gave me encouragement to take up again the work which a bad accident and a long period of enforced inactivity interrupted. The members of the Department of English of my university carried library books to me, Professor Franklin Rolfe and Professor James Phillips read drafts of early chapters, and Professor Alfred Longueil read the whole of the section on poetry. The librarians at the Huntington Library and at the University Library have been helpful, as always. The Research Committee of the University has provided typing assistance. For all of this help I am most grateful. Professor F. P. Wilson took time from busy days at Oxford to consider the section on drama, the librarians in the North Room of the

British Museum were generous with their help during a long summer, and the librarians made a hasty visit to the Bodleian profitable. For this British courtesy to a visiting American I am also most grateful. I can only hope so much kindness will not have been bestowed in vain.

Perhaps one word is necessary in regard to the transcribing of quotations from sixteenth-century texts. I have not altered spelling or punctuation except that I have observed modern usage in transcribing u and v, i and j. I have persisted, in spite of some friendly criticism, in using the form of the name of a Bible character which occurs in the poem or play being discussed. I have done so because the spelling has occasionally seemed significant to certain critics in determining the particular Bible used by the author.

LILY B. CAMPBELL

THE UNIVERSITY OF CALIFORNIA
LOS ANGELES
May 1957

INTRODUCTION

WHEN Milton turned to divine poetry, writing of 'the heaven-descended King' in his ode *On the Morning of Christ's Nativity*, he invoked the Heavenly Muse.[1] When he began *Paradise Lost*, pursuing 'Things unattempted yet in Prose or Rhyme', he again invoked the aid of the Heavenly Muse, joining with his plea an invocation to the Holy Spirit. From 1574, when Du Bartas published *La Muse Chrestiene* containing the poem *L'Uranie*, Urania the Muse of Astronomy had been taken over as the Christian Muse,[2] and as Milton began the Seventh Book of *Paradise Lost*, his description echoed the associations that had grown up about her:

> Descend from Heav'n *Urania*, by that name
> If rightly thou art call'd, whose Voice divine
> Following, above th' *Olympian* Hill I soar,
> Above the flight of *Pegasean* wing.
> The meaning, not the Name I call: for thou
> Nor of the Muses nine, nor on the top
> Of old *Olympus* dwell'st, but Heavenly born,
> Before the Hills appear'd, or Fountain flow'd,
> Thou with Eternal Wisdom didst converse,
> Wisdom thy Sister, and with her didst play
> In presence of th' Almighty Father, pleas'd
> With thy Celestial Song.

The consecrating of Urania to Heavenly tasks gave new inspiration to a movement already gathering momentum in the Christian world. The invention of printing had made possible the wide distribution of the rediscovered literature of the ancient pagan world. Translation, emulation, creation followed, and a great secular literature was coming into being.

[1] The change to divine poetry with the writing of his poem on Christ's nativity is recorded in Elegy VI, written to Charles Diodati. I have used throughout the edition of *Milton* prepared by Merritt Y. Hughes (New York, 1937) and quotations from Milton's Latin are given in the English translations of this edition. Milton's change to divine poetry is discussed by J. H. Hanford, *John Milton* (New York, 1949), but without recognition of the term *divine poetry*.

[2] See ch. IX.

CDP

The old romances too, found readers and imitators. It is not surprising that the need for an accessible Bible and a Christian literature became insistent.

It was Milton who was most eloquently to answer those who claimed precedence for the ancient classics because of their excellence and their antiquity when he represented Christ replying to Satan's praises of them:

> Or if I would delight my private hours
> With Music or with Poem, where so soon
> As in our native Language can I find
> That solace? All our Law and Story strew'd
> With Hymns, our Psalms with artful terms inscrib'd,
> Our Hebrew Songs and Harps in *Babylon*,
> That pleas'd so well our Victors' ear, declare
> That rather *Greece* from us these Arts deriv'd;
> Ill imitated, while they loudest sing
> The vices of their Deities, and their own
> In Fable, Hymn, or Song.

Little to profit or delight will be found in them when their 'swelling Epithets' are removed, and they

> Will far be found unworthy to compare
> With *Sion's* songs, to all true tastes excelling,
> Where God is prais'd aright, and Godlike men,
> The Holiest of Holies, and his Saints;
> Such are from God inspir'd, not such from thee;
> Unless where moral virtue is express'd
> By light of Nature not in all quite lost.[1]

The Hebrew prophets too, Milton's Christ claimed, better than the great pagan orators, taught 'What makes a Nation happy, and keeps it so'.

As Sidney summarized the arguments in defence of Poetry, as Raleigh summarized in his preface to *The History of the World* the claims of history as a guide to the present, so Milton summarized in these and like passages the arguments for a Christian literature based on the Bible, a new divine literature.

The beginnings of the movement which produced a divine

---

[1] *Paradise Regained*, Bk IV, ll. 331–52.

literature in England were halting and often awkward, but the progress toward its fulfilment is worth recording. It is my purpose, then, in this study to trace the movement in the sixteenth century which resulted in the poetry of Donne and Herbert and Milton and those others in the seventeenth century who praised God in nobler words and sounder rhythms.

If I were to undertake to trace the whole movement to make the Bible the guide to Christian living I should require more years than I can hope to live and more volumes than any printer would publish. In education Henry VIII decreed that the fundamentals of religion might be learned in English; Colet thought the boys at St Paul's school might learn their Latin through reading Lactantius, Prudentius, Proba, Sedulius, and Juvencus as well as the pagan classics. The colloquies of Cordier or Castellio were offered as substitutes for the *Flowers of Terence*. Hebrew and Greek knowledge was recognized as a pathway to the Scriptures. Rhetoric and logic were offered in textbooks with all the examples culled from the Bible. King James in Scotland made the Book of Revelation serve the purpose of instruction in civil government. Even the stratagems of war could be learned, some thought, from the Bible rather than from Frontinus. Indeed, there were attempts to make the Bible a complete and exclusive guide to every aspect of Christian living for states as well as individuals. But this guide must be made available in their own languages if men and states were to live by it.

That the translation of the Bible into languages familiar to the common people of all nations was, therefore, a major purpose of the reformation movements in England as well as on the continent of Europe does not need to be re-demonstrated here. That making these translations accessible to all who could read their native languages was pressed as a means of combating the monopoly claimed by the Roman Catholic Church for its right to serve as the only guide on the journey to an assured heaven is also not a matter for further dispute. What I propose to try to show is that both Catholic and non-Catholic writers turned to the Bible to find in Latin or in the vernacular a means of combating the influence of the revival of classical learning and the developing taste for pagan and secular story and song. The Jesuit school drama written in Latin was as much a part of the movement as were the divine sonnet sequences which appeared in the vernacular in various countries.

In England the first phase of the movement was represented by translation—of the whole Bible into prose, the poetic parts of the Bible into English verse. Next came the adapting of Bible story to the various literary genres as they became current in secular literature. Finally there was the free use of Bible story as foundation, ornament, or atmosphere in original creations. I am restricting this study to English poetry and drama in the sixteenth century, and to poetry and drama based directly on the Bible. I am excluding other devotional poetry as well as drama devoted solely to a polemical purpose.

The term *divine poetry* has, I think, been generally misunderstood, though it is a recurrent term in the sixteenth and seventeenth centuries. For instance, C. S. Lewis summarizing Sidney's *Apology for Poetry* represents Sidney's 'kinds' as 'the devotional, the philosophical, and the fictional'.[1] But Sidney did not use the word *devotional*; what he said was that among poets 'The chiefe both in antiquitie and excellencies were they that did imitate the inconceivable excellencies of GOD', and he instanced the writer of Job, Solomon in his Ecclesiastes and Proverbs as well as in his Song of Songs, Moses and Debora in their hymns, and David in his Psalms as such writers. Only in a very broad sense can all of these works be termed devotional, and Sidney called David's Psalms 'a divine Poem',[2] though the Psalms are of course devotional. Kathleen Tillotson says of Drayton that he is 'perhaps above all, a religious poet—not so much in his biblical poems as in his view of poetry. (He speaks of it always as a something hallowed, a divine power; and his most powerful images are, like Milton's, celestial and starry.)[3] But when Drayton published in *The Muses Elizium* poems recounting the Biblical stories of Noah and the Flood, of Moses, and of David and Goliath, he set them off in a separate section

[1] *English Literature in the Sixteenth Century* (Oxford, 1954), p. 344.
[2] See ch. VI.
[3] *The Works of Michael Drayton*, ed. by J. William Hebel, vol. v, ed. by Kathleen Tillotson and B. H. Newdigate (Oxford, 1941), p. xiv.

with a separate dedication calling them *divine poems*. Mrs Tillot-son says, however, that in spite of the invocation which opens 'Noahs Floud', it cannot be regarded as a religious poem.[1]

It is this use of *devotional* and *religious* and sometimes of *theological* which seems to me to cloud the fact that there was a movement to substitute divine poetry for the secular poetry which was coming off the presses in the sixteenth century, a movement to substitute Biblical story for secular story, to substitute a Christian mythology for a pagan mythology, as well as to substitute prayer and praise of the Christian God for poetry addressed to an unkind mistress. That it is the subject-matter of the poem or drama that makes it divine poetry or divine drama and not the religious or non-religious attitude of the author is implicit in the description of the kinds of poetry distinguished by Sidney. It is explicit in Peter Martyr's *Common Places*: 'betweene Poems divine and humane, this is the difference; that humane Poems doo set foorth the renoume of kings, princes, feelds, cities, regions, castels, women, marriages, and sometime of brute beasts. But divine Poems doo onlie sing of God, and celebrate him onlie'.[2] The *Refutation* by 'I.G.' of Thomas Heywood's *Apology for Actors* would, indeed, make divine drama worse than non-religious: 'The *Materiall* cause or matter of Playes is their Subject whereupon they speake and entreat, and that is two fould, either *Divine* or *Prophane*. If Playes be of *Divine* matter, then are they most intollerable, or rather Sacrilegious.'[3] That I.G.'s attitude was not that of the participants in the movement to create a divine literature is obvious, but it illustrates the point which I want to stress, that divine literature depends upon its subject-matter.

No one of the writers of divine literature doubted that it could and should be written in prose or poetry, in any and all of the metrical forms which were used in profane verse, in any and all of the literary genres which were currently in use. When Milton translated the Psalms, when he wrote his divine poetry as ode and epic and tragedy, when he turned to Urania

[1] *Drayton*, vol. v, p. 224.
[2] Peter Martyr Vermigli, *Common Places* (London, 1583), part 3, cap. 12.
[3] Reprinted with Heywood's work in *Scholars' Facsimiles and Reprints* (New York, 1941), with introduction and notes by R. H. Perkinson, p. 54.

as his Muse, he was following in the long-established tradition for the divine poet.

There were some who professed a desire to clothe their high message in plain and humble garb, but for the most part, they accepted what Thomas Nashe expressed, though they might not have accepted Thomas Nashe. Dedicating his *Christs Tears over Jerusalem* to Lady Elizabeth Carey, and noting that 'Fames eldest favorite, Maister Spencer, in all his writings he prizeth you', he said: 'Unworthy are wee of heavenly knowledge, if we keepe from her any one of her hand-maydes. Logique, Rethorique, History, Philosophy, Musique, Poetry, all are the hand-maides of Divinitie. She can never be curiously drest, or exquisitely accomplisht, if any of these be wanting.'[1] It will be apparent in the following pages that most of the writers of divine literature must have been well acquainted with these handmaids to divinity, for most of them had had an university education or had been well trained in music. That they lacked, many of them, that something more—call it divine fury or what you will—is only too apparent, but I am concerned here with the beginnings and the purposes which underlay the studied attempt to oppose the pagan and secular literature seeming to many good men in the sixteenth century to lead the people away from God.

I have chosen to trace rather a narrow path by which the movement came into being in England. There were many contributions which I have not recorded, but I think the path I have tried to describe is the most important one.

[1] Pub. 1593. Nashe says in his dedication: 'To write in Divinitie I could not have adventured, if ought else might have consorted with the regenerate gravitie of your judgement. Your thoughts are holy, holy is your life: in your hart lives no delight but of Heaven. Far be it I should proffer to unhallow them, with any prophane papers of them.'

PART I

DIVINE POETRY IN SIXTEENTH-CENTURY ENGLAND

CHAPTER I

THE FORERUNNER: SAVONAROLA

IT was in the sixteenth century that the Christian Bible came once more to stand forth in its glory, undimmed by its cloud of witnesses. In England as in the rest of Christendom the Bible itself had become almost lost in the multitude of interpretations, in the intellectual tangles of theological logic, in the rivalries of dispute over dogma. To the majority of the people it was an inaccessible and a forbidden book; inaccessible because only the learned could understand the Latin in which it was available, and forbidden even to those who could read Latin save only those duly authorized by the Church. In England, Knight records in his life of Colet, 'that Use and Study of the *Scriptures* was so low at that Time, and even in the University of *Oxford*, that the being admitted a *Batchelor of Divinity*, gave only Liberty to read the *Master of Sentences* [Pet. Lombard], and the highest Degree of *Doctor of Divinity*, did not admit a man to the Reading of the *Scriptures*'.[1] In Cambridge, too, Mullinger writes that the lecturers were not allowed to lecture on the Bible until they had lectured on the Sentences.[2]

The resurrection of the Greek and Roman past known as the Revival of Learning had brought first to Italy and then to all of western Europe and to England a new approach to all the arts and a new interest in human life as it is lived on earth. It had brought also the old pagan gods to the horizons of thought and pagan philosophies to rival the philosophy which was formulated in the theology of the Christian church. The invention of printing had made possible the dissemination of learning of every kind to others than the cloistered few and the small number having access to princely libraries. Even the spiritual shepherds of men turned their thoughts to secular affairs, to the enjoyment which their five senses could provide, to the worship in spirit and sometimes in fact of the pagan gods.

[1] Samuel Knight, *The Life of Dr John Colet* (London, 1724), p. 51.
[2] James B. Mullinger, *The University of Cambridge* (Cambridge, 1873), vol. I, p. 363, n. 2, and Index under *Bible*, p. 653.

Machiavelli is not generally chronicled among the reformers of the church, but he wrote that nothing could 'portend the ruine of our Church with more certainty, than that those who are nearest the Church of Rome (which is the head of our Religion) should have less religion than other people', adding that anyone comparing the current practice with the primitive foundation, would find that 'either utter destruction, or some great judgment was hanging over our heads'.[1] Those who were to lead the rebellion against the licentiousness of their time did in fact attempt to do just what Machiavelli suggested here, to go back to the source of their religious faith. They wanted to go behind the Sentences, behind all the niceties of dogma, to the Bible itself. They wanted to revisit the early fathers of the church and to proclaim anew a fresh and vigorous faith.

The luxury with which the Borgias clothed their debaucheries, the papal sanction given to war and to lust, the penetration of the influence of the pagan classics into every phase of life could but call forth eventually a revolt, and, like another John the Baptist, the friar Girolamo Savonarola[2] came from his Florentine monastery in the last decade of the fifteenth century, denouncing the evils of the life about him and crying for repentance lest destruction ensue both here and in the hereafter. Very rarely have men's hearts been so moved as they were by his words. Learning flourished, but religion was being destroyed, and the two things were associated in Savonarola's mind. To him a return to the Bible and its teaching was the only means of salvation. 'Go thou to Rome and throughout Christendom,' he exclaimed; 'in the mansions of the great prelates and great lords, there is no concern save for poetry and the oratorical art. Go thither and see, thou shalt find them all with books of the humanities in their hands, and telling one another they can guide men's souls by means of Virgil, Horace, and Cicero.' The clergy, he said, 'tickle men's ears with talk of Aristotle and Plato, Virgil and Petrarch, and take no concern

[1] Nicholas Machiavel, *The Discourses upon the First Decade of Titus Livius* in *Works* (London, 1720), p. 284.

[2] One of the best contemporary accounts of Savonarola is given in *The Historie of Guicciardini*, trans. by Geoffrey Fenton (London, 1599), Bk III (the first ed. was printed in 1579).

for the salvation of souls. Why, instead of expounding so many books, do they not expound the one Book in which is the law and spirit of life!'[1]

Yet in a work that seems to have been almost lost sight of, *Opus perutile de divisione ac ultilitate omnium scientiarum*, Savonarola showed that he would not altogether abolish the pre-Christian learning. 'There is', he wrote, 'a false race of pretended poets, who can do naught but run after the Greeks and Romans, repeating their ideas, copying their style and their metre; and even invoking the same deities, almost as though we were not men as much as they, with reason and religion of our own. Now this is not only false poetry, but likewise a most hateful snare to our youth.' Nevertheless, he recognized that 'even among the ancients, there be some that condemned vicious things, and extolled the generous deeds of great men: by these, poetry was turned to good use, and I have neither the right nor the wish to condemn them'. The safeguard that he would set up was 'a strong and healthy Christian training' before any study of the heathen poets was allowed.[2] It must be remembered too that it was he who saved the great Medician library deposited in the convent of Saint Mark's when its confiscation was threatened by Medici creditors. His was, indeed, the general attitude to be taken by those rebelling against the paganizing and secularizing of the intellectual life of Christendom.

In a practical way also Savonarola demonstrated the means by which the obnoxious practices of the times might be supplanted. At the time when Savonarola was at the height of his popularity as a preacher in Florence, the Florentine delight in carnivals and pageants was accentuated by Lorenzo the Magnificent, whose most famous invention was, according to Villari, the *Canti Carnascialeschi* 'to be sung in carnival masquerades of the triumph of death, troops of devils, or other whimsicalities of the time'. The songs are universally described as adorned with obscenities and vulgarities. In 1497 and 1498 Savonarola inspired a counter-celebration, known as the Burn-

[1] Pasquale Villari, *The Life and Times of Girolamo Savonarola* (London and New York, 1888), pp. 179–83.
[2] Villari, pp. 500–5. See also Piero Misciattelli, *Savonarola*, trans. by M. Peters (Cambridge, 1929), pp. 30–2 and 101–2.

ing of the Vanities. Burckhardt has described the celebration of
1497 as it took place on the Piazza della Signoria:

In the centre of it rose a high pyramid of several tiers....On the
lowest tier were arranged false beards, masks, and carnival disguises;
above came volumes of the Latin and Italian poets, among others
Boccaccio, the 'Morgante' of Pulci, and Petrarch, partly in the form
of valuable printed parchments and illuminated manuscripts; then
women's ornaments and toilet articles, scents, mirrors, veils and
false hair; higher up, lutes, harps, chessboards, playing cards; and
finally, on the two uppermost tiers, paintings only, especially of
female beauties, partly fancy-pictures, bearing the classical names of
Lucretia, Cleopatra, or Faustina, partly portraits of the beautiful
Bencina, Lena Morella, Bina and Maria de' Lenzi....When the pile
was lighted the Signoria appeared on the balcony, and the air
echoed with song, the sound of trumpets, and the pealing of bells.
The people then adjourned to the Piazza di San Marco, where they
danced round in three concentric circles. The innermost was composed of monks of the monastery, alternating with boys, dressed as
angels; then came young laymen and ecclesiastics; and on the outside, old men, citizens, and priests, the latter crowned with wreaths
of olive.[1]

To overthrow the *Canti Carnascialeschi* Savonarola composed
his *Laudi Spirituali* which Villari would place outside the field
of genuine art, for, he says, 'their metre, form and even almost
their ideas are suggested and determined by the very species of
poetry they were meant to supersede. The author set them to
the same music as the Carnival Songs, and followed the same
arrangement, while trying to substitute a word of faith or
religion for every one of their lewd expressions.'[2]

Savonarola was executed in 1498, but his influence lived on in
artists, the greatest of whom was Michelangelo, and in new
religious leaders, the greatest of whom was Martin Luther.[3] To

[1] Jacob Burckhardt, *The Civilization of the Renaissance in Italy* (Phaidon Press,
dist. by Oxford University Press, New York, 1950), pp. 295–6.

[2] Villari, pp. 506–7.

[3] That Luther claimed Savonarola as a forerunner of the Reformation is
argued from his preface to his edition of Savonarola's *Expositio ac Meditatio in
Psalmum Misereri Mei*, published probably in 1520 according to the British Museum
Catalogue. Misciatelli contests the claims (p. 208), finding him rather a precursor
of the Counter-Reformation. It is interesting to note that the Luther Memorial
at Worms still stands with Savonarola as one of the four figures grouped about
the central figure. See A. C. McGiffert, *Martin Luther* (London, 1911), p. 204,
for a description.

England the tenets of his teaching were carried directly or indirectly: the return to the Bible as the fountain of all truth, the limited acceptance of those pagan works which inculcated a sound morality both by precepts and examples, the use of popular secular forms of literature to carry new religious content. These were ideas and precedents which formed the basis of much of the new movement toward a Christian literature which was to develop during the succeeding century.

CHAPTER II

THE THEORIST: ERASMUS

THE problem which faced the Christian world when the great literature of the ancient Greeks and Romans was given new life through the rediscovery of old manuscripts and the dissemination of their contents by the new art of printing was essentially the same problem which had had to be faced at the time when Christianity first spread to the educated classes. Therefore, it was natural that the men of the Renaissance who were troubled about the influx of pagan literature and pagan ideas and ideals should turn again to those of earlier ages who had attempted to find the answer. Probably the most influential scholar in the sixteenth century and foremost among those bent on reclaiming the work of the ancient fathers of the church[1] was Erasmus of Rotterdam, Desiderius Erasmus as he was later to call himself. In the early summer of 1499 he journeyed to England, where he became the friend of John Colet and Thomas More. The lasting result of this friendship has been recorded most eloquently by Frederic Seebohm in his *Oxford Reformers* and by W. E. Campbell in his *Erasmus, Tyndale and More* and in many studies of the three individually. I shall not attempt to retell their story, but it is necessary to note here that it was the influence of Colet that directed the talents of the young humanist scholar toward matters of religion.

It was in 1496 that Colet, newly returned from Italy, began a course of lectures on Saint Paul's epistles which were, Seebohm says, 'so far as can be traced, the first overt act in a movement commenced at Oxford in the direction of practical Christian reform'.[2] Whether Colet had during his stay in Italy heard the preaching of Savonarola has never been determined, but what he set out to do in his exposition of the Pauline epistles

---

[1] P. S. Allen, *Erasmus* (Oxford, 1934), pp. 47-55 *et passim*. For lists of his editions of the ancient fathers see Allen, *Erasmi Epistolae* (Oxford, 1906-47), where these lists are added at the end of each of volumes 6 to 13.

[2] Frederic Seebohm, *The Oxford Reformers* (Everyman's Library ed., London, 1929), p. 2.

was the logical sequence of Savonarola's teaching.[1] To place the Bible before his hearers as 'a record of real events, and the lives and teaching of living men' instead of regarding it simply as an 'arsenal of texts' was Colet's aim, and such exposition of the Scripture as he gave brought it to bear upon men's daily lives and thoughts.[2]

When Erasmus went to England he was already known as a humanist, and his continued reputation has been largely based on works directed to other ends than that upon which his resolve centred after his first trip to England and his friendship with Colet. '"Erasmus" is the only name in all the host of humanists', Huizinga says, 'which has remained a household word all over the globe', and it is as a humanist that his fame has so long outlived him, but during his time in England he determined to devote himself thereafter primarily to theological studies.[3] Here he came in contact with scholars like Grocyn and Linacre learned in Greek. He realized his limitations if he were to enter upon the great work of his life, and like a true scholar he determined to perfect himself in Greek as a preparation for it.[4]

Long familiar with the works of the ancient fathers of the church and attracted especially to Saint Jerome, Erasmus knew the most famous of Jerome's letters in which he described the dream in which he had been 'caught up in the spirit and dragged before the Judge's judgment seat', and on being asked his condition, had replied that he was a Christian. The great Judge had answered, 'Thou liest, thou art a Ciceronian, not a Christian'.[5] Perhaps Colet did for Erasmus what the dream did for Jerome. At any rate, like Jerome, he brought the training and the talents of the humanist to the works of religion to which most of his later life was devoted.

At about this time Erasmus decided to edit the whole works

---

[1] On the question of Savonarola's influence see especially Seebohm, pp. 10–11, 21 and n. 1, and 97.
[2] Seebohm, p. 17.
[3] J. Huizinga, *Erasmus of Rotterdam* (London, 1953), pp. 33–40.
[4] W. E. Campbell, *Erasmus, Tyndale and More* (London, 1949), pp. 32–4.
[5] Jerome's Letter 22 as trans. by F. A. Wright (Loeb Classical Library, London, 1933), p. 127.

of Jerome, but a chance discovery in an old library near Louvain of Valla's *Annotationes* on the New Testament determined him to do what Jerome had done, to make a new translation of the New Testament into Latin.[1] Since Jerome's translation of the Bible was the authorized text of the Church, his undertaking was a hazardous one. In dedicating to Archbishop Warham in 1506 his translation into Latin of the *Hecuba* and the *Iphigenia in Aulis* of Euripides he wrote that he had decided to do these translations to test how far he had progressed in the study of both Greek and Latin 'in material difficult indeed, but not sacred; so that the difficulty of the undertaking might be useful for practice and at the same time if I made any mistakes these mistakes should involve only the risk of my talent and leave the Holy Scriptures undamaged'.[2]

In 1505 Erasmus succeeded in having Valla's manuscript work printed in Paris, not without an outcry against his bringing the work of a humanist scholar to the criticism of sacred literature. It was probably during his second stay in England from late in 1505 until the summer of 1506 that, spurred on by Colet, Erasmus made his initial translation of the New Testament. It was a propitious time for his undertaking, since he was then in friendly contact with Greek scholars as well as with those ecclesiastics like Warham who were to become his patrons. In 1509 he returned to England for the last of his extended visits, a visit which ended in 1514. Here he completed his *Praise of Folly* in the house of More, its Latin title *Moriae Encomium* furnishing opportunity for a scholarly pun. Here at times he lectured at Cambridge on divinity and on Greek. Most of his days and nights were, however, given over to his edition of the works of Jerome and to the preparation of the amended text of the New Testament, for he had decided to publish a Greek text and his notes along with his Latin translation. The work, says Huizinga, was 'inspired, encouraged, and promoted by Colet'.

A brief visit to England in 1515 was perhaps made in part to secure a copy of the translation of the New Testament which

---

[1] Campbell (p. 34) gives 1502 as the date; Huizinga (p. 57), 1504.
[2] Huizinga, pp. 81–91 and 204–5.

he had left there. At any rate the results of his many years of scholarly labour were evident when in 1516 both his New Testament and the first four volumes of the nine-volume edition of Jerome's works were published. The labour of other scholars contributed to this edition of Jerome's works (published 1516–20), but Erasmus was the general editor, and these first four volumes were those which contained Jerome's letters edited by Erasmus himself.[1]

Though Erasmus was translating the New Testament into Latin, thus offering a new Latin text to compete with the authorized text of the Catholic Church, his preface advocated making it available to all men, laymen as well as clerics, and to this end he would have it translated into the vernacular and made a part of their life in their songs and stories.[2] These ideas were later incorporated in a separate work which was printed in 1519 at Basel under the title *Paraclesis, id est, Adhortatio ad sanctissimum ac saluberrimum Christianae philosophiae studium* and which, translated into English by William Roye, appeared in editions of 1529 and 1540 as *An Exhortation to the Diligent Studye of Scripture.* I quote from the 1540 edition certain passages which were echoed constantly in the later writing on these subjects. Addressing 'the good and godly reader', Erasmus says:

I Remembre good reader, that at another tyme also in a certayn place, I have testifyed and knowledged my selfe, to be very farre dysagreynge in opynyon, from those whiche do thynke the laye men & suche as be not learned ought utterly to be kept far awaye from the readynge of the holy bokes and scryptures, to the which (as in the olde tyme, none but the preestes entred, unto the most holy and moste secrete places of the temple) they thynke none shuld be admytted: or suffered to have entreaunce but a fewe suche which have ben many yeres exercysed and beaten in the phylosophy of Arystotle and in the dyvynyte scolastycall, used within the scoles of the unyversytes.

Acknowledging that some parts of the Old Testament are not quite adapted to common understanding, he argues that the

[1] For Erasmus's comments on Jerome as expressed in his letter to Pope Leo X see J. J. Mangan, *Life, Character and Influence of Desiderius Erasmus of Rotterdam* (New York, 1927), vol. I, pp. 395–8.
[2] For the influence of Jerome evident in the ideas of Colet and of Erasmus see especially Seebohm, ch. XI, pp. 199–209.

gospels of the New Testament were written and taught to the unlearned as well as to the learned, and every man may select what will do him good:

Let us consydre what manner hearers Chryste hym selfe had, was it not a multytude gathered of all sortes, in the whiche were blynde, lame, beggers, tolle gatherers, Capytaynes of warre, artyfycers, women and children? Wyll he be greved that his wordes be redde of suche of whom he was contented to be herde when he dyd speake hym selfe? By my counsell and advyse, the ploughman and husbande-man of the countrey shall reade scrypture, the carpenter, the smyth, the mason, yea and harlottes also, and bawdes shall reade it and to be shorte, the Turkes also shall reade it. If Chryst dyd not kepe suche away from his owne voyce, I wyll not stop theym and kepe theym awaye from his bokes.[1]

Jerome had set a precedent when he had made a translation of the Bible into the familiar language, Latin. He had set another precedent when he incorporated in one of his letters which Erasmus edited a description by Paula of the little monastery at Bethlehem which she had helped Jerome to found. I quote Rand's translation of the passage:

In this little villa of Christ everything is rustic, and apart from the singing of Psalms, there is silence. The ploughman driving the share sings an *alleluia*. The sweating reaper diverts himself with Psalms, and the vine-dresser clipping the shoots with his curved pruning-knife hums some snatch from David. These are the songs in our district. These are the popular love-lays. This is what shepherds whistle; this is what heartens the tillers of the soil.[2]

The description of 'this little villa of Christ' is echoed by Erasmus in the *Paraclesis* as he writes that 'beynge of the same oppynyon & mynde, whiche saynte Hierome was of' he would rejoice exceedingly if it could be

that the ploughman holdynge the plough dyd synge somwhat of the mystycall Psalmes in his owne mother tonge yea and yf the wever, syttyng at his worke, dyd synge somewhat of the gospell, for his solace and comforte in his labours & moreover yf the mayster of the shyppe, syttyng faste at the sterne, do synge also somewhat of the

[1] Ff. d iiii and e ii *verso*.
[2] Letter 46 as trans. by E. K. Rand, *Founders of the Middle Ages* (Cambridge, Mass. 1929), p. 119.

same and for to make an ende yf the wedded wyfe, when she sytteth at her dystaffe, have some companyon, or kynneswoman nere unto her which doth reade and reherse somewhat herof unto her.[1]

Thus Erasmus not only challenged the Christian world to accept a fresh Latin translation from a new Greek text, but he would also free the Bible from the binding interpretations of the schoolmen by letting all men read it in their native languages and make it a part of their daily living in their songs and in their stories.

In 1517, even while he was at work amending his translation of the New Testament, Erasmus published the first of his Biblical paraphrases, that of Paul's Epistle to the Romans. It was the beginning of a series of paraphrases which in an English translation were incorporated in the paraphrase of the New Testament ordered in 1547 to be put in every parish church.

[1] F. g ii verso.

CHAPTER III

THE BIBLE AS ENGLISH LITERATURE: TYNDALE AND THE CATHOLIC OPPOSITION

I N his *History of the English Bible* Westcott writes: 'Before the end of the 15th century Bibles were printed in Spanish, Italian, French, Dutch, German and Bohemian; while England as yet had only the few manuscripts of the Wycliffite versions.'[1] That England in the next century had a printed Bible in English was primarily due to William Tyndale, who put into practice the ideas being promulgated by Colet and by Erasmus. The facts of Tyndale's early life are only vaguely known, being largely deduced from the account given by John Foxe in his *Actes and Monuments* familiarly known as his 'Book of Martyrs'.[2] We know, however, that he was granted the degree of B.A. in 1512 and M.A. in 1515 by Oxford University, and since Foxe speaks of him as 'brought up from a child in the University of Oxford' and as having been in Magdalen Hall as well as in Magdalen College, he cannot but have felt the lasting influence of Colet, who had left Oxford in 1505 when he was appointed Dean of Saint Paul's.[3] From Oxford Tyndale went on to Cambridge. His latest biographer, J. F. Mozley, thinks he moved there in 1519, but it may have been as early as 1516. At any rate, Erasmus's New Testament was known and was the subject of dispute in this university where Erasmus had taught from 1510 to 1514. At some time during his university years Tyndale was ordained, but when he left

---

[1] Brooke F. Westcott, *A General View of the History of the English Bible*, 3rd ed. revised by W. Aldis Wright (New York, 1922), p. 25.

[2] For accounts of Tyndale's life see J. F. Mozley, *William Tyndale* (London, 1937), and the earlier work which it does not entirely supersede, R. Demaus, *William Tyndale*, revised by R. Lovett (London, 1886). The Foxe account is quoted by Mozley, p. 12, and by Demaus, pp. 33–4. That Tyndale was also known as Hutchins, both names spelled with characteristic lack of uniformity, is an established fact. See especially Mozley, pp. 5–7.

[3] Seebohm, pp. 83–4.

the university life it was to go as schoolmaster to the young children of Sir John Walsh, though he is known to have done preaching also. While a member of this household Tyndale, desiring to answer the disputants at his employer's table with authority greater than his own, translated the *Enchiridion militis Christiani* of Erasmus,[1] which, read and used by 'his master and lady', caused 'the great prelates' to be less frequently invited to their house and to be made less comfortable when they did come, if we believe Foxe. It was a book to be issued in many English editions between 1533 and 1576.

With a letter from his friend and master addressed to Sir Harry Guildford, Tyndale went to London in 1523, hoping to translate the Bible into English under church authority, and hence trying to find a way through Guildford to the Bishop of London, Cuthbert Tunstall. It is significant that he took with him a translation of an oration of Isocrates to prove his ability to turn Greek into English. It would seem likely that he, like Erasmus, had wanted to test his own ability on 'material difficult indeed, but not sacred', before he undertook his ultimate task. But when through Guildford's intercession he was given the opportunity to plead his case before Tunstall, the bishop answered that his house was full, advising him that he could find employment elsewhere in London. While waiting to see Tunstall, he had, however, through some good fortune, preached a few sermons at Saint Dunstan-in-the-West, Fleet Street, and there a wealthy merchant, Humphrey Monmouth, heard him and became his friend. Monmouth took him as a guest in his house, and when he decided that the work upon which he had determined could not proceed anywhere in England, helped to make possible his removing to the continent.

Of the particulars of Tyndale's journeying in his efforts to find the means to accomplish his supreme undertaking there is no need to write here, but it is necessary to record the fact now apparently established that he went from Hamburg, his first stopping place, to Wittenberg. There he could find the riches of a university, and there he could consult with Luther, whose translation of the New Testament into German, pub-

---

[1] A careful account of the *Enchiridion* is given by Huizinga, pp. 49–54.

lished in 1522, was partly based on Erasmus's text. It must be remembered that the King of England was then engaged in a controversy with Luther which brought him from the Pope the title of Defender of the Faith. Erasmus himself had been drawn into the quarrel with Luther, but Tyndale drew from the works of both, though making his own translation from the Greek. Returning from Wittenberg to Hamburg to secure the money promised him from England, he at last set out for Cologne and there began the printing of the New Testament in 1525. Betrayed, he was forced to flee to Worms, where sympathy for his undertaking could be found, and in Worms the New Testament was printed in 1526. The octavo edition printed at Worms was without the prologue and glosses which appear in the Cologne fragment. In spite of the efforts of King Henry and Cardinal-Chancellor Wolsey, copies of both editions reached England in 1526, without, however, any indication of the translator. They were eagerly bought and as persistently destroyed by the authorities, and edition after edition was called for. Tyndale revised his work for the 1534 and the 1535 editions and proceeded to the translation of the Old Testament from the Hebrew, the Pentateuch being published in 1531, the book of Jonah probably in the same year, and the epistles from the Old Testament added to the 1534 edition of the New.

In 1528 Tyndale published *The Obedience of a Christian Man*, the book which Demaus describes as, next to his Bible translations, 'the book by which he was best known to his contemporaries, that which exerted the greatest influence upon those who were friendly to the Reformation, and which gave deepest offence to the authorities of the Church', yet King Henry was pleased with it, for it argued the supreme authority of the king in the state as well as the supreme authority of the Bible in the church.[1] Tyndale here opposed the authority claimed by the pope in the state and also the authority of those who claimed the right to give the people only an interpretation of the Bible rather than the Bible itself. He ridiculed the requirement for the doctor of divinity that he 'have been two yeres maister of

[1] Demaus gives the most comprehensive description of the work and its reception.

art' before he could study God's word, and threw scorn upon the variety of interpretations that were offered for the plain words of the Bible. As for the curates, he thought they knew nothing of what the Bible meant, arguing: 'If they will not let the lay man have the woorde of God in hys mother tounge, yet let the priests have it, which for a great part of them do understand no latine at all; but sing, and say and patter all day with the lips only, that which the hart understandeth not.' As for the English language not being fitted for the translation of Greek and Hebrew, he insisted that it agreed better with both tongues than did the Latin.

Two passages in Tyndale's prefatory address are of particular interest here, for they show that he, like Jerome and Erasmus, wanted to make the Bible the familiar accompaniment of life. The first finds precedent in the speech of Moses to the Israelites in the sixth chapter of Deuteronomy: 'Let these wordes which I commaunde thee thys day sticke fast in thine hart, & whet them on thy children, & talke of them as thou sittest in thine house, as thou walkest by the way, & when thou lyest downe, & when thou risest up, & binde them for a token to thyne hand, & let them be a remembraunce betwene thine eyes, & write them on the postes & gates of thine house.' But, Tyndale asks, 'How can we whette Gods word (that is, to put it in practise, use, & exercise) upon our children and housholds when we are violently kepte from it, and knowe it not?'[1] The second passage which I quote compares the popular secular reading of the day with that offered by the Bible:

this threatning and forbidding the laye people to reade the Scripture is not for love of your soules…in as much as they permitte and suffer you to read Robbin Hode & Bevis of Hampton, Hercules, Hector, and Troylus, with a thousand histories and fables of love and wantones, and of rybaudry, as filthy as hart can thinke, to corrupt the mindes of youth withall, cleane contrary to the doctrine of Christ and of his Apostles.

The fount from which Tyndale drew his arguments is indicated in his closing paragraph, which advises the reader that 'A thou-

[1] *The Obedience of a Christian Man* in *The Whole Works of W. Tyndall, John Frith, and Doct. Barnes*, printed by John Joye (London, 1573), pp. 101-2.

sand reasons moe might be made (as thou mayst see in *Paraclesis Erasmi*, & in his preface to the paraphrasis of Mathew) unto which they should be compelled to holde their peace, or to geve shamefull aunsweres'.[1]

This new emphasis on the Bible as the one book from which Christians should derive nourishment and the insistence upon its being made available to all men and women in their native tongues were concepts made familiar by the teaching of Savonarola and Colet, Saint Jerome and Erasmus, and were those which determined the creation of an English Bible and the attempt to substitute it for the secular and pagan reading then popular.

These works of Tyndale brought the answer of Sir Thomas More usually referred to as the *Dialogue against Tyndale*, which was published in 1528 and summarized the Catholic position. Reviewing the regulations which had followed the heresies attendant upon Wycliffe's earlier version of the Scriptures, More used the traditional arguments: Adam's being prohibited the tree of knowledge, Moses's talking with God on the mountain top and bringing the law down to the people, Paul's division of the church into teachers and hearers, Plato's prohibiting young men from disputing even temporal laws. He warns:

And thus in these matters, if the common people might be bold to claim it, as ye say, and to dispute it; then should ye have the more blind the more bold, the more ignorant the more busy, the less wit the more inquisitive, the more fool the more talkative of great doubts and high questions of holy scripture, and of God's great and secret mysteries—and this, not soberly of any good affection, but presumptuously and unreverently at meat and at meal. And there, when the wine were in and the wit out, would they take upon them with foolish words and blasphemy to handle holy scripture in more homely manner than a song of Robin Hood.[2]

The issues apparent in the long fight over the translation of the Bible continued to be those apparent in the More–Tyndale controversy: whether the Bible should be translated at all; whether if it were to be translated it should be translated in-

[1] P. 104.
[2] *The Dialogue concerning Tyndale*, by Sir Thomas More, ed. with introd. by W. E. Campbell and an essay by A. W. Reed (London, 1927), p. 246.

dependently, without the authority of the church; whether it should be freely read by all, laymen and clerics alike. But of the history of this conflict and of the progress of the Bible in English I cannot treat here. Tyndale was to suffer martyrdom in 1536, but just one year later the Bible in English was legalized and, as Westcott records, 'by far the greater part of his translation remains intact in our present Bibles'. Of supreme importance, it was Tyndale's influence which 'decided that our Bible should be popular and not literary, speaking in a simple dialect, and that by its simplicity it should be endowed with permanence'.[1]

In 1582 the principle of fighting fire with fire was demonstrated when English Catholics were offered a New Testament, the title of which describes clearly its purpose:

The New Testament of Jesus Christ, Translated faithfully into English, out of the authentical Latin, according to the best corrected copies of the same, diligently conferred with the Greeke and other editions in divers languages: With arguments of books and chapters, annotations, and other necessarie helpes, for the better understanding of the text, and specially for the discoverie of the corruptions of divers late translations, and for clearing the controversies in religion, of these daies: in the English College of Rhemes.

The preface answers those arguments which had been advanced for the opening of the Bible to everyone, and the answer often comes as a direct reply to those who continued to repeat the ideas and the words of Erasmus and Tyndale. This can be seen when it is asked whether the reader can think

that our forefathers suffered every schole-maister, scholer, or Grammarian that had a little Greeke or Latin, straight to take in hand the holy Testament: or that the translated Bibles into the vulgar tonges were in the handes of every husbandman, artificer, prentice, boies, girles, mistresse, maide, man: that they were sung, plaied, alleaged, of euery tinker, taverner, rimer, minstrel: that they were for table talke, for alebenches, for boates and barges, and for every prophane person and companie. No, in those better times men were neither so ill, nor so curious of them selves so to abuse the blessed booke of Christ: neither was there any such easy meanes before printing was invented, to disperse the copies into the handes of euery man, as now there is.

[1] Westcott, p. 158.

It is in point here to quote one more passage from the preface, one that gives clear evidence of the growth before 1582 of a literature based on the English Bible as well as evidence of the opposition to it:

> Looke whether the most chast and sacred sentences of Gods holy word, be not turned of many, into mirth, mockerie, amorous ballets & detestable letters of love and lewdnes: their delicate rimes, tunes, and translations much encreasing the same.

CHAPTER IV

THE FIRST ENGLISH SONG BOOK: LUTHER AND COVERDALE

MILES COVERDALE had worked with Tyndale as a fellow-exile in Hamburg; like Tyndale, he had visited Luther in Wittenberg; and when in 1535 he published the first complete Bible in English, his translation clearly reflected Tyndale's version so far as Tyndale had been permitted to go. Coverdale's Bible was dedicated to King Henry VIII with good wishes extended also to his 'dearest just wyfe, and most vertuous pryncess, Quene Anne'. Anne Boleyn had been a faithful advocate of a Bible in English, and whether her advocacy was prejudicial to Coverdale's cause or no, the Bible of Coverdale, in which the King had showed great interest, appeared without the notation on the title-page of its being printed with the King's licence, and Anne became the first of the King's wives to die on the scaffold. Yet the Bible was not suppressed, and the dedication with the queen's name changed to *Jane* reappeared in the next edition.[1] Finally in 1537 the so-called Matthew's Bible bore on its title-page the King's licence. The printed Bible in English had become legal.

Coverdale's contribution to the new movement for a divine literature in English went beyond his publication of the first complete English text of the Bible, however, for he published also what seems to have been the first rival collection of songs in open opposition to the popularity of secular verse in English. Not only were old romances and tales of Robin Hood along with the still older writings of pagan antiquity finding favour, but also the new toys of amorous verse and secular song from the continent were furnishing inspiration and patterns to English writers. The courtiers at Henry's court took up the fashion of composing lyrics and, as Chambers notes, 'the making of "balletes" was by no means left to such professional exponents

---

[1] Coverdale's disappointment is discussed in the Introduction to *The English Hexapla* (London, n.d.), pp. 23–4.

of the art as William Cornish of the Chapel Royal and John Heywood. Henry himself made them, and it was the last nail in the coffin of Anne Boleyn that she turned his attempts to derision. The courtiers took up the fashion; Anne's brother Lord Rochford, Thomas Lord Vaux, Lord Thomas Howard, Sir Francis Bryan, Sir Anthony Lee.'[1] And of course there were Sir Thomas Wyatt and Henry Howard, Earl of Surrey, whose names are almost the only ones familiar today. But the writing and singing of songs was not confined to the court. Ballads of the popular sort were also being written as well as sung by those who were not likely to be aware of the 'courtiers' trifles' written in imported verse forms.

How early the printing of the new poetry began remains uncertain. Until recent scholarship unearthed fragments of two earlier collections of lyric poetry in England, *A Boke of Balettes* and *The Courte of Venus*, it was customary to count the *Songes and Sonnettes* published by Tottel in 1557 as the first great landmark in the progress of lyric poetry during the English Renaissance. Yet these two earlier works or similar ones yet undiscovered must have been published during earlier Tudor reigns,[2] for we have evidence in the opposition they roused.

Over and over again we hear those who would offer a substitute for secular song quoting the Apostle Paul's words:

And be not drunk with wine, wherein is excess; but be filled with the Spirit; speaking to yourselves in psalms and hymns and spiritual songs, singing and making melody in your heart to the Lord (Eph. v. 18, 19).

Let the word of Christ dwell in you richly in all wisdom; teaching and admonishing one another in psalms and hymns and spiritual songs, singing with grace in your hearts to the Lord (Col. iii. 16).

And almost as often we hear the like admonition of James: 'Is any merry? let him sing psalms' (Jas. v. 13).[3] Saint Jerome

---

[1] E. K. Chambers, *Sir Thomas Wyatt and Some Collected Studies* (London, 1933), p. 99.

[2] The discovery of fragments of these early works is recounted by Chambers, *ibid.* pp. 111–16 and especially notes 1 and 2 on p. 113, and pp. 207–27.

[4] Unless otherwise stated, I have used quotations from the King James or Authorized Version of the Bible in this work where no question of wording seems significant.

had recorded the habit of making psalms the accompaniment of daily life in his 'little villa of Christ', Erasmus had been 'of the same oppynon & mynde, which saynte Hierome was of' as he hoped it might come to pass that labours of the plough-man, the weaver, the master of the ship, the housewife might be accompanied by Biblical song and story. Tyndale had echoed the words of Erasmus in pleading his own hopes for Christen-dom. Savonarola had set a precedent in having his spiritual songs sung to the tunes of the carnival songs which he wished to displace.

As I have said, probably the greatest of those who acknow-ledged the leadership of Savonarola was Martin Luther, to whose work Coverdale was largely indebted. Certainly Luther followed the example set by Savonarola when he came to the task of creating new divine songs for the German people and having them sung to popular tunes. The problem of creating a rival to secular song was one that he long considered, and it is recorded in the *Colloquia Mensalia*:

> *Luther* bade his Harper (at that time) plaie such a lesson as David plaid, I am persuaded (said he) if David now arose from the dead, so would hee much admire, how this Art of Musick is com to so great and an excelling height. Shee neuer came higher than now shee is. How is it (said Luther) that in *Carnalibus*, wee haue so many fine *Poëmata & Carmina*,…*but* in *Spiritualibus*…wee have such old and rotten things.[1]

Luther set about solving his problem systematically, as is evident in his letter to Spalatin:

> There is a plan afoot to follow the example of the prophets and fathers of the early Church and compose for the common people German psalms, that is spiritual songs, so that the Word of God may remain among the people in the form of song also. We are seeking every-where for poets, and since you are gifted with such knowledge of the German language and command so elegant a style, cultivated by much use, I beg that you will work with us in the matter…I wish that you would leave out all new words and words that are only

---

[1] Martin Luther, *Colloquia Mensalia*, trans. by Capt. Henrie Bell (London, 1652), p. 500. For a history of the work see Preserved Smith, *Luther's Table Talk: A Critical Study* (New York, 1907).

used at court. In order to be understood by the people, only the simplest and commonest words should be sung, but they should also be pure and apt and give a clear sense, as near as possible to that of the Psalter.

In 1524 the book of spiritual songs was published, two years after the German translation of the New Testament, Luther's preface explaining that he greatly desired 'the youth, who certainly should and must be trained in music and other proper and useful arts, to have something whereby they may be weaned away and freed from the love ballads and worldly (carnal) songs, and instead of these learn something wholesome and beneficial'.[1]

The Catholic Church had, of course, used song in its services, but the hymns and sequences were in Latin and were sung by the priests and choristers. Luther's hymn book was written in the vernacular, and the hymns could be sung by the whole congregation in the services of the church or by those who wished them as accompaniment to the round of their daily living.

Miles Coverdale, like Luther, was the first to give his country-men a complete Bible. Like Luther also he was the first to offer to his countrymen a collection of songs to rival the new secular poetry. Apparently some time before 1538[2] his *Goostly Psalms and Spirituall Songes* was printed, and most of the pieces in his collection have been traced to Luther's German originals. He prefaced his work by three quotations, the one from Colossians and the one from James (already quoted here) and one from Psalm cxlvi. The *envoy* 'To the Boke' announced his purpose:

[1] The letter is quoted by F. Eby, *Early Protestant Educators* (New York and London, 1931), pp. 156–7, from the translation by Preserved Smith and C. N. Jacobs in *Luther's Correspondence and Other Contemporary Letters*. For Luther's preface see *Works of Martin Luther*, printed for the United Lutheran Church in America (Philadelphia, 1932), vol. VI, pp. 283–4.

[2] Attached to the copy of Coverdale's work which I saw in the Bodleian Library, where it was on loan from the Queen's College as part of the Music Exhibition, is a manuscript note dated 11.12.29. from Lieut.-Col. Isaac, signed F.S. Isaac, which says, 'The boke of the goostly psalms has preliminary matter, including Coverdale's preface, printed in a different and later type, than the psalms and music. The psalms begin at a¹. Both words and music are in J. Rastel's type which is worn. The ink on a¹–f is faded. The omission of "ad imprimendum solum" in the colophon puts the date of the printing before the act of 1538.'

Go lytle boke, get the acquaintaunce
Amonge the lovers of Gods worde
Geve them occasyon the same to avaunce
And to make theyr songes of the Lorde
That they may thrust under the borde
All other balettes of fylthynes
And that we all with one accorde
May geve ensample of godlynes.

The prefaced address to 'the Christen reader' followed closely the plea of Erasmus:

would God that our mynstrels had none other thynge to playe upon, nether our carters & plow men othe thynge to whistle upon, save Psalmes, hymnes, and such godly songes as David is occupied with all. And yf women syttynge at theyr rockes, or spynnynge at the wheles, had none other songes to passe theyr tyme withall, than soch as Moses sister, Elchanas wife, Debora, and Mary the mother of Christ have song before them, they shulde be better occupied, then with hey nony nony, hey trely loly, & soch lyke fantasies.

His purpose was made further explicit:

to geve oure youth of Englonde some occasion to chaunge theyr foule & corrupte balettes into swete songes and spirituall Hymnes of Gods honoure, and for theyr owne consolacion in hym, I have here (good reader) set out certayne comfortable songes grounded on Gods worde, and taken some out of the holy scripture, specyally out of the Psalmes of David, At whom wolde God that oure Musicians wolde lerne to make theyr songes: & that they which are disposed to be mery, wolde in theyr myrth folowe the councell of saynt Paule and saynt James and not to passe theyr tyme in naughty songes of fleshly love and wantonesse, but with syngnge of Psalmes and soch songes as edifye, & corrupte not mens conversacyon.

'As for the comen sorte of balettes which are now used in the world,' Coverdale asked, 'Corrupte they not the manners of yonge persones? Do they not tangle them in the snares of unclennesse?' And he gave a particular warning to the courtier not to rejoice in naughty songs.

The *Dictionary of Hymnology* describes the contents of the Coverdale book: 'Following Luther's large-hearted adoption of materials from many sources, it contains Psalm versions, paraphrases of Latin hymns, and fifteen other hymns.'[1] Airs were provided to which the poems were to be sung, but it is to be noted that, instead of using the new verse forms being introduced from Italy and France, Coverdale imitated the German originals of the poems. The stanzas of four, seven, nine, ten, and thirteen lines striving for an iambic pace are arranged with a variety of rhyme schemes, with occasionally 'Kirieleyson' and 'Alleluya' as refrains. Though the 'balettes' were, as he confessed, 'rude in songe and ryme', the purpose with which he sent them forth and the precedent which they established make them significant in the history of the creation of a divine literature. That Coverdale published in 1545 an abridgement of Erasmus's *Enchiridion* is but one indication of that writer's influence in his work.

Certainly by 1542 the popularity of romantic story and love poetry was sufficient to cause Thomas Becon in his *Golden Boke of Christen Matrimonye* to offer the Psalms and 'godly songs' as an antidote, for advising 'How daughters and maydens must be kept', he wrote:

lette them not reade bokes of fables, of fond and lyght love, but call upon God to have pure hartes and chaste....Bokes of Robyn Hood, Beves of Hampton, Troylus, & such lyke fables do but kyndle in lyers lyke lyes and wanton love....If ye delyght to synge songes ye have the Psalmes and many godly songes & bokes in Englysh right frutefull & swett.

He was bitter that now 'to synge vayne songes of rybaudry, is called good pastyme'.

Becon saw the singing of the Psalms, not as isolated for periods of devotion, but as the proper accompaniment of all the activities of daily life, for he notes in *Davids Harpe* (published also in 1542):

Would God that all men of honour would nourish such minstrels in their houses, as David is, and that might sing unto them both at dinner and supper, yea, and at all other times, these most sweet and delectable songs of David! so should both they and all their family

---

[1] John Julian (London, 1915), pp. 264–70. The article on Coverdale is by H. L. Bennett. A. F. Mitchell in his Introduction to the Scottish Text Soc. edition of *A Compendious Book of Godly and Spiritual Songs* (Edinburgh and London, 1897) discusses the relation of Coverdale's book to the Scottish work.

be disposed to live more virtuously than many be now-a-days, and be provoked to leave their pompous, gallant, wicked, venereal, fleshly, beast-like, and unclean manner of living. Would God also that all fathers and mothers, all masters and mistresses, would bring up their children and servants in the singing of these most godly songs! Again, would God that all schoolmasters and teachers of youth would, instead of Virgil, Ovid, Horace, Catullus, Tibullus, Propertius, &c., teach these verses of David! For so should they not only obtain eloquence, but also divine erudition, godly knowledge, spiritual wisdom, and increase in all kind of virtue.[1]

It is noteworthy too that he here wishes to substitute scripture for the great Latin classics in the schoolroom.

Becon, in dedicating *The New Pollecye of Warre* to Sir Thomas Wyatt, offered it in part 'forasmuch as ye have ever hitherto earnestly embraced not only the studies of human letters, but also the grave exercises of divine literature'. Chambers comments on Becon's attack on the *Court of Venus* as a 'filthy' book in the 1564 edition of his works that he does not appear conscious that one of the contributors was the Sir Thomas Wyatt to whom he dedicated the book on war in 1542, but Chambers was unaware that the *Golden Boke of Christen Matrimonye* had been published in 1542 and again in 1543, and that Becon in these early editions had written vigorously against the new secular poetry.[2]

[1] Parker Soc. edition of *The Early Works of Thomas Becon* (Cambridge, 1843), p. 267.
[2] *S.T.C.* nos. 1723 and 1724. Why Chambers failed to note these earlier editions is a mystery.

CHAPTER V

THE PSALMS AS ENGLISH POETRY UNDER EDWARD VI

THE courtiers at Henry the Eighth's court were indeed, much as Chambers said, given to the writing of 'balettes', but literary historians have been curiously affected with a critical astigmatism which makes them generally disregard a massive component of the lyric poetry which they wrote. Yet the courtiers, as well as those about the court who cannot be styled courtiers but who were attached to the court by some more or less official position, were producing a quite considerable amount of sacred poetry and sacred song, and those about the young Edward VI when he came to be king followed the habit enthusiastically. To give a complete account of this poetry would take a volume about as large as Julian's *Dictionary of Hymnology*, and I can here undertake only the more humble task of attempting to show the spirit in which the ideal was maintained which had been set by the example of Jerome in his 'little villa of Christ' and by Savonarola in his Spiritual Songs, and proclaimed by Erasmus and Tyndale. Coverdale had followed Luther in setting forth his work, but the great stream of English divine poetry during the century did not spring from Germany, for English poetry in general did not find its models there.

Padelford has summed up the contributions of the Earl of Surrey and Sir Thomas Wyatt, 'the most distinguished poets of the early Renaissance school', saying that 'Attentive readers of the contemporary French, Italian, and Spanish poets and emulous of their achievements, they modernized English prosody and experimented successfully with poetry of various types'.[1] Even C. S. Lewis, who refuses to use the word *Renaissance*[2] except in quotation marks, and who classes Wyatt and

---

[1] F. M. Padelford, *The Poems of Henry Howard, Earl of Surrey*, revised edition, *University of Washington Publications: Language and Literature*, vol. 5 (Seattle, 1928), p. 44.

[2] *English Literature in the Sixteenth Century* (Oxford, 1954), pp. 55–6.

Surrey among the 'drab' poets, does concede that 'the grand function of the Drab Age poets was to build a firm metrical highway out of the late medieval swamp'.[1] At any rate, recent critics agree with Padelford that the 'greater credit for achieving these reforms must be given to Sir Thomas Wyatt rather than to the younger poet'.[2] Both poets made their contribution to divine poetry, and here I think that of Wyatt must again be considered as more important than that of Surrey.

In 1542 Becon, as we have already seen, commended Wyatt as one who had 'embrased not only the studies of humaine letters, but also the grave exercises of divine literature'. Since Wyatt died in 1542, his poetry obviously pre-dated that year, but his divine poetry was not published as far as we know until 1549, when I. Raynold and John Harrington printed *Certayne Psalmes chosen out of the Psalter of David commonlye called the vii Penytentiall Psalmes, drawen into englysche meter by Sir Thomas Wyat Knight.*[3] The work is quite different from Coverdale's. Coverdale wanted the people to sing songs of Godly content instead of the 'naughty songs' he was hearing; Wyatt put the Psalms into the stream of English literature, using the verse forms which he had brought from the continent to England.

In 1527 Wyatt had travelled to Italy as a member of an embassy to the papal court, and it has been popularly assumed that it was this visit which inspired him to introduce into English verse the sonnet, *terza rima*, and *ottava rima*. When he became acquainted with the Italian prose version of the Penitential Psalms of Aretino which were published in 1536 is

---

[1] P. 237.

[2] P. 44. See also Kenneth Muir, *Collected Poems of Sir Thomas Wyatt* (London, 1949), pp. xvii–xviii, and E. M. W. Tillyard, *The Poetry of Sir Thomas Wyatt* (London, 1929), p. 55.

[3] The name is spelled *Harryngton* in this edition, but his son's (Sir John's) is usually spelled with one *r*. The manuscript sources for Wyatt's poems are summarized by Tillyard, pp. 51–2 and 149, but all accounts are indebted to Miss A. K. Foxwell's *Study*. In her edition, *The Poems of Sir Thomas Wiat* (London, 1913), vol. II, p. 133, she stated that no copy of the 1549 edition was extant, and Tillyard echoed the statement, p. 52. However, two copies are registered in the *S.T.C.* (no. 2726) as in Cambridge libraries. I have not seen a copy but am indebted to Professor William Jackson for information concerning it and Muir records the title, p. 275. No. 2727 is apparently a ghost. Miss Foxwell chose to use the spelling Wiat throughout her work.

uncertain, but it was on the plan devised by Aretino of setting
these Psalms in a narrative framework that he constructed his
own arrangement. However, Miss Foxwell says that 'Aretino
ceases to become a model in the substance of the Psalms. Then
Wiat relies upon the English version, and keeps close to the
Great Bible, or to the 1530 Psalter',[1] the prose Psalter which
according to the colophon had been 'Emprinted at Argentine'
(perhaps Strassburg), and the title-page of which records it as
translated after 'the text of ffeline' (Martin Bucer). The impetus
to this particular task was probably furnished by Wyatt's visit
as part of an embassy to the French Court in 1539, for it was
then, Miss Foxwell says, that 'on the occasion of the Emperor's
passing through France to the Netherlands, C. Marot presented
these Psalms to Charles V'.[2]

It seems well at this moment to turn briefly to consider the
contribution of Clement Marot, a poet who turned to reform
and ultimately to Calvinism, rather than a reformer who turned
to poetry; an expert in 'courtiers' trifles', who established the
Psalms as great poetry in the vernacular. It will be remembered
that Marguerite of Angoulême, later Queen of Navarre, the
sister of François of France, had been, with her brother,
sympathetic to the reforming movement in religion, and though
she never left the Catholic Church, had been less yielding than
he to political pressures in regard to the products of that movement. Anne Boleyn had been one of her maids of honour, and
Anne's daughter, the little Princess Elizabeth, later translated
one of her poems into English as *A Godly Medytacyon of the
Christen Sowle*, seen into print in 1548 by John Bale[3] with a
dedication to the translator. A metrical version of Psalm xiv
was appended. Marguerite wrote Biblical dramas which, with
'Le Miroir' and other poems, were published as *Marguerites*

---

[1] Foxwell, *Poems*, vol. II, p. 136. Another possible source was proposed by
H. A. Mason, 'Wyatt and the Psalmes', London, *Times Lit. Sup.* 27 February
1953, p. 144.

[2] Foxwell, vol. II, p. 135.

[3] Bale wrote in his dedication: 'I receyved your noble boke ryght frutefully
of you translated out of the frenche tunge into Englysh. I receyved also your
golden sentences out of the sacred scriptures, with no lesse grace than lernynge
in foure 1 oble languages, Latyne, Greke, Frenche, & Italyane, most ornately,
fynely, & purely with your owne hande.'

[*Pearls*] *de la Marguerite*, and Clement Marot was for a time *valet de chambre* to her before he became *valet de chambre* to her brother King François.

When Marot's *Psaumes de David* was published with a dedication to King François, the humanist scholar is apparent in his proclaiming God as David's Apollo, the Holy Ghost as his Calliope, heaven as his Parnassus, and when he measures David's poems against those of Homer and Horace. However, when he follows this dedication by an address '*Aux dames de France*' we hear once more the familiar plea of Erasmus:

> O bien hereux qui veoir pourra
> Fleurir le temps, que l'on orra
> Le laboureur à sa charrue,
> Le charretier parmy la rue,
> Et l'artisan en sa boutique,
> Avecques un pseaume ou cantique
> En son labeur se soulager!
> Heureux qui orra le berger
> Et la bergere au boys estans
> Faire que rochers & estangs,
> Après eulx chantent la haulteur
> Du sainct nom de leur Créateur![1]

Marot's Psalms were set to music popular in that day, and they became the rage at court and in the country. Margaret Walker Freer recorded some of the queer alliances: 'Diane de Poitiers sang the psalm commencing with the words "*Du fond de ma pensée*" set to the popular dance tune, "*Le Branle de Poitou*"; and Catherine de Medici, in allusion to her husband's infidelities, profanely appropriated the sixth psalm, arranged to the air "Des Bouffons", "Ne veuilles pas, ô Sire, etc."'[2] François accepted the dedication, and the Psalms maintained their popularity in spite of the Sorbonne and many of the clergy. The modifications that they had to undergo after Marot fled to Geneva, Calvin's theories about church music, and Bèze's

[1] See Waldo S. Pratt, *The Significance of the Old French Psalter Begun by Clement Marot in 1532. Papers of the Hymn Society*, no. 4 (New York, 1933). I have quoted from *Les Oeuvres de Clement Marot*, ed. J. Plattard (Paris, 1931), vol. v, pp. 195, 200. On Spenser and Marot see *The Shepheardes Calendar*, ed. W. L. Renwick (London, 1930), pp. 176, 180, 220.

[2] *The Life of Marguerite d'Angoulême, Queen of Navarre, Duchesse d'Alençon and De Berry* (Cleveland and London, 1895), p. 278.

contributions are not in place here, but the manner in which a vernacular Psalter had its beginnings in France has a bearing on the history of the translation of the Psalms into English.

Tillyard says that Wyatt wrote his English poems in Italian or French forms 'to show that an English poet could compete with the foreigner on his own ground', and that when he translated the Psalms he matched himself with Marot and Aretino.[1] Since Wyatt did not publish his version of the Seven Penitential Psalms himself, and the dedication comes from their publisher, John Harrington, the only basis on which we can build any surmise as to his intent is the general tone of the poetry, together with the sonnet written by Surrey and inscribed as a preface to them in the manuscript used by Miss Foxwell in her edition of his poetry, from which I quote:[2]

> The great Macedon that out of Persë chasyd
> Darius, of whose huge power all Asy rang,
> In the riche arke of Homers rymes be placyd,
> The fayned gestes of Hethen Prynces sang.
>
> What holly grave, what wourthy sepulture,
> To Wyates Psalmes shud Christians then purchase?
> When he dothe paynte the lyvely faythe, and pure:
> The stedfast hoope the swete returne to grace
>
> Of just Davyd, by parfite penytence:
> Where Rewlers may se in a myrror clere
> The bitter frewte of false concupiscence,
> From Jewry bought Uryas deathe full dere.
>
> In Prynces hartes goddes scourge yprynted depe
> Myght them awake out of their synfull slepe.

Wyatt wrote a prologue in *ottava rima* to each of the seven Psalms, the prologues forming a narrative to give significance to the Psalms, as can be seen in this first stanza of the first prologue:

> Love to gyve law unto his subject hertes
> Stode in the Iyes of Barsabe the bryght,
> And in a look anone hymsellff convertes
> Cruelly pleasant byfore Kyng David syght;

---

[1] Tillyard, p. 22.

[2] The Penitential Psalms are printed in vol. I, pp. 203–50, Psalm xxxvii in the preceding pages 197–202. Muir separates the Sackville sonnet from the Wyatt Psalms, pp. xxxiii, 203–26.

> First dasd his Iyes, and forder forth he stertes
> With venemed breth, as sofftly as he myght
> Towcht his sensis, and over ronne his bonis
> With creping fyre, spasplid for the nonis.

Love enters through the eyes as Plato would have it, and Wyatt tells of David's lust, of his sending 'Urye' to his certain death, of the prophet Nathan's chiding 'By murder for to clok Adulterye', and of David's repentance, so that,

> His harpe he taketh in hand to be his guyde,
> Wherewith he offereth his plaintes, his sowle to save.

The sixth of the Psalms closes with the prophetic hope that the Lord will redeem Israel, and the seventh prologue takes the theme offered by the word *redeem*, departing from Aretino's prose link, to picture David 'As in a traunce' foreseeing the coming of Christ to effect his salvation.

Surrey's sonnet compared David with Homer, Wyatt's seven prologues in *ottava rima* told David's story, and it remained for the seven Psalms rendered in *terza rima* to complete this offering of divine poetry in the verse forms newly imported from Italy and established in secular poetry for long years thereafter. Wyatt also translated Psalm xxxvii in *terza rima*, seemingly having decided upon this form as that most appropriate to the songs of David.

Surrey's fame rests chiefly upon his use of a sonnet form which Shakespeare perfected and upon his introduction of blank verse in his translation of two books of the *Aeneid*, but he did not use these metrical patterns in his translations from the Bible of the first five chapters of Ecclesiastes and of four Psalms—viii, lv, lxxiii, and lxxxviii. In these he used poulter's measure, except in Psalm lv, where he experimented with an unrhymed hexameter verse. Surrey's translations are very free, and the last three are very personal. Psalms lxxiii and lxxxviii have each a prologue which emphasizes their personal application, and it is worthy of note that Surrey, a member of a great Catholic family, was here writing his translations as a means to expressing his own grief, not as a means to furnishing a rival poetry to pagan and secular verse. Yet in the prologue to Wyatt's Psalms, he had contrasted the superior claims of poetry for Christians of these songs of David over 'Homer's rymes', which 'The fayned gestes of Hethen Prynces sang'. The defenders of putting the Psalms into English all claimed that in the Psalms could be found guidance for men's lives as well as a response to every emotional need. It is in this way that Surrey used them, as a very present help in time of trouble. The exception is found in Psalm viii, which asks in other words, 'What is man, that thou art mindful of him?' as he rehearses the wonders which the Lord has wrought. It is not, I think, right to call it, as Surrey's latest biographer calls it, 'polite verse',[1] but it was possibly written before serious ills befell him, because translating the Psalms was a habit at court. Surrey was brought to trial and executed in January, 1547. During the preceding time of his imprisonment he turned to the Psalms, addressing the prologues of two of them to particular men, one to George Blage, with whom Surrey had the quarrel which precipitated his trial, and the other to Sir Anthony Denny, one of the secretaries of the King, 'who must have had a hand in Surrey's downfall'—so Padelford describes them. To Blage he wrote in the prologue to Psalm lxxiii:

> But now, my Blage, myne errour well I see;
> Such goodlye light King David giveth me.

To Denny he addressed the prologue which concluded:

> My Deny, then myne errour, depe imprest,
> Began to worke dispaire of libertye,
> Had not David, the perfyt warriour, tought
> That of my fault thus pardon shold be sought.

C. S. Lewis says that Surrey's religious works 'are, of course, not good', and finds their significance in that he was 'trying to reform poulter's measure'. It seems to me that in the face of danger and death Surrey was more likely to seek courage and consolation in the spiritual message of the Psalms than to try to reform the poulter's measure, but I am not a poet.[2]

That there were many others besides Wyatt and Surrey who were translating the Psalms in prose and poetry is apparent to anyone who reads the *Short-Title Catalogue* or who seeks the

[1] Edwin Casady, *Henry Howard, Earl of Surrey* (New York, 1938), p. 208, n. 53.
[2] Padelford, pp. 42–3. Lewis, p. 232.

records of unpublished works, but the most important of the translations were those which were to be set to music, as were the great number of lyrics at the time. Of the long history of psalmody in England I cannot speak here, but of the beginnings of the movement to have the English metrical versions of the Psalms sung, it is necessary to take note, and those beginnings centre about Thomas Sternhold. The way in which his life parallels that of Marot has often been noted, for he was groom of the chamber to Henry VIII and to Edward VI, as Marot was to Marguerite and to François I, and his versions were first sung at court as were those of Marot. Puttenham wrote that 'king *Henry* the 8, her *Majesties* father, for a few Psalmes of *David* turned into English meetre by Sternhold, made him groome of his privy chamber & gave him many other good gifts'.[1] Anthony à Wood gave another account, saying that 'he became so scandaliz'd at the amorous and obscene Songs used in the court, that he forsooth turn'd into English meteer 51 of *Davids Psalms*, and caused musical notes to be set to them, thinking thereby that the courtiers would sing them instead of their sonnets, but did not, only some few excepted'.[2]

There has been some cavilling about Wood's statement by the more sceptical of modern critics,[3] but this is what Sternhold said when he dedicated his work to Edward VI, in whose reign it was apparently first printed:[4]

Seyng furdre that youre tender and godlye zeale doeth more delyght in the holy songes of veritie than in any fayned rymes of vanitie, I am encouraged to travayle furdre in the sayed boke of psalmes, trustyng that as your grace taketh pleasure to hear them song sumtimes of me, so ye wil also delight not onely to see & read them your selfe, but also to commaund them to be song to you of others, that as ye have the Psalme it selfe in youre mynde, so ye may judge myne endevoure by your eare.

[1] G. Gregory Smith, *Elizabethan Critical Essays* (London, 1904, 1937), vol. II, p. 17.

[2] *Athenae Oxonienses* (London, 1691), vol. I, col. 62.

[3] Hallett Smith, 'English Metrical Psalms in the Sixteenth Century and their Literary Significance', *Huntington Library Quarterly*, vol. IX, pp. 249–71, and 'The Art of Sir Thomas Wyatt', pp. 323–55.

[4] The *S.T.C.* gives as conjectural the date 1547 for *Certayne Psalmes chosen out of the Psalter of David, & drawen into English Metre by Thomas Sternhold grome of the kinges magesties Roobes.*

No one, I think, has noticed the reference which goes far to confirm Wood's account to be found in William Baldwin's dedication to the same king of his metrical version of *The Canticles or Balades of Salomon* [The Song of Songs] published in 1549:

> Would god that suche songes myght once drive out of office the baudy balades of lecherous love that commonly are indited and song of idle courtyers in princes and noble mens houses. They are not fine ynough sum will answer: well then woulde I wish that such fine felowes would becum course ynough for suche course matters. The coursest frise best pleaseth the finest of them in winter. And I doubt not but theyr colde soules shoulde be kept warme with these course songes, if in the winter of theyr frosen faythe, & clumsed charitie, they woulde tunably to syng them.

Baldwin is known to have been working on plays and pastimes presented at the court of Edward VI during the Christmas season of 1552–3, and it is reasonable to suppose that as he writes of Sternhold to the king in 1549 he knows whereof he speaks:

> I speake not this of these balades alone, but of all other of lyke matter: as psalmes, and himnes: In which the apostle woulde have them rejoice, to be exercised. To whiche your Majesty hath alredy geven a notable ensample, in causyng the psalmes brought in to fine englysh meter, by youre godly disposed servaunt Thomas Sternholde, to be song openly before your grace in the hearyng of all your subjectes. Which good example, I beseche GOD all your subjectes may have grace to follow.

It would seem probable that in a Tudor court the courtiers' taste would follow the king's. However, Sternhold did not write his metrical versions of the Psalms in the verse forms of courtly verse, as Wyatt did, but in ballad measures. As Julian says, common metre became almost a consecrated measure, three-quarters of the Psalms composed by him or his followers, Hopkins and Norton, being composed in this metre.

Most critics have agreed with Thomas Fuller that these translators were 'men whose piety was better than their poetry; and they drank more of Jordan than of Helicon', but nevertheless he thought that their verses 'go abreast with the best poems of those times',[1] and John Playford said of their verse that 'it was ranked with the best *English* Poesie at that time'.[2]

That the original purpose of Sternhold's work was not lost sight of is attested by *The Whole Booke of Psalmes* with all its accretions, published by John Daye in 1562 which states on the title-page that it is 'very mete to be used of all sortes of people privately for their solace & comfort: laying apart all ungodly Songes and Ballades, which tende only to the norishing of vyce, and corrupting of youth'. The title-page, it should be noted, bears too the quotations from James and from Paul to the Colossians.[3]

Another musician about the court of Edward VI as a member of the Chapel Royal was William Hunnis, whose *Certayne Psalmes drawen into English meter* was printed in 1550 by the widow of John Herforde for John Harrington, the John Harrington who had in 1549 printed Wyatt's Penitential Psalms. Hunnis in this edition is called servant to Sir William Herbert, but from sometime between 1550 and 1553 he became a member of the Chapel Royal. Most of his work falls, however, in the reign of Elizabeth, to be discussed in the next chapter. This early volume of 1550 contained only a few Psalms in common metre, together with certain Biblical songs, and the *Complaint of a Sinner.*[4]

William Forrest, a Catholic who wrote a sympathetic poem about Queen Katherine and was later chaplain to Queen Mary, also wrote versions of the Psalms which should be noted here, though they were not printed till the nineteenth century, for

---

[1] Julian, p. 857; Hallett Smith, p. 250.

[2] *Psalms & Hymns* (London, 1671) in prefatory 'Original of Singing Psalms in Metre'.

[3] A manuscript note on the 1560 edition in the British Museum catalogue says the copy is not complete, but pieced.

[4] Mrs C. C. Stopes in *William Hunnis and the Revels of the Chapel Royal: Materialen zur Kunde des älteren Englishen Dramas*, vol. 29 (Louvain, 1910). Mrs Stopes collected practically all the information available at that time about the *Court of Venus*, the beginnings of English psalmody, and other related matters. About Hunnis she remains our chief authority, though she is inclined to credit him with more poems and dramas than have generally been thought to be his. See also her article 'The Metrical Psalms and the *Court of Venus*', *Athenaeum*, 24 June 1899, pp. 784–6.

he dedicated his work to the Duke of Somerset, Protector to King Edward, and his dedication noted the change that had taken place in court music in his time and paid tribute to Sternhold:

> Instead of balades dissonaunte and light,
> Godly Psalmes receaved are in place,
> Conveyde in meatre of numbre and feete right,
> As unto ryme apperteyneth the grace,
> Sung to the vyall, lute, treble or base,
> Or other instrument, pleasinge to the eare,
> With whiche commutation ought each man to beare.
>
> The first that so endevored his payne
> (As I have herde, and perfectlye doe knowe)
> Was Thomas Sterneholde, by Atropos slayne,
> The pyked beste of Psalmysters rowe,
> Whois stepps dyverse attemptethe to followe,
> And dothe full well, worthye of highe prayse;
> God contynue them in their godlye wayse![1]

The first to publish the whole *Psalter of David translated into Englysh metre* was Robert Crowley, best known today for having printed in 1550 three editions of *Piers Plowman*. His edition of the *Psalter* was printed by himself in 1549 and, besides including the whole Psalter, he printed 'all the canticles that are usually songe in the church'. Crowley's version was made from the translation of Leo Juda, and it provided for all the poems to be sung to 'a note or song of .iiij. partes, which agreth wyth the letre of this Psalter'. The address 'To the Christian Reader' stated his purpose 'to move the to delyte in the readynge and hearynge of these Psalmes, wherein lyeth the most precious treasure of the christen religion'.[2]

In 1553 Frances Seager published *Certayne Psalmes selected out of the Psalter of David, and drawen into English Metre, with Notes to every Psalme in .iiij. partes to Synge.* The work was dedicated to Lord Russell (later the second Earl of Bedford), the author terming himself 'his lordships humble orator'. A poem was

---

[1] For other work of Forrest see ch. XI.

[2] For accounts of Crowley, see Christina H. Garret, *The Marian Exiles* (Cambridge, 1938), and Albert Paul, *Robert Crowley: Puritan, Printer, Poet* (Manchester, 1937), a lecture to the Presbyterian Historical Society of England.

appended, 'A Discription of the lyfe of man, the world, and vanities thereof' in the common metre. When in 1557 Seager published the book by which he is best known, *The Schoole of Vertue and Booke of Good Nourture for Chyldren and Youth to Learne theyr Dutie By*, Robert Crowley was joint author and seems to have contributed the second section of the book. Seager was one of the contributors to the *Mirror for Magistrates*, but it is by his courtesy book rather than by his psalmody or his *Mirror* tragedy that he is remembered. That he and Crowley were joint authors of this work and that they both published translations of the Psalms is a point of interest, as is the fact that one dedicated his translations to Lord Herbert, the other to Lord Russell, for it will, I think, become apparent that the creation of a Biblical literature was to a great extent undertaken by those about the court and those who were attached in some way to the leading figures of the court where the monarch was sympathetic to such activity.

CHAPTER VI

THE PSALMS AS ENGLISH POETRY UNDER ELIZABETH I

THE reign of Mary, 1553–8, inevitably produced a hiatus in the publication of Biblical song in the English language, but the publication of miscellanies of predominantly secular verse—and love poetry at that—proceeded apace, with Tottel issuing the volume of *Songes and Sonnettes* in June of 1557 and following it with a second edition in July of the same year. The *Court of Venus* was licensed in 1557–8, but one or more editions had certainly been printed earlier, for in 1550 John Hall had attacked it by name, linking it with 'other bookes of lecherous Ballades'. The publication of such miscellanies went steadily on after Elizabeth became Queen and provide the great storehouse of Elizabethan lyric poetry known to all students of literature. Tottel's book was issued in six new editions by 1587, *The Paradise of Daintie Devises* in nine editions between 1576 and 1609, and there were others to crowd the book-stalls before Francis Davison published in 1602 *A Poetical Rhapsody*, called by Hoyt Hudson 'the last of the Elizabethan miscellanies'.[1] A broadside by Thomas Brice in 1561–2 shouted the indignation of the righteous:

What meane the rimes that run thus large in every shop to sell?
With wanton sound, and filthie sense, me thinke it grees not well
We are not Ethnickes we forsooth, at least professe not so
Why range we then to Ethnickes trade? come bak, where will ye go?
Tel me is Christ, or Cupide Lord? doth God or Venus reigne?
And whose are we? whom ought we serve? I aske it, answere plaine
If wanton Venus then go forth, if Cupide, keep your trade
If God, or Christ, come bak the best, or sure you will be made
Doth God? is he the Lord in deed? and should we him obey?[2]

---

[1] For later reference see Arthur Dent, *The Plaine Mans Pathway to Heaven*, first published in 1601. I have seen the 1603 edition. A summary of facts concerning 'Elizabethan Miscellanies' is found in J. W. Hebel and Hoyt H. Hudson, *Poetry of the English Renaissance 1509–1660* (New York, 1929), pp. 947–50.

[2] 'Against filthy writing / and such delighting' in the Heber Collection of Broadsides and Ballads now in the Huntington Library.

For some reason it was *The Court of Venus* that among all the miscellanies was attacked by name, perhaps because its very title flaunted its wares and gave offence. At the end of Elizabeth's reign it was still being decried by the godly. It remained for Hall, however, to provide an anti-body to the work which as early as 1550 he had castigated.[1] This he did in *The Court of Vertue: contaynyng many holy songs, sonnets, psalmes and ballettes*, which was published in 1565. Nine muses appropriate for help to a Christian poet are called upon: virtue, faith, love, hope, wisdom, temperance, patience, constancy, and meekness or humility. The three Christian graces (Arete, Spes, and Charitas) are also invoked, though their functions would seem somewhat to overlap those of the muses. At any rate, apparently confident of the assistance of this noble hierarchy, Hall ventured into vision literature, probably with Sackville's 'Induction' published in the 1563 edition of the *Mirror for Magistrates* in mind. Twice he dreams, and at last as Hope, Love, and Vertue come to him, Vertue recites the evil that men are doing because they have forsaken God's word:

> Such as in carnall love rejoyce,
> Trim songes of love they wyll compile,
> And synfully with tune and voyce,
> They syng their songes in pleasant stile,
> To Venus that same strompet vyle:
> And make of hir a goddes dere,
> In lecherie that had no pere.
>
> A booke also of songes they have,
> And Venus court they do it name,
> No fylthy mynde a songe can crave,
> But therein he may finde the same:
> And in suche songes is all their game.
> Whereof ryght dyvers bookes be made,
> To nuryshe that most fylthy trade.
> [She then charges him]
> That thou thyne exercise doe brynge,
> To make a boke of songes holy,
> Godly and wyse, blamyng foly.

[1] *A court of Venus Moralized* was entered to Richard Field in 1568, but is apparently not known otherwise.

Accordingly Hall produced a Christian miscellany, many of the pieces being provided with melodies to which they could be sung, and on occasion offering an arrangement for four-part singing. Certain Psalms, songs from the Bible, a portion of Ecclesiasticus, pious poems for all occasions, wisdom sayings were offered—everything rendered in a variety of metres, and all constituting regrettable poetry to set up as a rival volume to the growing number of miscellanies. The most striking venture is the attempt to write what Chambers calls 'spiritual parodies' of certain popular songs, noting especially parodies of Wyatt's 'My lute, awake', 'My pen, take pain', and 'Blame not my lute'.[1] It may be worth seeing how Hall goes about it in the most popular of the three:

> Blame not my lute though it do sounde
> the rebuke of your wicked sinne
> but rather seke as ye are bound
> to know what case that ye are in:
> And though this songe doe sinn confute,
> and sharply wyckednes rebuke:
> blame not my lute.

More important than a miscellany of sacred and moral verse to rival the secular poetry which was so rapidly increasing was the renewed publication, after Elizabeth was safely on the throne, of the metrical version of the Psalms begun by Sternhold and continued by others. John Daye's title-page still bore the admonition to lay aside 'all ungodly Songes and Ballades, which tend to the nourishing of vyce and corrupting of youth'. The work had a long and honourable history, well summarized by John Playford in the next century:

> The whole Book of *Psalms* being thus translated into *English* Metre, and having apt *Tunes* set to them, was used and Sung only for Devotion in private Families; but soon after by permission, brought into the *Churches*, being printed and bound up with the Books of *Common-Prayer* and *Bibles*, with allowance to be Sung before *Morning* and *Evening Service*, and also before and after *Sermons*: And for many Years, this part of *Divine Service* was *Skilfully* and *Devoutly* performed, with delight and Comfort by many Honest and Religious people.[2]

[1] See ch. IV, n. 1 on p. 28.

[2] 'Original of Singing Psalms in Metre' in his *Psalms & Hymns in Solemn Musick* (London, 1671). See also his *Introduction to the Skill of Musick* (1674).

No less a person than Matthew Parker, Archbishop of Canterbury, was the author of another *Whole Psalter* published by Daye in 1567, an edition to which Thomas Tallis, a famous Catholic musician, contributed tunes.[1] Parker's translations were more venturesome than those of the Sternhold book, for he used not only the old ballad metres now sanctified as the metres of hymnology but also stanzas made up of lines of unequal length arranged in a variety of rhyming patterns. A quotation from 'Henrie Haward Earle of Surrie in his Ecclesiastes' appears rather surprisingly in the extensive prefatory material, but to the theme of this study, Parker's poem 'Of the vertue of Psalmes' is specially pertinent. I quote two stanzas:

> Depart ye songes: lascivious,
>   from lute, from harpe depart:
> Geve place to Psalmes: most vertuous,
>   and solace there your harte.

> Ye songes so nice: ye sonnets all,
>   of lothly lovers layes:
> Ye worke mens myndes: but bitter gall,
>   by phansies pevish playes.

William Hunnis, who had translated 'certayne Psalmes' published during the reign of Edward VI, turned again to divine poetry during the reign of Elizabeth, when he could describe himself as 'one of the Gentlemen of her Majesties honourable Chappel, and maister to the children of the same'. In 1583 *Seven Sobs of a Sorrowfull Soule for Sinne* was published, adequately described on the title-page as 'Comprehending those seven Psalmes of the *Princelie Prophet* DAVID, commonlie called Poenitentiall; framed into a forme of familiar praiers, and reduced into meeter'. But Hunnis was now venturing into broader fields, for the title-page also recorded additional poetry: 'his Handfull of Honisuckles; the Poore Widowes Mite; a Dialog betweene Christ and a sinner; divers godlie and pithie ditties, with a Christian confession of and to the Trinitie'. Neither the routine translations of the Psalms in common metre nor the religious poems seem to a modern reader to

[1] Concerning the date of composition see H. L. Bennett in Julian's *Dictionary*, p. 917.

deserve the ten editions of the work which were offered between 1583 and 1629.[1]

Other gentlemen of the Chapel Royal were publishing divine poetry, set to music that has received from later generations more appreciative notice than has that of William Hunnis, and among them all William Byrd ranks supreme. Of him E. H. Fellowes has said that by many authorities he 'is regarded not only as the greatest of all Tudor musicians, but the greatest English composer of all time'. Since church music is outside the limits set for this study, Byrd's church music (regarded as his best) cannot be considered here, but it is necessary to mention his *Psalmes, Sonets, & Songs of Sadnes and Pietie*, which was published in 1588. Byrd urged everyone to learn to sing, his final reason being that 'the better the voyce is, the meeter it is to honour and serve God therewith: and the voyce of man is chiefly to be imployed to that end'. The ten Psalms which are set to music for five-part singing were written in common metre and are of more interest to the musician than to the historian of literature, but they represent the effort to popularize the general singing of divine songs as the madrigals were being sung. Among the other pieces are the story of Susanna written in a six-line stanza and a lullaby sung by Mary when Herod threatens the life of the child Jesus. In 1589 Byrd published another collection, *Songs of Sundrie Natures*, containing the Penitential Psalms and Psalm 121 (all in common metre but with different musical settings), Susanna with new music, two Christmas carols, and other varied sacred works, some in prose.[2]

That Sidney's translation of the Psalms had to wait until the nineteenth century to be published and that Spenser's translation of the seven Penitential Psalms was allowed to be lost, while inferior poets found a popular audience for their offerings,

---

[1] I have seen the 1597 edition. See Stopes, ch. XVI, especially pp. 209–18 concerning the bibliographical problem in considering this work. See also above, ch. V, n. 2 on p. 43.

[2] For accounts of Byrd see E. H. Fellowes, *William Byrd* (London, 1936), and his preface in *The English Madrigal School* (London, 1920), vol. XIV. A view of Byrd with his Catholic associates is given in *John Gerard: The Autobiography of an Elizabethan*, trans. by Philip Caraman (London and New York, 1951). It is interesting to note that Father Gerard while in prison suffered from hearing 'lewd songs and Geneva hymns' (p. 77).

is a sad fact. That both great writers not only translated the
Psalms but went beyond these translations to other divine
works is, however, evidence of the developing movement
which reached its greatest glory in Milton.

Sidney's comment on the Psalms in his *Apology for Poetry*
presents the best introduction to his own English versions, for
it is both scholarly and personal. He recognized them as poetry,
as showing in their metrical form and in their rhetorical devices
the characteristics of true poetry, as well as in their penetrating
to that inner truth which makes them prophetic:

Among the Romans a Poet was called *Vates*, which is as much
as a Diviner, Foreseer, or Prophet,...And may I not presume a
little further, to shew the reasonablenes of this worde *Vates*? And
say that the holy *Davids* Psalmes are a divine Poem? If I doo, I shall
not do it without the testimonie of great learned men, both auncient
and moderne: but even the name Psalmes will speake for mee, which,
being interpreted, is nothing but songes. Then that it is fully written
in meeter, as all learned Hebricians agree, although the rules be not
yet fully found. Lastly and principally, his handeling his prophecy,
which is merely poetical. For what els is the awaking his musical
instruments; the often and free changing of persons; his notable
Prosopopeias, when he maketh you, as it were, see God comming in his
Majestie; his telling of the Beastes joyfulnes, and hills leaping, but
a heavenlie poesie, wherein almost hee sheweth himselfe a passionate
lover of that unspeakable and everlasting beautie to be seene by
the eyes of the minde, onely cleered by fayth?

Speaking of the three *kinds* of poetry, Sidney saw the Psalms as
one among the poetical parts of the Bible and recognized their
peculiar fitness to express men's thoughts in moments of joy
or sadness:

The chiefe both in antiquitie and excellencie were they that did
imitate the inconceivable excellencies of GOD. Such were *David* in
his Psalmes, *Salomon* in his song of Songs, in his Ecclesiastes, and
Proverbs, *Moses* and *Debora* in their Hymnes, and the writer of *Job*;
which, beside other, the learned *Emanuell Tremelius* and *Franciscus
Junius* doe entitle the poeticall part of the Scripture....In this kinde,
though in a full wrong divinitie, were *Orpheus, Amphion, Homer* in
his hymnes, and many other, both Greekes and Romaines: and this
Poesie must be used, by whosoever will follow S. *James* his counsell,
in singing Psalmes when they are merry: and I know is used with

the fruite of comfort by some, when, in sorrowful pangs of their death-bringing sinnes, they find the consolation of the never-leaving goodnesse.[1]

Sidney died in 1586, mourned as few have been mourned, and leaving his work unfinished. He had translated forty-three of his English Psalms, his sister, the Countess of Pembroke, completing the task he had undertaken. When the whole work was first published in 1823, from a manuscript transcribed by John Davies of Hereford, as a volume of the *Early English Poets* series, the title-page described the poems as 'translated into divers and sundry kindes of verse, more rare and excellent for the method and varietie than ever yet hath been done in English'. Yet only rarely has the modern historian of literature in considering Sidney's versification recognized that in his Psalms he was attempting metrical experiments just as he was in his Arcadian poems.[2] Generally using the iambic foot, he tried out a great variety of rhyme schemes with varied line lengths. Thus he used the *terza rima* rhyme scheme with a five-foot line in Psalm vii and with a four-foot line in Psalm xxx, he used a six-foot line with a rhyme royal structure in Psalm xviii, he experimented with tail rhyme, he tried an extra syllable as the rhyming syllable, he wrote a thirteen-line stanza in hexameters using only one rhyme.[3] Hallett Smith has identified fourteen of the forty-three as fashioned in imitation of metrical patterns used in the Marot–Bèze Psalter and others as using the rhyme scheme of the French original though varying the line pattern. The general idea of doing the translations in a variety of meters may also have come to Sidney from Marot, as Professor Smith suggests, but he did the Arcadian poems in a variety of metres, and Sidney was not the first in England to use variety in translating the Psalms.

The dignity and beauty of the Authorized Version is a

---

[1] G. G. Smith, vol. I, pp. 154–5 and 158.

[2] For the exception see Hallett Smith, 'English Metrical Psalms in the Sixteenth Century and their Literary Significance', *Huntington Library Quarterly*, vol. IX, pp. 248–71, and John Buxton, *Sir Philip Sidney and the English Renaissance* (London, 1954), pp. 152–5. Buxton (p. 114) notes that Byrd set two funeral songs for Sidney and one of his songs from *Astrophel and Stella* to music.

[3] Sidney, *Complete Works*, ed. A. Feuillerat (Cambridge, 1923), vol. III, pp. 187–246.

haunting memory as we listen to any of the metrical translations, but here is Sidney's opening stanza for the familiar Twenty-third Psalm:

> The Lord, the Lord my shepheard is,
> And so can never I
> Tast missery.
> He rests me in greene pasture his:
> By waters still, and sweete
> Hee guides my feete.

Sidney's interest in divine literature, as I have said, went beyond the Psalms, for he had begun the translation of *A Worke concerning the Trewnesse of the Christian Religion* by Philippe de Mornay, which was turned over to Arthur Golding to complete, and he had made a translation of part of the great divine work of Saluste du Bartas. Of this last I shall write later in considering the influence of the French poet on English writers of the time.

In 1600 Sir John Harington was writing to the Countess of Bedford, 'I have sent you heere the devine, and trulie devine translation of three of Davids psalmes, donne by that Excellent Countesse and in Poesie the mirrois of our Age', and it was in such terms that the Countess of Pembroke and her works were referred to by many.[1] She not only completed the translation

---

[1] N. E. McClure in *The Letters and Epigrams of Sir John Harington* (Philadelphia, 1930), p. 87. McClure has given in his Introduction the best available account of the relationship of the five John Haringtons prominent in this period. This Sir John and his father collected in manuscript a large number of poems by contemporary authors (p. 44 and n. 1) and, like his father, Sir John tried in 1592 to set up a private printing press. He sent his translations of 'Selected Psalms' to King James in 1612, desiring apparently to dedicate them to him. He noted the assistance given him in 'the resolucion of all doubtfull places' by Launcelot Andrewes, Bishop of Ely (Letters 61 and 62, pp. 142–4). His death in 1612 probably accounts for his failure to see these Psalms in print, but Thomas Park in *Nugae Antiquae* (London, 1804), vol. i, p. xxiv, says that 'His entire version of the Psalms' was in the collection of Francis Douce. Among the works printed from the assembled MSS. by him and his father in *Nugae Antiquae* are Surrey's Ecclesiastes and three of his Psalms, two of those by the Countess of Pembroke, and three of his own (vol. i, pp. 339–71, 403–10). Sir John paid tribute to the Countess's Psalm versions in an epigram (McClure, p. 310).

Since this book was written Ian Grimble's *The Harington Family* has been published in London and New York, giving much information about the family, but little about the publication of the Psalms. See pp. 75–164, especially pp. 90–1, 119, 193, 194.

of the Psalms, she wrote *A POEM on Our Saviour's Passion*, and most important of all she became famous as a patroness of religious literature.

Sir John Harington himself during the reign of King James undertook to translate the Psalms and sent them to the King for criticism. So many were those who put Psalms into English metre, and whose work now exists only in manuscript or is known by some reference to it, that we must conclude that the number of the devout who sought consolation or a pathway to heaven by this means was very great indeed. Even royalty turned to the task, but King James was the only royal author to have his versions published, and publication did not come until after his death. What remain can now be regarded as chiefly of interest to the historian of literature and, sometimes, of interest to the history of prosody. Nevertheless, it is of great importance to recognize that there was, centring about the metrical translation of the Psalms, a concerted movement to displace the new love poetry and the newly popularized pagan literature by a poetry founded on the Bible. The theme of all those who made their offerings continued to be that of Richard Rowlands's *Odes in Imitation of the Seven Penitential Psalms*, printed at Antwerp in 1601:

> The vaine conceits of loves delight
> I leave to *Ovids* arte,
> Of warres and bloody broyles to wryte
> Is fit for *Vergils* parte.
>
> Of tragedies in doleful tales
> Let *Sophocles* entreat:
> And how unstable fortune failes
> Al Poets do repeat.
>
> But unto our eternal king
> My verse and voyce I frame
> And of his saintes I meane to sing
> In them to praise his name.

CHAPTER VII

THE WORKS OF SOLOMON AS ENGLISH POETRY

FROM that which 'the learned *Emanuell Tremelius* and *Franciscus Junius* doe entitle the poeticall part of the Scripture',[1] Sidney noted particularly '*David* in his Psalmes, *Salomon* in his song of Songs, in his Ecclesiastes, and Proverbs, *Moses* and *Debora* in their Hymnes, and the writer of *Job*', as the 'chiefe both in antiquitie and excellencie'.[2] Other English writers of the sixteenth century also claimed for this Biblical poetry precedence in time as well as an inherent pre-eminence, and they cited authority for their claims. Thus Thomas Lodge wrote:

Beroaldus can witnes with me that David was a poet, and that his vayne was in imitating (as S. Jerom witnesseth) Horace, Flaccus, and Pindarus; sometimes his verse runneth in an Iambus foote, anone he hath recourse to a Saphic vaine, and *aliquando semipede ingreditur*. Ask Josephus, and he wil tel you that Esay, Job, and Salomon voutsafed poetical practices, for (if Origen and he fault not) theyre verse was Hexameter and pentameter. Enquire of Cassiodorus, he will say that all the beginning of Poetrye proceeded from the Scripture.[3]

Thomas Churchyard added marginal notes of comment to his *Musicall Consort of Heavenly Harmonie*: 'David sung the Liricke verses to his harp and these ebrue songs consisted of divers and unequall numbers, sometimes in Iambicks running other while'; 'Jeremiah wrote his funerall lamentations in saphycks long before Simonides the Greeke poet'; 'Isaias wrote sacred Odes & holie verses'; 'The song of Sydrack and his fellowes in the hot flame was in verses'; 'Moises by some is thought the first deviser of verse, and his sister Marie devised the exameter'.[4] Ben Johnson in *Timber* made the genealogy specific: 'Poesy... had her original from heaven, received thence from the

---

[1] Isaac Baroway, 'Tremelius, Sidney and Biblical Verse', *Modern Language Notes*, vol. XL (1934), pp. 145–9.   [2] G. G. Smith, vol. I, p. 158.
[3] G. G. Smith, vol. I, p. 71.   [4] Published in 1595.

Hebrews, and had in prime estimation among the Greeks, transmitted to the Latins and all nations that professed civility'.[1]

When, during the years when Edward VI was king, the Psalms were being put into English metres, other of these poetical parts of the Bible were inevitably attracting the efforts of poets and would-be poets, and the Song of Songs (or the Song of Solomon) offered a particular challenge—not only because of its poetic lure. Preachers as well as poets were contestants in the fray that was raging about this book of the Bible, and the poetic versions of the sixteenth century cannot be understood without reference to the theologians. The theological battle over it centred about Sebastian Castalio and John Calvin. When Castalio declared it 'a filthy and wanton book', he was, on Calvin's insistence, refused the pastorate which he sought, and in 1544 was commanded to leave the city where he taught a small school. This was not the end of his difficulties, but of his further fortunes in his fight with Calvin over whether the church had the right to punish heretics with death we are not concerned here. The account given by Theodore de Bèze must, however, be further noted in so far as it concerns this book, for Bèze was not only Calvin's friend and successor but also the poet who had continued the work begun by Marot of translating the Psalms into French. Bèze wrote that Castalio 'did turne or rather overthrowe and confounde the whole Bible', and 'He did set before his translation of the Bible, an Epistle dedicated to the late good king Edwarde of England, whereby under colour of preaching Charitie, he overthroweth the auctoritie of the Scripture, as darke or unperfect'.[2]

[1] See also Baroway, 'The Bible as Poetry in the English Renaissance', *Jour. of English and Germanic Philology*, vol. XXXII (1933), pp. 447–80, and 'The Hebrew Hexameter: A Study in Renaissance Sources and Interpretation', *E.L.H.* vol. II (1935), pp. 66–91.

[2] *A Discourse…conteyning in briefe the Historie of the Life nd Death of Master John Calvin*, trans. by I. S. (London 1564), A viii^v–Bi^r. In 1587 John Harmar, professor of Greek at Oxford, published a translation of Bèze's sermons on the first three chapters of this controversial book, dedicating his translation to Leicester at whose command he had made it. Bèze in this work begins by saying there are persons who think the book should be reserved for those mature in the thinking of the church as well as persons who think it should be fully accepted as one of the canonical books. See Willeston Walker, *John Calvin* (1906), pp. 288–91, in *Heroes of the Reformation* series for an account of the quarrel.

The Great Bible, first published in 1539 by Whitchurch, gave the title of the book as 'The Ballet of Balettes of Salomon: called in Latin *Canticum Canticorum*'. This was the text on which William Baldwin, the first of the Song's poetic translators, based his *Canticles or Balades of Salomon, phraslyke declared in Englyshe Metres* published in 1549. It will be remembered that the *Boke of Balettes*, the very existence of which was not discovered until the twentieth century, had been published and offered a secular prototype. The very word *ballad* or *ballette*, used in the translation of the early Bibles, gave offence to Catholic critics, who considered it a profane word, used as if the translators were rendering Demosthenes rather than a holy work, 'as if it were a ballet of love between Salomon and his concubine, as Castalio wantonly translateth it'.[1] Baldwin, like other apologists, admits that 'No doubt but it is an hie and misticall matter, and more darkely hyd than other partes of the scripture, by means of the wanton wordes: which also cause many to deny it to be Gods wurde'. But he adds: 'Whose errour to redresse is the chief cause why I have medled with the matter.'[2] Using Origen and Anselm as his authorities, he explains that it is really a prophecy in which are figured 'Christe the brydegrome accompanied with his frends, good bishops and teachers: And the catholike churche his spouse accompanied with damoysels, young christen soules'.[3]

'Yf comparyson may be made in the holy gostes wrytinges', this book contained 'the principall balades of holy scripture', so Origen thought, and Origen according to Erasmus was 'the best skylled of all the doctours in understanding the holy scriptures'. Furthermore, Erasmus in dedicating his paraphrase of Matthew to the Emperor Charles, had set a precedent by which Baldwin justified his presenting this work to King Edward, a work which contained such songs as he hoped 'myght once drive out of office the baudy balades of lecherous love that commonly are indited and song of idle courtyers in

---

[1] Gregory Martin, *A Discoverie of the manifold corruptions of the Holy Scriptures by the Heretikes of our daies* (Rheims, 1582), and the answer by William Fulke, *A Defence of the sincere and true translations of the holie Scriptures into the English Tong* (London, 1583). [2] From 'To the reader'.
[3] From the dedication to King Edward VI. See ch. v, p. 42.

princes and noblemens houses'. In the crusade for such songs Baldwin gives place to Sternhold in words which I have quoted earlier.[1]

Baldwin printed the work himself in the shop where the Great Bible was printed, the colophon attesting him to be 'servaunt with Edwarde Whitchurche', and he printed each of the eight chapters from the Great Bible as a preface to his metrical versions of the songs which make up the chapter. For each poem he gives the text (not from the Great Bible) and the 'argument', which is of course the symbolic meaning as he understands it. All this machinery is unimportant, however, in comparison with the fact that Baldwin was clearly trying to compete with the courtiers whose 'baudy balades' he disapproved of. That his purpose far exceeded his ability to perform will not be denied by anyone, but the variety of his experiments is astonishing. He tortured the sense of each passage to make it conform to his theological interpretation; he tortured his sentences to make them conform to the verse form he had decided to achieve. He wrote in an iambic measure for the most part, or at least that seems to be the metre at which he aimed, but he arranged it in lines of three, four, five, or six feet in stanzas ranging from a simple ballad measure to one such as this which he fashions upon the text, 'I waked thee up among the apple trees wher thy mother conceyved thee, where thy mother brought thee into the worlde':[2]

> Emong the apple trees, I waked thee up my spouse,
> Where as thou sleptest in sin, in sin original,
> Which Eva, by the frute she plukt fro the apple bowes,
> Brought on her whole posteritie,
> Whiche are condemned al,
> For theyr parentes iniquitie,
> And for theyr owne unryght.

The other three stanzas continue the elaboration of the passage, and the other poems are no better, but the fact that Baldwin tried to depart from the ballad measures of Sternhold and to experiment with line length, rhyme schemes, and refrains,

---

[1] From the dedication to King Edward VI. See ch. v, p. 42.
[2] Part of ch. 8, verse 5, in the Authorized Version numbering.

indicates that he was attempting to make a body of English divine song, however unfitted he was for the task. That he saw himself opposing the courtiers who were making love songs at the court he states explicitly.

In 1575 there was published *A Misticall Devise of the Spirituall and Godlye Love between Christ, the Spouse, and the Church or Congregation* by one Jud Smith. Actually Jud Smith paraphrased only the fifth and sixth chapters of the book of Solomon, using common metre as Sternhold had used it. He adds in the same metre 'A Coppie of the Epistle that Jeremye sent unto the Jewes' which forms the last chapter of the apocryphal book of Baruch, and—in long metre—the ten commandments, together with some prose works. What is interesting in the work is not the poetry but the address 'To the christian Reader' which is written by John Wharton[1] and gains added significance by putting Chaucer along with Ovid in the opposition:

For surely (gentle Reader) if thou covit to heare anye olde bables, as I may terme them, or stale tales of Chauser, or to learne how Acteon came by his horned head? If thy mynde be fixed to any such metamorphocall toyes, this booke is not apt nor fit for thy purpose. But if thou art contrary wise bent, to heare, or to reade holsome documentes, as it becometh all Christians, then take this same: For thou shalt fynde it sweeter (as the Prophet sayeth) then the honye or the honye combe. [He added the usual plea:] Would to God that all our rebald songes were abrogated and cast quit away, and that we would once call to mynde this sweete saying of our Lord God. (O that my people would have harkened unto mee.) Therefore let us followe the good consail of the Apostle, that is: To cast awaye the workes of darknesse, and put on the Armour of lyght, which lyght is the true worde of the most hiest; as David in his Psalmes writeth. Thy worde is a Lanterne unto my feete, & a lyght unto my path.

Dudley Fenner, publishing *The Song of Songs*[2] in 1587, addressed 'the right worshipfull companie of the Marchant

---

[1] The *S.T.C.* lists only one work by him, *Whartons Treasure*, published in 1577, and described as 'an invective against usurers'.

[2] He says his work was half printed before another book turned this into English metre, but I do not know to what book he refers. He speaks also of the other songs of the Bible which with the Psalms and the 'Lamentations of Jeremie' for the most part are already 'Turned with varietie both of Frenche and Englishe tunes'.

adventurers' who had called him 'to the woorke of the Minis-
terie' among them:

That whereas you doe ordinarilie eare you depart from the table
both at noone & at night, admonishe your selves by singing some
spiritual songs, & do with great desire heare the arguments and
doctrine of the same, brieflie opened unto you by anie Minister which
shalbe present: this may be as a suply unto you for the often absence
of the minister.

The picture of the Merchant Adventurers singing their spiritual
songs as they sit around after meals and listen to their exposition
by any minister present needs to be viewed against the picture
offered by Thomas Morley as the young Philomathes describes
his initial venture into society:

But supper being ended, and Musicke bookes, according to the
custom being brought to the table: the mistresse of the house
presented mee with a part, earnestly requesting mee to sing. But
when after manie excuses, I protested unfainedly that I could not:
everie one began to wonder. Yea, some whispered to others, de-
maunding how I was brought up: so that upon shame of mine ignorance I go nowe to seeke out mine olde frinde master *Gnorimus*,
to make myselfe his scholler.[1]

The Merchant Adventurers expand the picture to let us see a
social custom transformed into a religious service as an accompaniment to meals taken together, but the contribution to English
literature made by the offering of their minister can be passed over.

Spenser's version of Solomon's song has not survived, and
we must suppose that it was unknown to Meres,[2] for he chose as
the English representative of those writers who turn the Bible
into verse Gervaise Markham's *Poem of Poems. Or, Sions Muse
...divided into eight Eclogues*. Markham was a relative of the
Haringtons, father and son, to whom we are indebted for the
preservation of Wyatt's Psalms, as I have already recorded.[3]
He was a prolific writer and wrote in a great variety of literary
forms, and I think it is significant that he dedicated this work
to Elizabeth, the daughter of Sir Philip Sidney. Saying that, since
he had become a prentice to the Muses, he found poesy which

---

[1] Thomas Morley, *A Plaine and Easie Introduction to Practical Musicke* (London,
1597), p. 1.   [2] G. G. Smith, vol. II, p. 323.
[3] See p. 35, n. 3. The elder John Harington married as his second wife
Isabella Markham. See McClure, pp. 5 and 283. See also Grimble, pp. 92–101.

he had so much revered 'created but as a hand-maide to attend Divinitie, and that as Poesie gave grace to vulgar subjects, so Divinitie gave glorie to the best part of a Poets invention'. Like the others of the orthodox, he considers the poem a series of dialogues between Christ and the Church, pedantically *Thaumatos* and *Ecclesia*. That he considers that he has written a series of eclogues in a variety of stanza forms gives his composition at least some grounds for differentiating it from the others.

Michael Drayton began and ended his poetic career with divine poetry. When in 1591 he published *The Harmonie of the Church* he evidently intended a more complete offering of the 'poetical part of the Bible' than had been presented in English verse. He did not translate the Psalms of David or the other books of Solomon, however, but did include 'The Most Excellent Song Which Was Salomons'. To the whole of the Harmonie he prefixed a dedication to Lady Jane Devereux and an address 'To the curteous reader' which makes the usual plea for these songs as offering delight to any true Christian. 'I speak not of *Mars*, the god of Wars', he wrote, 'nor of *Venus*, the goddesse of love, but of the Lord of Hostes, that made heaven and earth: Not of Toyes in Mount *Ida*, but of triumphes in Mount *Sion*: Not of Vanitie, but of Veritie: not of Tales, but of Truethes'.

Like most of his translations, that of Solomon's song was based on the Geneva Bible, Mrs Tillotson has decided.[1] Except for the eighth chapter which is written in septenary couplets, it is written in poulter's measure, and a few lines from a familiar passage may illustrate Drayton's poetic talent which rarely rose above the undistinguished but as rarely degenerated into doggerel:

Who's she I doo behold, so like the morning cleare,
Or like the Moon, when towards the ful, in pride she doth appear,
Bright as the radiant raies, that from the Sun descend,
Or like an Army terrible, when Ensignes they extend.[2]

[1] Vol. v of *The Works of Michael Drayton*, ed. J. W. Hebel (Oxford, 1941), prepared by Kathleen Tillotson and B. H. Newdigate after the death of Professor Hebel, offered introductions and notes to all his poems. See pp. 1 and 2. The *Harmonie* is printed in vol. 1, pp. 1–43 (published in 1931).
[2] Ch. 6, verse 10.

Drayton translated the other songs of the Bible into a variety of metres, seven in septenary couplets, seven in pentameter quatrains with varying rhyme schemes, one in tetrameter quatrains with lines rhyming in couplets, three in the metre of *Venus and Adonis*.[1] As he began his poetic life with divine poems, so he ended it with another set, of divine narrative poems, which will be considered later.

Next among the works of Solomon translated into English should perhaps be considered the book of Proverbs. In 1550 there was published *Certayne chapters of the proverbs of Salomon drawen into metre by T. Sternholde*, but the same year saw another edition of the same work, the indignant title-page of which I quote in full: *Certayn chapters taken out of the Proverbes of Salomon, wyth other chapters of the holy Scripture, & certayne Psalmes of David, translated into English metre, by John Hall, Which Proverbes of late were set forth, Imprinted and untruely entituled, to be thee doynges of Mayster Thomas Sternhold, late grome of the Kynges Majesties robes, as by thys Copye it maye be perceaved.*

As might be expected, the author urged the Christian reader to:

exercyse thy selfe in synging, ryming, and talking of the Proverbes of Salomon, and Psalmes of David, & other Chapters of the holy Scripture, as is contayned in this lytle boke, or the workes of other men more learned, whych for theyr doynges have as moche deserved to be commended, as he, what soever he was that made the court of Venus, or other bokes of lecherous Ballades, the whych have bene a greate occasion to provoke men to the desyre of synne, where as in these workes thou shalt learne to fle from evyl company, from dronckenes & dronkards, from covetousnes & slouthfulnes, from wrathe and envy, from whoredom & all the subtyle behaviours of whores, from pryde, yea & finallye from al wickednes & sinne....

Again he attacks the *Court of Venus* in particular in his pious hope for godly girls:

I wold to god these gygolat gerles were as apte to learne vertous thinges, as they be to mock & floute men, & to take them at the worst, or as wel learned in vertue & godlines, as they be in the court

---

[1] All selections are from the Old Testament and the Apocrypha.

of Venus, & as they be in dyinge of theyr heyre yelow, & then to brayde & curle it with bodkins & laye it out to be sene, & to paynte their faces, in doyng of the which they bloot & put out the ymage of God.

To the Psalmist's injunction to sing unto the Lord a new song, John Hall imagines 'oure Englishmen' replying:

...We have songes made by wyse & learned men in the court of Venus, thou art gods minstrel, & makest melody wyth spiritual songes to hys prayse, but we wyl sing songes of love to the goddes of lechery....

Quoting text after text as authority for the divine command to sing psalms, Hall laments again that 'in our myrth it is manifest what our doynges are, for our songes are of the court of Venus, yea, and rather worse'. To the main body of his work, the translation of Proverbs, Hall added metrical versions of the sixth chapter of the Book of Wisdom, the ninth of Ecclesiasticus, the third of the second Epistle to the Thessalonians, and certain Psalms. It is significant of the lack of consideration given to divine poetry by modern literary historians that this work has only been mentioned by them because it indicated that the *Court of Venus* had been previously published.[1]

That the attempts to render wisdom literature into English verse should result in poetry which can only be compared with that by which older generations learned the multiplication tables, the number of days in the month, and the capitals of the states is not surprising. The value of rhyme as an aid to memory has always been recognized, of course, and it may be worth noting here that among the Heber collection of broadsides and ballads is to be found *A most excellent new dittie, wherein is shewed the saage sayings, and wise sentences of Salomon: wherein each estate is taught his dutie, with singular counsell to his comfort and consolation. To the tune of Wigmores Galliard.*

The third of Solomon's works mentioned by Sidney was Ecclesiastes, and I have already noted Surrey's translation which, though not printed, was well enough known to be quoted by Archbishop Parker in his edition of the Psalms. Like

[1] See p. 28, n. 2.

Surrey's versions of certain Psalms, it was made by him to echo his own life's problems. Padelford wrote that 'The chapters from Ecclesiastes lend themselves to that elegiac strain which has ever been so near the surface in the English temperament,[1] and Surrey's adaptation of these chapters to the sentiments uppermost in his mind is a sixteenth century expression of that poignant sense of the illusion of boastful heraldry and of pomp and glory'. The translation is very free, and the verse is again poulter's measure. Soon to die on the scaffold, Surrey could well exclaim:

> Like to the stereles boote that swerves with efery wynde,
> The slipper topp of worldely welthe by crewell prof I fynde.
> Skace hath the seade, whereof that nature foremethe man,
> Received lief, when deathe him yeldes to earth wher he began.[2]

Today all but unknown, Henry Lok was once sufficiently recognized to be allowed to offer his tribute of praise to James in a sonnet in *His Majesties Poeticall Exercises* and to dedicate his poem to Queen Elizabeth. According to the editor of *New Poems by James I of England*, he had spent most of his life as 'an envoy or political intelligencer', and having been guilty of intrigues with Bothwell and John Colville, he was out of favour by the time James did become indeed king of England and was in considerable difficulties thereafter.[3] His mother was the A.L. who had been Anne Vaughan, and who had translated into English verse Calvin's *Sermons upon the Songe that Ezechias made after he had bene sicke* and had also made some verses 'in the manner of a Paraphrase after the 51 Psalm of David'.[4] Such a mother would have found pleasure in her son's book which bore the comprehensive title of *Ecclesiastes, Otherwise Called the Preacher. Containing Salomons Sermons or Commentaries (as it may probably be collected) upon the 49 Psalme of David his father. Compendiously abridged, and also paraphrastically dilated in English poesie, according to the analogie of Scripture, and consent of the most approved*

---

[1] Padelford, p. 42.
[2] Padelford, p. 102. Translation of ch. 3, verses 1–4.
[3] Westcott, pp. xlii and xliii.
[4] A. B. Grosart, *Miscellanies of the Fuller Worthies Library* (printed for private circulation, 1871), vol. II, p. 395.

writer thereof. It was dedicated to Queen Elizabeth, to whom
he addressed a prefatory sonnet, and it may be of interest that
among the prefatory poems in the volume is one by John Lyly
also addressed to the Queen. The high purpose of the work is
fittingly proclaimed:

> The heavenly words of holy *Davids* sonne,
> Who over Israels race sometimes did raigne,
> Wherewith to vertue he his subjects wonne,
> Whilst in Jerusalem he did remaine,
> And to instruct them thus did not disdaine.
>> Those words, no vaine discourse it is I write,
>> Pend by a Prince, as God did them indite.

The method by which Lok 'compendiously abridged, and
also paraphrastically dilated in English Poesie' a text may be
illustrated by his version of a phrase in the ninth verse of the
twelfth chapter of the book. The phrase, printed in the margin,
reads 'And searched forth, and prepared many parables'. This
is what he makes of it in the double stanza in which part of the
poem is translated.

> His heavenly Muse with wings of zeale did fly
> Above the common pitch of earthly men,
> And so inflamed were his thoughts thereby
>> With holy liking of his love as then,
>> That he could not containe his gratefull pen.
>
> In thousand songs and five his powers did try,
> The prayses of his sacred soules delight,
> In whom sweet peace and love he did espy,
> Which from him, love of world did banish quight,
>> Among the which that song of songs by name
>> Describes her beauties, did him so inflame.

Lok in characteristic fashion varied the metre in this work,
using rhyme royal, the popular six-line stanza, and this hybrid
twin. With Ecclesiastes were printed, rendered into septenary
couplets, the Lord's Prayer and five Psalms, Psalm cxix being
arranged in twenty-two parts. Also with a separate title-page is
included a reprint of the 1593 volume of sonnets, *Sundry*

Christian Passions, which I propose to consider later, but it is perhaps interesting to note that both volumes were printed by Richard Field, Shakespeare's first printer.

In 1596 there was published also the apocryphal book The Wisdom of Solomon put into the six-line stanza by Thomas Middleton. It is very awkwardly done. Indeed, Solomon fared rather worse at the hands of the poets than did his father David.

OTHER BOOKS OF THE BIBLE AS ENGLISH POETRY

ENGLISH poets and would-be poets more often turned to the translation of the works of the two royal poets, David and Solomon, than to other books of the Bible, but there were occasional offerings of some interest. A very comprehensive task was that undertaken during the reign of Edward VI, when the ventures of Sternhold and Baldwin and others testify to his sympathy, for William Samuel started to put the whole Bible into metre. Identifying himself as 'servaunt to the Duke of Somerset his grace', and dedicating it to Anne, the wife of the Protector, he first published in 1551 *The Abridgemente of Goddes Statutes in Myter*. It was printed by Robert Crowley for Robert Soughton, and it will be remembered that Crowley had himself produced the first metrical version of the complete Psalter. This early work of Samuel is apparently extant only in the copy at the Huntington Library and is not registered in the *Short-Title Catalogue*. The dedication indicates that it is intended as the beginning of a great work, the purpose of the whole being here recorded:

My mynd is that I wold have my contrey people able in a smale some to syng the hole contents of the byble, & where as in tymes past the musicians or mynstrells, wer wont to syng fained myracles, saints lives, & Robin hode, in stede thereof to sing, undoutyd truthes, canonycall scryptures, and Gods doynges. I have also begon the same order that I intend to kepe as where a boke hath thyrtye, fortye, or fyfthtye chapters, to devyd it into fyttes, or partes, that it shall not be to tedyous to the reader, synger, or hearer, to have the boke in practys....The abrygement of Gods acts or statutes I do call it because it is a summe or short rehersal of things done at large in the Byble booke, whych may be called the kyng of al kinges actes.

That Samuel was not the worst of the poets of his time may be seen from his opening verses.

> Almyghty God dydde make the heaven,
>   the Lyght the firmament:
> The sun, the mone, the stars the beasts,
>   with soules to fleeyng bent.
> The earth the sea and al therein
>   all thys hys word dyd make
> Wyth man made last and yet set fyrst
>   his wyll on them to take.

That he pursued his intention is evidenced by the publication in 1569 of *An Abridgement of all the Canonical Books of the Olde Testament*, described adequately as 'written in Sternnolds meter by W. Samuel Minister'.

A similar project was undertaken by Henoch Clapham in *A briefe of the Bible, drawne first into English Poësy, and then illustrated with apte Annotations*, the apt annotations almost submerging the tiny trail of poetry through the pages. The annotations, in fact, control the format of the page, the lines of verse being divided so that they form a mere trickle in the centre of the prose. Yet the book must have had some appeal to the faithful, for originally printed in Edinburgh in 1596, it was later printed in England, four editions in all being printed.

These are, I think, the only attempts at so large, not to say monstrous, an undertaking. One of the more modest undertakings was that of Christopher Tye, Doctor of Music, master of the chapel boys at Ely, and like Sternhold a gentleman of the Chapel Royal during Edward's reign. He is said to have been Edward's music master.[1] In the play *When You See Me, You Know Me*, published in 1605,[2] he comes to life as his work is proffered to young Prince Edward. Since the author of the play was Samuel Rowley, and Rowley is thought to have been Tye's grandson, the passage is illuminating. Henry is king, and Edward is prince, the hope of the Tudor dynasty. When Tye enters the scene, Edward greets him as his 'music lecturer', and as they discuss the place of music in life, Tye gives a very

---

[1] Henry Davey in the *D.N.B.* quotes Burney's judgment of Tye: 'Perhaps as good a poet as Sternhold, and as great a musician as Europe could then boast.' I have taken my facts from this article.

[2] I have used the Malone Society Reprint, ed. by F. P. Wilson (Oxford, 1952). The quoted lines are numbered 2083–98.

eloquent speech in its defence. After the performance of music
by instruments and then by voices, the dialogue continues:

> *Prince.* I oft have heard my Father merrily speake,
> In your hye praise, and thus his Highnesse sayth,
> England, one God, one truth, one Doctor hath
> For Musicks Art, and that is Doctor *Tye*
> Admir'rd for skill in Musicks harmonie.
> *Tye.* Your Grace doth honor me with kind acceptance,
> Yet one thing more, I doe beseech your Excellence
> To daine, to Patronize this homely worke,
> Which I unto your Grace have dedicate.
> *Prince.* What is the Title?
> *Tye.* The Acts of the holy Apostles turn'd into verse,
> Which I have set in severall parts to sing,
> Worthy Acts, and worthily in you remembred
> *Prince.* Ile peruse them, and satisfie your paines,
> And have them sung within my fathers Chappell:
> I thank yee both.

The *both* refers to Tye and Cranmer, and Cranmer as they
depart hails the prince, 'The hope of *England*, and of learnings
praise'.

Rowley was probably telescoping historical events here as
elsewhere in his play, for it was in 1553 when Edward was king
that there was published with the dedication to the king *The
Acts of the Apostles, translated into Englyshe Metre...wyth notes
to eche Chapter, to synge and also to play upon the Lute*. The title-page
added that it was 'very necessarye for studentes after theyr
studye, to fyle theyr wyttes, and also for all Christians that
cannot synge, to reade the good and Godlye storyes of the
lyves of Christ hys Apostles'. Verses to the King rather naïvely
acknowledge that writers have made versions of Psalms and the
'booke of Kynges: / Because they se, your grace delyte / In
such like Godlye thynges'. And his subjects will do as he does.
His hope is that the king, when he takes up his lute, 'In stede
of songs, of wanton love' will play these songs, and he has
provided music for the first two stanzas of each of the fourteen
chapters of his version. Tye's music is praised by historians of
music, but Tye remained firmly committed to the text, as the
first stanza will show.

In the former, treatyse to thee
Deare frende, Theophilus:
I have written, the veritie
Of the Lord Christ Jesus.

Among Tye's unpublished works is one that should be mentioned because it illustrates the habit which persisted of using secular song for divine purposes. Three leading musicians of the time John Shepherd, John Taverner, and Tye all wrote masses on the song 'Western wind, why dost thou blow?' Taverner's rather than Tye's is given particular praise, but Tye is the only one of the three to publish a poetic work also.

Another member of the Chapel Royal during Edward's reign was William Hunnis, whose early translations of certain Psalms I have already discussed. During the time that Mary was on the throne, he had been in trouble in connection with plots against her and had been in prison. After Elizabeth became queen, he came back to his place in the Royal Chapel, was made Master of the Children in 1566 to succeed Richard Edwardes, and continued to receive favours from Elizabeth until his death in 1597.[1] The first work published after his return was *A Hive Full of Hunnye: Containing the Firste Booke of Moses, called Genesis*, printed by Thomas Marshe in 1578. Marshe was continuing to publish the *Mirror for Magistrates*, and in 1587 a long prefatory poem was introduced by Thomas Newton, who in 1581 had been responsible for the publication of *Senaca his Tenne Tragedies*, also printed by Marshe. Wood calls Newton Hunnis's crony, and in the congratulatory poem prefixed to the *Hive* Newton speaks of the interludes and poems Hunnis had written earlier 'for Youthful humours meete', and comments that now in the winter of his age he treats of higher things. Since *Genesis* was put into the alternating three and four foot lines of the common metre of psalmody, and adhered as closely to the text as did the *Actes of the Apostles*, Newton could well praise the author for his work in lines which to us convey some misgiving.

[1] See p. 43, n. 4, for references to Mrs Stopes's work. See also E. K. Chambers, *Elizabethan Stage* (Oxford, 1923), vol. II, pp. 34–41, and vol. III, pp. 349–50. The *Hive* was dedicated to the Earl of Leicester.

In curraunt meeter, roundlie coucht, and soundly taught withall
As they which Text with Verse conferre, full soone acknowledge shal.
Great thankes (no doubt) thou hast deserv'de of all that thyrst for
    grace,
Syth thus thou Minced hast the Foode, which Goodmen all embrace.
The holy Ghost, from whom thou doost this Heavenly Honnie Sucke,
Direct thy Minde, and to thy Penne alotte most happy Lucke.

Perhaps the reason for the pedestrian verse may be found in
Hunnis's address to the reader:

> Looke not for fyled Wordes and Termes,
>   nor Phraze that Poetes chuse:
> It is forbidden in this Woorke,
>   as thing not meete to use.

At any rate, it was an explanation often offered by the divine
poets. What this work lacked in beauty it made up in the
paraphernalia of authority. Each chapter is prefaced by the
argument, and the margins are used for expository comments,
moral lessons to be derived from the text, and pedigrees of the
sons of Noah, of Abraham, and of Jacob.

The next work of his to be recorded in the *Short-Title Catalogue* is *Hunnies Recreations*, published in 1595. The title-page
proclaimed that it contained 'foure godlie and compendious discourses', the first representing God telling of Adam's banish-
ment, the others—'Christ his Crib', 'The Lost Sheepe', and
'The Complaint of Old Age'—are not our immediate concern.
But to these discourses were 'newly adjoyned these two notable
and pithie Treatises: The Creation of the first Weeke [and] The
life and death of Joseph'. The 'Joseph' was somewhat revised,
but for the rest Hunnis simply drew upon the *Hive* for his
Biblical story. Of his translation of the seven Penitential
Psalms and its publication with some minor poems I have
written earlier, but I must note again that he reprinted the
Newton poem in this, the last of his publications.

Thomas Drant, Archdeacon of Lewes,[1] is better known because of the reference to him in the Spenser–Harvey correspondence than because of his contributions to literature; yet be-

[1] See G. G. Smith, vol. 1, pp. i–lv and 372–3, for a discussion of Drant and his
rules.

cause his *Medicinable Morall*, published in 1566, illustrates clearly
the attitude of the Christian humanist in the movement to create
a divine literature it is of special interest. Here he put in juxta-
position two books of Horace's satires 'Englished according to
the prescription of Saint Jerome, *Quod malum est, muta.* | *Quod
bonum est, prode.*' and 'The wailings of the Prophet Hieremiah,
done into Englyshe verse'. To explain his making companion
pieces of the works of the two authors he says:

> *Horace* was excellent good in his time, a muche zelous controller of
> sinne, but chiefly one that with sharpe satyres and cutting quippies,
> coulde wel displaie and disease a gloser. The holy Prophete *Jeremie*
> dyd rufully and waylingly lamente the deepe and massie enormities
> of his tymes, & earnestly prognosticate and forspeake the sorie and
> sower consequents that came after, and sauce with teares the hard
> plagues that had gone before.
> Therefore as it is mete for a man of god rather to wepe then to
> jest: and not undecent for a prophane writer to be jesting and merie
> spoken: I have brought to passe that plaintive Prophete *Jeremie*
> shoulde wepe at synne: and the pleasant poet *Horace* shoulde laugh
> at synne.

The methods to be used in translating a profane writer and
a divine writer Drant conceives to be quite different. In para-
phrasing Horace, he says he cut out the vanity and superfluity,
made a general moral from his private carping, Englished the
poetry according to the demands of our vulgar tongue rather
than of his, removed his obscurity, sometimes bettering his
matter, mending the similitudes, but not altering the sense or
at least the purpose of the work. But when he makes Jeremiah
speak English, he does not take such liberties:

> That thou mightest have this ruful parcel of scripture, pure &
> sincere, not swarved or altered: I laid it to the touchstone, the native
> tongue. I waited it with the *Chaldie Targum*, & the *Septuaginta*.
> I desired to jumpe so nigh with Hebrue, that it doth erewhile deforme
> the vayne of the Englysh: the proprieties of that language, & ours,
> being in some speeches so muche dissemblable.

The first verse of Lamentations is thus tendered:

> How sytts the Citie desolate,
> so populous a place?

> The ladye of so many landes,
> Becumbe in wydowes case.
> The Princes of the provinces,
> her tribute nowe must paye.

In 1568 Drant translated the *Epigrams and Spirituall Sentences* of Gregory of Nazianzus, and he put Ecclesiastes into Latin verse in 1572, but in 1567 he had also published a translation of Horace's *Art of Poetry*, his epistles and satires. And he did not neglect his sermonizing while he occasionally turned to English or Latin original verse; he said so.

Another poetic version of *The Lamentations of Jeremie* was published in 1587, the dedication by Christopher Fetherstone saying that he had had the verses given to him by a friend (unnamed), but that he himself had made the prose translation of the works from Latin into English together with the annotations of Tremelius. Whether the unnamed friend added the music for his verses is not indicated, but the music seems to have determined the arrangement of the poetry. Stanzas of eight lines of common metre are grouped by the demands of the musical units. The verse follows the text rather mechanically, but the music might be interesting.

CHAPTER IX

DU BARTAS AND
KING JAMES AND THE
CHRISTIAN MUSE

THE most obvious way in which to create a divine poetry in English was to translate the 'poetical part of the Bible' into English verse. There were attempts to put other parts of the Bible into verse, as I have indicated, but they were few and generally feeble. I have tried, therefore, to show particularly how the spread of secular ballads and songs called forth a rival poetry translated from the works of David and Solomon and from the lyrics scattered through other parts of the Bible. Putting Bible song into currently popular English verse forms was not the whole of the effort, however, for writers were moved to the creation both of ballads based on Bible stories and—of supreme importance—to the creation of a massive store of devotional poetry. I have omitted any discussion of ballads because the manner of recording them and dispersing them makes it almost impossible to cite specific evidence concerning the purpose for which they were composed. I have also omitted any discussion of the devotional poetry which was to form such a large part of English literature for the reason that it is corollary to my subject, which is to show how the Bible was introduced into English literature as the result of a determined movement in the sixteenth century.

Bible story, as well as Bible song, was to be put into contemporary form, and it was being presented in dramas to be played on street corners, in banqueting halls, and in public theatres, of which I propose to give an account in the second part of this book. But many earnest men were determined to show that the Bible also offered better stories for poetic narratives than were offered in translations or adaptations of Homer and Virgil, Boccaccio and Bandello, Ovid and Musaeus, Ariosto and the compilers of the chivalric romances. The list which Louis

Zocca has compiled is staggering, and he does not tell all.[1]
Thomas Ascham was moved to exclaim:

These be the inchantementes of *Circes*, brought out of *Italie*, to
marre mens maners in England; much by example of ill life, but
more by preceptes of fonde bookes, of late translated out of *Italian*
into English, sold in every shop in London, commended by honest
titles the soner to corrupt honest maners, dedicated over boldlie to
vertuous and honorable personages the easelier to begile simple and
honest wittes....I know when Gods Bible was banished the Court,
and *Morte Arthure* received into the Princes chamber....And yet
ten *Morte Arthures* do not the tenth part so much harme as one of
these bookes made in *Italie* and translated in England.[2]

Stephen Gosson wrote his 'pleasant invective against Poets,
Players, Jesters and such like Caterpillers of a Commonwelth'
in his *Schoole of Abuse*, and the attacks on the newly popular
books of stories were to call forth the defences of poetry on
which we today rely for much of our knowledge of the literary
scene in Elizabethan England.

Since the new poetry based on Bible story was written with the
avowed purpose of offering a substitute for the pagan and
secular poetry then current, it was written in the popular forms
of its rival. I have thought, therefore, that I could best demonstrate its methods by discussing it in terms of poetic genre
rather than by considering it chronologically. I propose, then,
to trace the Biblical stories as they were shaped into tales and
epics, mirrors, erotic poems or epyllia, and sonnet sequences,
since these were poetic types that emerged in English literature
in the sixteenth century with distinctive characteristics.

Before I turn to these matters, however, I must record the
acceptance of a new Muse for divine poetry, a Muse whose aid
could be invoked in its writing and to whom its votaries could
offer their tribute of praise. The Muse was Urania, and she was
introduced to the world of divine poetry in a work entitled
La Muse Chrestiene.[3] The author was Saluste du Bartas, and
his book, epochal in Christian poetry, contained three poems,

---

[1] Louis R. Zocca, *Elizabethan Narrative Poetry* (New Brunswick, N.J., 1950).
[2] G. G. Smith, vol. 1, pp. 2, 4.
[3] In this chapter I have used much of the material I presented in 'The Christian
Muse', printed in the *Huntington Library Bulletin*, no. 8 (Cambridge, Mass., 1935).

two of great importance: *La Judit*, a divine epic, and *L'Uranie*, a poetical plea for and a defence of divine poetry.

These two poems and *Le Triomfe de la Foi* were published in 1574 at Bordeaux, and were republished in 1579 at Paris in a volume *Oeuvres Poetiques* containing a new address to Marguerite, Queen of Navarre, with a slightly altered account of the writing of *La Judit* in the Address to the Reader.[1] It was from this second edition that Thomas Hudson, a musician at the court of King James of Scotland, 'Englished' *The Historie of Judith in Forme of a Poeme, Penned in French, by the noble Robt. G. Saluste, Lord of Bartas*, which was published in 1584 at Edinburgh. Du Bartas had given an account of his reasons for undertaking its composition:

Beloved *Reader*, it is about fourtene years past since I was commanded by the late Illustrate and most vertuous Princesse *Jean, Queen of Navarre*, to reduce the *Historie of Judith*, in forme of a *Poeme Epique*, wherein I have not so much aimed to follow the phrase or text of the byble, as I have preased (without wandring from the veritie of the Historie) to imitate *Homer* in his *Iliades*, and *Virgill* in his *Æneidos*, and others who have left to us workes of such like matter: thereby to render my worke so much the more delectable. And if the effect hath not answeared to my desire, I beseech thee to laye the fault uppon her who proposed to me so meane a *Theame* or subject, and not on mee who could not honestly disobeye. Yet in so much as I am the first in *Fraunce*, who in a just *Poeme* hath treated in our toung of sacred things, I hope of thy favour to receive some excuse, seeing that things of so great weight cannot be both perfectly begunne and ended together.[2]

Du Bartas thus announced that it was by the command of Jeanne, the daughter of Marguerite of Navarre, that he undertook to put the Biblical story of Judith into the form of the classical epic, claiming, much as Milton claimed in later years, that in so doing he was undertaking 'Things unattempted yet in Prose or Rhyme', since he was the first in France, 'who in a just *Poeme* hath treated in our toung of sacred things'.

[1] I have established Hudson's use of the second edition of *Judit* by comparing the versions of the address to the readers printed in *The Works of Guillaume De Salluste Sieur Du Bartas*, 3 vols. ed. by U. T. Holmes, Jr., J. C. Lyons, and R. W. Linker (Chapel Hill, 1935), vol. I, pp. 212–13 and 215–16. For an account of Du Bartas's work see pp. 10, 13–15.

[2] The letters from the King to Du Bartas are printed pp. 203–4.

The new apostle of divine poetry was introduced into English letters by no less a person than King James of Scotland, who ordered the translation, as Hudson informs us in his dedication to the King:

AS your Majestie Sir, after your accustomed & verteous maner was sometyme discoursing at Table with such your Domestiques, as chaunced to bee attendant.

It pleased your Highnesse (not onely to esteeme the pereles stile of the Greeke HOMER, and the Latin VIRGIL to be inimitable to us, whose toung is barbarous and corrupted:) But also to alledge partly throw delite your Majest. tooke in the Hautie stile of those most famous Writers, and partly to sounde the opinion of others, that also the loftie Phrase, the grave inditement, the facound termes of the French Salust (for the like resemblaunce) could not be followed, nor sufficiently expressed in our rude and impollished english language. Wherein, I more boldly then advisedly (with your Majest. lycence) declared my simple opinion.... But rashly I alledged that it was nothing impossible even to followe the footsteppes of the same great Poet SALUST, and to translate his vearse... succinctlie, and sensibly in our owne vulgar speech. Whereupon, it pleased your Majestie (among the rest of his workes) to assigne me, *The Historie of Judith*, as an agreable Subject to your highnesse, to be turned by me into English verse.

It was, however, the other divine poem in *La Muse Chrestiene* which was responsible for the title given to the first French volume, for *L'Uranie* elevated the Muse of Astronomy into the place she held henceforth as the Muse of Christian poetry. More flattering than the royal command which elicited the English translation of *Judith*, was James's personal introduction of the new Muse into English literature by including both the French original and his own translation, *Uranie*, in *The Essayes of a Prentice*, which was published, like Hudson's *Judith*, in 1584 at Edinburgh by Thomas Vautrollier.

In his address 'To the favorable Reader', James in his often decried 'king's English' explained his evangelical purpose:

Having oft revolved, and red over...the booke and Poems of the devine and Illuster Poëte, *Salust du Bartas*, I was moved by the oft reading & perusing of them, with a restles and lofty desire, to preas to attaine to the like vertue. But sen (alas) God, by nature hathe refused me the like lofty and quick ingyne, and that my dull

Muse, age, and Fortune, had refused me the lyke skill and learning,
I was constrained to have refuge to the secound, which was, to doe
what lay in me, to set forth his praise, sen I could not merite the lyke
my self. Which I thought, I could not do so well, as by publishing
some worke of his, to this yle of *Brittain* (swarming full of quick
ingynes,) as well as they ar made manifest already to France...
preferring foolehardiness and a good intention, to an utter dispaire
and sleuth, I resolved unadvysedly to assay the translating in my
language of the easiest and shortest of all his difficile, and prolixed
Poems: to wit, the *Uranie* or heavenly Muse, which, albeit it be not
well translated, yet hope I, ye will excuse me...sen I neither ordained it, nor avowes it for a just translation: but onely set it forth,
to the end, that,...some quick sprited man of this yle, borne under
the same, or as happie a Planet, as *Du Bartas* was, might by the
reading of it, bee moved to translate it well, and best, where I have
bothe evill, and worst broyled it.

Since Urania entered poetry not only as the Muse of Christian
poetry but also as the promulgator of what had been growing
up as the central doctrine of Christian poetry accepted henceforth by its artist practitioners, it is necessary to outline here
the poem of Du Bartas. I am using James's translation. First,
Du Bartas speaks of his early poetry written to gain gold and
honour, wanton song in honour of Cupid, and of his ambition
to dress the old Greek scene in French. Then he tells of Urania's
appearing to him, and he describes her nine-voiced mouth, her
sevenfold crown, and her azure gown, the hem adorned with
the constellations.

> Her porte was Angellike with Angels face,
> With comely shape and toung of heavenly grace.

Announcing herself, she pleads:

> O *Salust*, Gods immortals honour sing:
> And bending higher *Davids* Lute in tone
> With courage seke you endles crowne above.

Bewailing the base uses to which poetry has been put, she
proclaims the theory of the divine inspiration of the poet. That
poetry cannot be written by art or learning but can be written
by him within whom that holy fire burns bright though he be
without learning is proved by Homer and Ovid and David.
Then she renews her plea to him to turn to divine poetry.

Sen verse did then in heaven first bud and blume,
If ye be heavenly, how dare ye presume
A verse prophane, and mocking for to sing,
Gainst him that leads the starrie heavens the ring?
Will ye then so ingrately make your pen,
A slave to sinne, and serve but fleshly men?
Shall still your brains be busied then to fill
With dreames, ô dreamers, every booke and bill?
Shall Satan still be God for your behove?
Still will ye rive the aire with cryes of love?
And shall there never into your works appeare
The praise of God, resounding loud and cleare?

Because of the power of poetry to imprint in us good or evil
Plato would not have poets in his commonwealth, but Urania
argues it is their shameless rhymes that have caused poets to
be looked down upon and their works to be forbidden. Poets
would be revered instead of disdained if they sang of holy things
as did David, Moses, Judith, Deborah, and Job. Satan, 'who
can seame / An Angell of light', stirred up his gods and priests
to emulate the song of the blessed.

Urania bids the poet look to the horn of plenty, the rich
storehouse, the boundless ocean, the deep spring of heavenly
subjects that await the singer, and she proclaims the power of
high subjects to create high poetry, of immortal subjects to
make immortal verse:

From subjects base, a base discours dois spring,
A lofty subject of it selfe doeth bring
Grave words and weghtie, of it selfe divine,
And makes the authors holy honour shine.

Therefore, she urges:

Let not your art so rare then be defylde,
In singing *Venus* and her fethred chylde:
For better it is without renowne to be,
Than be renownde for vyle iniquitie.

And she again begs him to consecrate his song to singing the
miracles of Scripture, to prefer the Holy Ghost to Pegasus.
She promises Salust fame if he will heed her counsel. Moved
by her speech, he afterwards could only think himself blessed

if he might but touch the crown she bore in her hand, though he might never wear it.

From Hesiod to Natalis Comes, Urania had received her meed of praise as the Muse of Astronomy, and in the early sixteenth century Giovanni Pontano had given the title *Urania* to his great work in Latin hexameters on the heavens, to which he appended a series of Christian poems or hymns. This work was repeatedly published and probably gave to Du Bartas the title for his poem. It was in this poem of Du Bartas, however, that Urania entered the scene as the Muse of Christian poetry.

L'Uranie not only provided a Muse for Christian poetry; it gave unity and direction to the whole movement in which many had taken part. The tenets of the movement seemed now firmly established:

(1) Poetry must be reclaimed from the base uses to which it had been put.

(2) Poetry must be recognized as a heavenly gift, not the result of study and learning.

(3) The first poetry was divine poetry, the poetry of the Bible, but later writers used poetry for profane purposes.

(4) The high subject will bring about a worthy style.

(5) Biblical story must be substituted for pagan mythology: the dove of the Holy Ghost for Pegasus, Noah's flood for Deucalion's, etc.

(6) Better material for poetry lies in the history of faith's effects than in old classical stories.

(7) Poetry should give profit with its pleasure.

(8) Eternal fame can come only to the poet who writes of eternal things.

That these principles represent in part a Christianizing of classical theory is apparent, for however much its advocates believed in the divine fury or divine inspiration as the *sine qua non* of poetry, most of them had been exposed to considerable learning.

In dedicating to Queen Elizabeth *The First Part of the Catalogue of English printed Bookes* Andrew Maunsell wrote in 1595:

When as the Lord by miracle sent his holy spirite upon his Apostles at Jerusalem, he sent them withall (for the propagation of the Gospell) the gift of Tongs, that the strangers there gathered together, heard every man in his own tongue, the wonderful works of God. So now by ordinarie meanes for the furtherance of the same, hath hee given not onely his holy spirit to your sacred Majestie, and godly subjects, but also the gift of Tongues. Whereby it is come to passe (through the blessing of God, and your most godly and peaceable government) that whatsoever excellent knowledge of God, or godlynesse in anie language, we have it in some measure in our owne.

Certainly the divine poets accepted Du Bartas as the special agent through whom a new message came to them, and they called upon their knowledge of languages to serve in setting it forth.

As I have said, the King of Scotland, who was then in communication with those in England who shared his hope that he would be King of England, was the first on that island to provide Bartas's work with an English tongue. In May of 1587, Du Bartas himself came by way of England to Scotland, apparently in answer to the enthusiastic invitation of King James expressing his desire to see Urania's secretary.

In spite of the presumptions of James's letter, it would seem that when Du Bartas arrived in Edinburgh, he did not come wholly as a divine messenger for, according to Sir James Melville, he came also as the agent of the King of Navarre. Melville states that Mr Peter Yong and Colonel Stuart had just returned from their sally into Denmark to look over a prospective bride for His Majesty. They reported themselves as pleased with the Danish princess, and James sent off another embassy:

These Ambassadours were not well imbarked, when Monsieur *Dubartas* arrived here to visit the King's Majesty, who, he heard, had him in great esteem, for his rare Poesie set out in the *French* Tongue. He would not say that he had a secret Commission to propose the Princess of *Navarre* as a fit marriage for His Majesty, but that the King of *Navarre*'s Secretary willed him, seeing he was to come this way, as on his own head, to propose the said marriage. Monsieur *Dubartus*'s Qualities were so good, and his Credit so great with his Majesty, that it appeared if the Ambassadours had not already made Sail, that their Voyage should have been stayed for that Season.

Du Bartas pressed the matter of the marriage, and Melville and his brother were sent to view the Princess of Navarre and to bring home her picture. Melville gives a most amusing account of James's having finally taken the pictures of the rival princesses with him into retirement for fifteen days to seek the counsel of God in the matter. He emerged thinking that God had advised in favour of Denmark. Time had passed, and Du Bartas had gone home.[1]

James, nevertheless, continued to translate Du Bartas. *His Majesties Poeticall Exercises*, published in 1591 in Edinburgh, had three sections in addition to its prefatory material. The first included James's translation of 'The Exord, or Preface of the Second Week of Du Bartas', 'The Translators Invocation', and his translation of *The Furies* of Du Bartas. The second section was, except for a solitary sonnet, given over to James's own poem, *The Lepanto*, in which he seems to have set out to write another *Jerusalem Delivered*. The third section consisted of a French translation by Du Bartas of *The Lepanto* and a flattering poem by the translator to the royal author. Each section contained an address by the author to the reader. In the first James praises Du Bartas; in the last Du Bartas praises James. The whole work constitutes a most admirable record of literary reciprocity.[2]

There can be little doubt in the mind of anyone who reads the ponderous utterances of the King that he rather fancied himself in the role of successor to both David and Solomon as a king on whom God had bestowed his special grace and wisdom, and as penman to the Holy Ghost. In 1593 Gabriel Harvey, who also spoke ponderously, contrived to flatter both King and poet:

And now whiles I consider what a Trompet of Honour Homer hath bene to sturre up many woorthy Princes, I cannot forget the

---

[1] *The Memoires of Sir James Melvil of Hal-Hill: . . . now published from the Original Manuscript*, by George Scott, Gent. (London, 1683), pp. 176–7.

[2] A. F. Westcott, *New Poems by James I of England* (New York, 1911), discussed the group of poets about the King. On Hudson see pp. xxxviii–xl. He also published fragments of other translations of Du Bartas made by King James, pp. 54–8. The first of these fragments had been previously published by R. S. Rait in *Lusus Regius*.

woorthy Prince that is a Homer to himselfe, a Golden spurre to Nobility, a Scepter to Vertue, a Verdure to the Spring, a Sunne to the day, and hath not onely translated the two divine Poems of Salustius du Bartas, his heavenly Urany, and his hellish Furies, but hath readd a most valorous Martial Lecture unto himselfe in his own victorious Lepanto, a short, but heroicall, worke, in meeter, but royall meeter, fit for a Davids harpe—Lepanto, first the glory of Christendome against the Turke, and now the garland of a soveraine crowne....The afore-named Bartas (whome elsewhere I have stiled the Treasurer of Humanity and the Jeweller of Divinity), for the highnesse of his subject and the majesty of his verse nothing inferiour unto Dante (whome some Italians preferre before Virgil or Homer), a right inspired and enravished Poet, full of chosen, grave, profound, venerable, and stately matter, even in the next Degree to the sacred and reverend stile of heavenly Divinity it selfe; in a manner the onely Poet whome Urany hath voutsafed to Laureate with her owne heavenly hand, and worthy to bee alleadged of Divines and Councellours, as Homer is quoted of Philosophers and Oratours....What a judgement hath that noble youth, the harvest of the Spring, the sapp of Appollos tree, the diademe of the Muses, that leaveth the enticingest flowers of delite, to reape the fruites of wisdome?[1]

The youth maintained his role of royal author to the end, writing of education and politics and religion to be acclaimed as wise a king as Solomon and translating the Psalms of David to complete his claim as another divine poet.[2]

[1] G. G. Smith, vol. II, pp. 265–6.
[2] In 'The Author to the Reader' James speaks of hoping to present 'my APOCALYPS, and also suche nomber of the Psalmes as I have perfited', as he hopes for encouragement in finishing the task. See D. Harris Willson, *King James VI and I* (New York, 1956), ch. IV, 'The Harp of David', and pp. 81–4.

CHAPTER X

DU BARTAS AND ENGLISH POETS

THE political flirtations between the young Scots king and the Englishmen who shared at least tentatively his hopes for the English crown in the indeterminate future have often been recounted by historians, but the literary associations of the King with such groups have not been adequately explored. At the political centre of an English group until his death was Robert Dudley, Earl of Leicester. The central figure as far as literature was concerned was his nephew, Sir Philip Sidney. It will be remembered that one of the tutors of King James was George Buchanan, a man famous for his contribution to the new divine drama because of the Latin plays written while he was a schoolmaster in France, and one who continued to make his contribution to divine literature by translating the Psalms into Latin. With this English group Buchanan exchanged ideas on political matters, and when Sidney went to the continent, he carried a letter from Buchanan to Languet, who was to become one of the most important influences in his life. James's favourite, the Master of Gray, was Sidney's friend, and Westcott concluded that Sidney and James 'were on friendly terms and that communication had passed between them'. James contributed to the Cambridge volume of laments at Sidney's death, and Sidney certainly shared the King's interest in Du Bartas.[1]

Sidney died in 1586, but on 23 August, 1588, there was entered on the Stationers' Register to William Ponsonby, after notice of payment for registering the *Arcadia*, a record of a like

---

[1] See James E. Phillips, 'George Buchanan and the Sidney Circle', *Huntington Library Quarterly*, vol. XII (1948), pp. 23–55. A. F. Westcott, *New Poems* (pp. xviii–xxi), records Buchanan's influence on James, and (pp. lxxi–lxxxi and 88) discusses the relation of James and Sidney. He prints the English version of the King's sonnet on Sidney's death, p. 29. John Buxton (pp. 50–63) gives an account of Buchanan's friendship with Hubert Languet and of Languet's influence on Sidney and (p. 52) notes the impression Sidney made on Henry of Navarre when they met in Paris in 1572. A. W. Osborn, *Sir Philip Sidney en France* (Paris, 1932), discusses Sidney and Du Bartas, pp. 35, 36, and 66.

payment for registering 'A translation of *SALUST DE BARTAS*. Done by ye same Sir P. in the Englishe'. Of the fate of this work I shall write later. Here I want to call attention to the close relationship of Sidney's plea for divine poetry in his *Apology for Poetry* to that of *L'Uranie* of Du Bartas. In discussing the dearth of good English lyric poetry, Sidney wrote:

> Other sorts of Poetry almost have we none, but that Lyricall kind of Songs and Sonnets: which, Lord, if he gave us so good mindes, how well it might be imployed, and with howe heavenly fruite, both private and publique, in singing the prayses of the immortall beauty, the immortall goodnes of that God who gyveth us hands to write and wits to conceive; of which we might well want words, but never matter; of which we could turne our eies to nothing, but we should ever have new budding occasions.

He shows the kinship of his ideas to those of Du Bartas also as he replies to the reiterated objection that poetry ensnares its readers in evil:

> how much it abuseth mens wit, trayning it to wanton sinfulnes and lustfull love: for indeed that is the principall, if not the onely abuse I can heare alledged....Grant, I say, what soever they wil have granted; that not onely love, but lust, but vanitie, but (if they list) scurrilitie, possesseth many leaves of the Poets bookes: yet thinke I, when this is granted, they will finde theyr sentence may with good manners put the last words foremost, and not say that Poetrie abuseth mans wit, but that mans wit abuseth Poetrie.

Like Du Bartas Sidney answers Plato:

> *Plato* therefore (whose authoritie I had much rather justly conster then unjustly resist) meant not in general of Poets...but only meant to drive out those wrong opinions of the Deitie (whereof now, without further law, Christianity hat taken away all the hurtful beliefe), perchance (as he thought) norished by the then esteemed Poets. And a man need goe no further then to *Plato* himselfe to know his meaning: who, in his Dialogue called *Ion*, giveth high and rightly divine commendation to Poetrie...especially sith he attributeth unto Poesie more then my selfe doe, namely, to be a very inspiring of a divine force, farre above mans wit, as in the aforenamed Dialogue is apparant.[1]

When Sidney turns to ask why England was not then producing poets and honouring them in spite of the fact that it 'certainly

---

[1] G. G. Smith, vol. i, pp. 201, 186–91, 192, 194.

in wit ought to passe all other', he instanced as patrons of poetry elsewhere King Robert of Sicily, King Francis of France (the brother of Marguerite of Navarre), and King James of Scotland, and 'So piercing wits as George Buchanan'. In defending plays, he instances 'The tragedies of *Buchanan* [which] doe justly bring forth a divine admiration'.

The relations of Spenser with Leicester and Sidney and the Countess of Pembroke have so often been anatomized by so many that I shall not repeat the evidence which can be found in almost any life of Spenser, but I must bring to mind the fact that for a time he was of that circle which had its political centre in Leicester and its literary centre in Sidney.[1] When in 1579 *The Shepheardes Calender* was published by 'Immerito', it was dedicated to 'the noble and Vertous Gentleman most worthy of all titles of learning and chevalrie M. Philip Sidney'. By 1591, when the volume of *Complaints* was printed, Edmund Spenser was no longer 'unkent', for the first three books of the *Faerie Queene* had been published and 'Immerito' had ventured to dedicate his work to Queen Elizabeth in his own name. In the volume of *Complaints, Virgils Gnat* was said to have been 'Long since dedicated' to Leicester 'late deceased', and *The Ruines of Time*, dedicated to the Countess of Pembroke, was offered as atonement for his tardy memorializing of Sidney, whom he called 'the Patron of my young Muses'. Spenser acknowledged 'the Straight bandes of duetie' by which he was tied to him. If Sir Calidore, the Knight of Courtesy in Book VI of the *Faerie Queene*, represents Sidney as very many have thought, the tribute to him who 'did steale mens hearts away' is greater than any words of dedication, but that Spenser knew and admired Sidney no one can doubt, not even the scholars who dispute what to many seem simple statements of fact.

What the impetus was that made Spenser turn to divine poetry no one can say, but before the publication of his *Complaints* he had written a good deal of such poetry. He may have been led to it by his contribution of four unrhymed sonnets from the Book of Revelation in the translation of *A Theatre*

---

[1] See, for instance, A. C. Judson, *The Life of Edmund Spenser* (Baltimore, 1945), ch. VIII and pp. 149–50.

for Worldlings by the Flemish refugee poet Vander Noodt. At any rate, his printer, Ponsonby, in addressing the reader in the *Complaints* volume said that in addition to the poems there assembled, Spenser had witten 'sundrie others, namelie *Ecclesiastes*, and *Canticum canticorum* translated.... Besides some other Pamphlets looselie scattered abroad: as *The dying Pellican, The howers of the Lord, The sacrifice of a sinner, The seven Psalmes*, &c.' which he hoped to publish. But these works have never yet been found.[1]

During the time that Spenser must have been writing this considerable body of divine poetry Sidney was translating the Psalms and Du Bartas; Gabriel Harvey, Spenser's particular friend, was praising King James and Du Bartas, and *L'Uranie* had introduced the new Muse sponsored by King James. That Spenser too was interested in Du Bartas is shown by Harvey's record of his praise: 'M. Spenser conceives the like pleasure in the fourth day of the first Weeke of Bartas. Which he esteemes as the proper profession of Urania'.[2]

And Spenser, in 'L'Envoy' to the *Ruines of Rome*, after praising '*Bellay*, first garland of free Poësie / That *France* brought forth', adds his tribute to another French poet:

> And after thee, gins *Bartas* hie to rayse
> His heavenly Muse, th'Almightie to adore.

Furthermore, it seems to me impossible to dissociate the Urania speaking in the *The Teares of the Muses* and the Urania of Du Bartas. Spenser's Urania bewails the love of blindness and ignorance which makes men dwell in darkness. Certainly she is the Christian Muse as she recounts the fruits of knowledge:

> Through knowledge we behold the worlds creation,
> How in his cradle first he fostred was;
> And judge of Natures cunning operation,
> How things she formed of a formlesse mas:
> By knowledge wee do learne our selves to knowe,
> And what to man, and what to God wee owe.

[1] All references are to *The Works of Edmund Spenser: The Minor Poems*, ed. by C. G. Osgood and H. B. Lotspeich (Baltimore, vol. I (1943), vol. II, (1947)).

[2] G. C. Moore Smith, *Gabriel Harvey's Marginalia* (Stratford-upon-Avon, 1913), p. 161. There are many references to Du Bartas in which Harvey links Du Bartas with the great ones of all time. See especially pp. 115, 137, 168.

From hence wee mount aloft unto the skie,
And looke into the Christall firmament:
There we behold the heavens great *Hierarchie*,
The Starres pure light, the Spheres swift movement,
The Spirites and Intelligences fayre,
And Angels waighting on th'Almightyies chayre.

And there with humble minde and high insight,
Th'eternall Makers majestie wee viewe,
His love, his truth, his glorie, and his might,
And mercie more than mortall men can vew.
O soveraigne Lord, O soveraigne happinesse
To see thee, and thy mercie measurelesse.

Such happiness have they that do embrace
The precepts of my heavenlie discipline,
But shame and sorrow and accursed case
Have they, that scorne the schoole of arts divine.
And banish me, which doo professe the skill
To make men heavenly wise, through humbled will.

It is bewildering to find Harold Stein insisting that Spenser
could not have referred to Du Bartas in 'L'Envoy' to the
Teares of the Muses as a 'heavenly' poet on the basis of his
Urania.[1] It is even more puzzling to find W. L. Renwick
annotating the envoy to his *Ruines of Rome* by a reference to
L'Uranie of Du Bartas and then commenting on the 'Urania' of
the *Teares of the Muses*:

> This is typical of the mixed origins of Spenser's philosophy,....Here
> Spenser summarizes the content of philosophical studies, forgetting
> for a moment the Muse of Astronomy in his pleased recollections
> of the Bible, Cicero, Christian theology, natural philosophy, and
> ethics.[2]

It should be remembered also that Spenser refers to the
Countess of Pembroke as Urania in *Colin Clouts Come Home
Again* because in her mind 'All heavenly gifts and riches locked
are'—a reference certainly not intended to suggest the Countess
of Pembroke as a woman wise in the ways of astronomy.

---

[1] *Studies in Spenser's Complaints* (New York, 1934), pp. 63-4.
[2] Ed. *Complaints* (London, 1928), p. 215.

Dedicating his *Fowre Hymnes* to Margaret, Countess of Cumberland, and Mary,[1] Countess of Warwick, Spenser wrote:

Having in the greener times of my youth, composed these former two Hymnes in the praise of Love and beautie, and finding that the same too pleased those of like age and disposition, which being too vehemently caried with that kind of affection, do rather sucke out poyson to their strong passion, then hony to their honest delight, I was moved by the one of you two most excellent Ladies, to call in the same. But being unable so to doe, by reason that many copies thereof were formerly scattered abroad, I resolved at least to amend, and by way of retraction to reforme them, making instead of those two Hymnes of earthly or naturall love and beautie, two others of heavenly and celestiall.

It has frequently been noted that Spenser is at least inconsistent in publishing the two early hymns on love and beauty with the later divine poems, and since there is no record of their previous publication, scholars have recently tended to regard the four hymns as a literary unit.[2] The dedication must then be looked upon as an integral part of the whole, its substance repeated in the second stanza of *An Hymne of Heavenly Love*:

> Many lewd layes (ah woe is me the more)
> In praise of that mad fit, which fooles call love,
> I have in th'heat of youth made heretofore,
> That in light wits did loose affection move.
> But all those follies now I do reprove,
> And turned have the tenor of my string,
> The heavenly prayses of true love to sing.

The hymn proper tells the Christian story in its glory, the invocation to the Holy Spirit pleading for that heavenly aid which is necessary to him:

> Yet O most blessed Spirit, pure lampe of light,
> Eternal spring of grace and wisedome trew,
> Vouchsafe to shed into my barren spright,
> Some little drop of thy celestial dew,
> That may my rymes with sweet infuse embrew,
> And give me words equall unto my thought,
> To tell the marveiles by thy mercie wrought.

---

[1] Renwick identifies the lady as Anne, rather than Mary, who was Countess of Warwick. Church had made the identification previously.

[2] Edwin Greenlaw was, I believe, the first to advance this theory in 'Spenser's Influence on *Paradise Lost*', *Studies in Philology*, vol. xvii, pp. 320–59.

Here then in this hymn he uses the formula of *L'Uranie*. Repenting his 'lewd layes', he turns to heavenly themes. Invoking the Holy Spirit as his muse, he recites the Christian story. Finally, he pleads that earth may lift eyes to heaven, attaining, through the contemplation of Christ and his love, to heavenly thoughts and inspiration.

In *An Hymne of Heavenly Beautie* Spenser again invokes the 'most almightie Spright, / From whom all guifts of wit and knowledge flow', and he conducts the reader finally to the very throne of God:

> There in his bosome *Sapience* doth sit,
> The soveraine dearling of the *Deity*,
> Clad like a Queene in royall robes, most fit
> For so great powre and peerelesse majesty.
> And all with gemmes and jewels gorgeously
> Adornd, that brighter then the starres appeare,
> And make her native brightnes seem more cleare.
>
> And on her head a crowne of purest gold
> Is set, in signe of highest soveraignty;
> And in her hand a scepter she doth hold,
> With which she rules the house of God on hy,
> And menageth the ever-moving sky,
> And in the same these lower creatures all
> Subjected to her powre imperiall.

The rest of the hymn describes the bliss which comes to one who is allowed by God to behold Heavenly Beauty or Sapience, and the willingness with which he puts away the false beauties that have heretofore fed his senses.

When it is remembered that Heavenly Beauty is personified as Venus Urania in Ficino, the following comment by Professor Renwick on Spenser's Sapience suggests another link in the chain of reference: 'Spenser had to find a parallel to or substitute for Venus capable of support by Christian authority. In Ficino he found Heavenly Beauty identified with Sapience, and he found Sapience in his Bible.'[1] In Du Bartas Spenser could have found a description of Urania which merged with

---

[1] Renwick, *Daphnaida and other Poems* (London, 1929), p. 212.

that of Venus Urania and justified a Sapience who 'rules the house of God on hy, / And menageth the ever-moving sky'.

Professor Fletcher thought Sapience should be identified as the Holy Ghost,[1] and it may be noted that after the Muse of astronomy was taken over as the heavenly Muse, the invocations to her employed very often the same language as those addressed to the Holy Spirit. Often, indeed, both were invoked in a continuous passage, a typical instance occurring in *Saint Peters Ten Teares*, where the unknown author, after bidding 'Imaginarie Muses' to be gone, seeks aid in writing his poem:

> Imaginarie *Muses* get you gone,
>   And you of *Ideas* idle company:
> That place your Paradice in *Cetheron*,
>   And call upon the Nimphes of *Thessalie*.
> Restraine your haughtie metaphorick lines:
> For reverent truth your glory undermines.
>
> The Throne of Heaven is her holy hill,
>   Whence flowes the Spring of saving health:
> In steed of birdes Archangels sing her will,
>   The Temple is her loue, and peace her wealth.
> O sacred sweete, and sweetest sacred substance:
> Unloose the Springs of *Peters* poore repentance.
>
> And thou O holy Ghost and sacred spirit,
>   Faire milke white Doue, unto the meekest lambe:
> The minister of heaven, the Lord of merit,
>   The gladdest messenger that ever came.
> Infuse thy grace so sweetly in mine eares,
> That I may truely write Saint Peters Teares.[2]

King James prayed 'To make the holie Spreit my Muse', and in the next century Samuel Austin more definitely besought that 'Thy Spirit bee my Urania'.[3]

Meanwhile a French and Latin edition of *L'Uranie* was published in 1589. In 1605 Joshua Sylvester added an English

---

[1] J. B. Fletcher, 'A Study in Renaissance Mysticism: Spenser's Fowre Hymnes', *Publications of the Modern Language Association*, vol. XXVI, pp. 452–75.

[2] Printed in 1597.

[3] *His Majesties Poeticall Exercises* (Edinburgh, 1591), fol. H 2ʳ, and *Austins Urania or the Heavenly Muse* (London, 1629), p. 7.

translation of *Urania* to the other translations of Du Bartas he had made, dedicating it to Mistress Jone Essex:

URANIA (noblest of the learned NINE)
Coming from Heav'n to call my Muse from Earth
From Loves, loose Sonnets, & lascivious Mirth,...

His translation continued to be published in editions of his work, and *Urania* became the familiar accompaniment of divine literature in the seventeenth century, sometimes used as a title, sometimes addressed as the appropriate Muse, often associated with the Holy Spirit in the writer's thought, and appearing in *Paradise Lost* to confound the modern critic.

CHAPTER XI

POEMS ABOUT BIBLICAL HEROES

THE divine epic as well as the Muse of divine poetry entered English literature through the work of Du Bartas, but there had been attempts earlier to popularize the accounts of the heroes in Bible story. I have already noted *The Life and Death of Joseph* which William Hunnis extracted from his translation of Genesis to include in his later work.[1] *The Holie Historie of King David* which was published by John Marbecke (or Merbecke) in 1579 might likewise be considered under the head of 'translations', but Marbecke has treated it as a narrative poem written in heptameter couplets, beginning with the sixteenth chapter of the First Book of Kings (the First Book of Samuel in the King James version):

> When as the Lord out of his sight had Saul the king reject,
> Unto the Prophet Samuel his worde he did direct.

He wrote it and gave it to the press, he said, because he 'regarded that such histories as Gods spirite hath left and commended unto us in the sacred Scriptures, might be advanced before, and infinitely farre above those vayne, unstable, and most unfruitfull devises...proceeding from the pen of man'. Furthermore, he intended 'to impayre hereby the credite as well of all leude lying legends of unsound saints, consecrated and canonized in the high court of *Rome*'.

Marbecke was the musician chosen by Cranmer to furnish the music for his first prayer book. He had been sentenced in 1543 to die for his heretical beliefs and had escaped apparently because of his reputation as a musician. In later life he seems to have given up his music for religion, and he is now known chiefly because of his music for the first prayer book and because of having made the first *Concordance* to the English Bible.[2] How early he had celebrated King David in his poem there is no way of judging.

[1] See ch. VIII.
[2] An account of Marbecke's religious works other than his *David* is found in R. M. Stevenson, *Patterns of Protestant Church Music* (Duke University Press, 1953), pp. 24–40.

In addition to the isolating of portions of the Bible which had been turned into verse and which recounted the adventures of Biblical heroes, there were few poems about Biblical heroes written in England before the arrival of Du Bartas in translation.

In 1619 Michael Drayton, addressing the reader, gave an explanation of the word *legend* which he was applying to poems he had begun to publish in 1593 and which is of interest in the study of the epic in this period:

The word *Legend*, so called of the Latine Gerund, *Legendum*, and signifying,...things specially worthy to be read, was anciently used in an Ecclesiasticall sense, and restrained therein to things written in Prose, touching the Lives of Saints.... To particularize the Lawes of this Poeme, were to teach the making of a Poeme; a Worke for a Volume, not an Epistle. But the principall is, that being a *Species* of an *Epick* or Heroick Poeme, it eminently describeth the act or acts of some one or other eminent Person; not with too much labour, compasse, or extension, but roundly rather, and by way of Briefe, or *Compendium*.[1]

If we accept Drayton's explanation of what constitutes a heroic poem, it is possible to consider poems written about a hero, in whatever way they are labelled, as related to the epic. Such as I have found, however, are more clearly related to the saint's legend than to the formal epic until Du Bartas's work is known. The earliest of the kind I know is *The History of Jacob and his Twelve Sons*, first printed about 1510, but still being reprinted in 1570. It is really a twofold legend, of Jacob and of Joseph. Written in rhyme royal, it is yet an amazingly naïve poem to find new readers as late as 1570, though perhaps worthy of note is its emphasis on the truth of the story as opposed to contrived fable, the last stanza admonishing

> Now ye that shall this Book see or read
> Doo not think that it is contrived of any fable
> For it is the very Bible indeed
> Wherin our faith is grounded ful stable.

Another *History of Joseph*, begun twenty-four years before it was finished in 1569, was written by William Forrest, chaplain to Queen Mary. I have mentioned him earlier as one who wrote

---

[1] *The Works of Michael Drayton*, ed. J. W. Hebel (Oxford, 1932), vol. II, p. 382.

translations of the Psalms, and I note his continued interest in divine poetry under Queen Elizabeth because I want to point out once more that the movement did involve Catholic writers throughout the century. Forrest's poem was not printed until the Roxburghe Club rescued it, and indeed its chief interest aside from its having a Catholic author lies in its reference to Chaucer, Lydgate, and Gower in the verses prefaced to the first part, and in its reference to Alexander Barclay and the Earl of Surrey in the dedication to the Duke of Norfolk, Surrey's son, in the second part. The poem was written in rhyme royal and the two parts dealt with Joseph's troubles and Joseph's felicity.[1]

In another Catholic poem, written like Forrest's work in two parts and on a subject which suggests the saint's legend, we find unmistakable evidence of the author's knowledge of the classical epic. The poem is *The Life and Death of Mary Magdalene*, and it too was not published until the Early English Text Society printed it in 1899.[2] The author, apparently a Thomas Robinson, was, it seems to me, a not inconsiderable poet, but whether he was the Thomas Robinson who was Dean of Durham under Queen Mary, and whether he wrote the piece before 1569, as the editor thinks, I am not at all sure. The difficulty in determining the date comes from the fact that dedicatory lines in the prologue of the Harleian manuscript version were addressed to Lord Henry Clifford, and the Lord Henry Clifford who was the second Earl of Cumberland died in 1569. Yet this prologue in a long defence of poetry refers to 'Cydney, glory of his time', and to 'Harrington among our noble Peares' as one of the poets of later years. The editor seems to have been a bit confused, for he thought the reference to 'Cydney' must be to Sir Henry Sidney, Philip's father, a man not thought of as contributing to poetry, and he annotated 'Harrington' by a summary of the life of James Harrington who was born in 1611.

[1] See ch. v. Prologues and extracts from *Joseph* were appended to Forrest's *History of Grisild*, ed. W. R. Macray (Roxburghe Club, London, 1875). The manuscript exists in the Bodleian Library (F. Madan and H. H. E. Craster, *A Summary Catalogue of Western Manuscripts* (Oxford, 1924), vol. VI, p. 98) and I have seen it reproduced on MLA Rotograph 308. Forrest's second Griselda was Queen Catherine, divorced wife of Henry VIII.

[2] Ed. H. Oscar Sommer. For his discussion of the authorship see his Introduction and compare the Notes on p. 71.

Whoever was the author, *The Life and Death of Mary Magdalene* presents an interesting mixture of saint's legend, formal epic, and Renaissance ornament. It is written in the eight-line stanza of Chaucer's *Monk's Tale*, the stanza called by King James *ballat royal* and prescribed by him for treating high and grave subjects, especially those drawn out of learned authors. The editor describes it as 'most probably one of the last legends of saints written in England', and the life of Mary is used mainly as the framework for allegory; yet it is clearly concerned to follow the traditional epic structure. The first two stanzas state the theme or proposition, the third and fourth offer the invocation to him 'that all enlightens', the story begins *in medias res* with a description of the Palace of Pleasure in which Mary dwells, the loveliest of the attendants upon Aphrodite. Epic similes are strewn about, and epithets abound. The most striking parts of the poem, however, are the long descriptions of the Palace of Pleasure, the Cave of Melancholy, and the Palace of Wisdom, calling to mind Sackville and Spenser as well as the *Castle of Perseverance*. Only at the end of the poem does Bible story prevail over allegory, and classical story rather than scriptural story provides the ornament and sets the moods throughout.

When in 1584 Thomas Hudson published his translation of Du Bartas's *Judit*, he introduced the divine epic into *English* literature, as I have stated before, though it was published in Edinburgh. Thomas Hudson was an Englishman, a musician, a 'violar', who had been attached to the household of King James from the time the King was a baby, and who rose to be Master of the Scottish Royal Chapel. The printer, Vautrollier, was an English printer then publishing in Edinburgh. King James had instructed Hudson to translate the poem into English. It was repeatedly republished in England in the early years of the seventeenth century.[1]

In Italy Biblical epics[2] had been written in Latin some time

---

[1] James Craigie's introduction to his edition of Hudson's poem, *Scottish Text Society*, 3rd ser. vol. 14, gives the fullest available account of Hudson's life with adequate comments on the poem.

[2] R. A. Sayce, *The French Biblical Epic in the Seventeenth Century* (Oxford, 1955), pp. 49–56. All the early chapters of this book are helpful in understanding the initial ventures which came to fulfilment in the seventeenth-century epic.

before Du Bartas wrote his *Judit*, most notably Sannazzaro's *De partu Virginis* (1526), Vida's *Christiad* (1535), and Fracastorius's *Joseph* (1555), and it is of some importance to the English divine epic that Du Bartas went for his models to Homer and Virgil and Ariosto (though the name of Ariosto was dropped from later editions), rather than to these earlier Latin works, for it was Hudson's *Judith* and later the translations of the *Divine Weeks and Works* which were to influence the divine epic of the seventeenth century in England.

Judith was divided into six books, each book preceded by a prose summary. It opened with an echo of the familiar *Arma virumque cano*:

> I sing the vertues of a valiant Dame,
> Who in defence of *Jacob* overcame:
> Th'*Assyrian* Prince, and slew that *Pagan* stout,
> Who had beset *Bethulia* walles about.

The statement of the theme or proposition was followed by an 'invocation of the true God', as the marginal note points out, and this in turn by a dedication to James substituted for Du Bartas's dedication. The invocation asks that God

> With sacred furie fill my hart at length.
> And with thy *Holy* sprite, my sprite enspire.

The story begins *in medias res*. The antecedent action is only gradually made known and, as James Craigie, the modern editor, has pointed out, the situation is not made clear until the fifth book. There are long speeches, descriptions of battles and sieges, a catalogue of places. There are long epic similes, epithets in abundance, exclamations and moralizing passages. Pagan story and pagan mythology are freely used to furnish literary ornament, as are Bible stories. Judith habitually occupies herself with embroidering tales of Lot's wife, of Susanna, of Joseph, and of Jephtha's daughter. But as she goes in to Holophernes, the tapestries which she can see are telling stories of Sardanapalus, of Cyrus, of Xopyrus. Judith's beauties are inventoried as lavishly as Solomon or Petrarch might prescribe, though with modest omissions, and the culmination of the description is reached in a comparison suggesting more of classical than of Biblical learning:

> In short, this *Judith* was so passing faire,
> that if the learned *Zeuxis* had been thaire,
> And seene this Dame, when he with pensile drew,
> the *Croton* Dames, to forme the picture trew
> Of her, for whome both *Grece* and *Asia* fought;
> this onely patron chief he would have sought.[1]

Du Bartas had been apologetic for writing his *Judit* on '*un si stérile sujet*', saying he had but complied with the command of a great personage in so doing. When he went forward to his next epic, he advanced to greatness if, as his *Uranie* had declared, a great subject makes a great poem, for he undertook to write an epic on the creation of the world, publishing in 1578 *La Sep- maine, ou Creation du Monde*.[2]

It was inevitable that, with the royal patronage of King James, Du Bartas should become a much-translated poet, and his *Divine Weeks and Works* became a part of English literature as it was translated, day by day, and section by section. *The First Week* was also translated into Latin to make immortality certain. The first of the translators to put it into English was, however, Philip Sidney, the entry for whose work in the Stationers' Register in 1588 I have earlier recorded. Whether he undertook the translation because of a friendship with the poet or because of a desire to join in the godly enterprise initiated by King James there is no evidence. In any case his political and religious and literary relationships would have made him the proper translator for the most Christian poet. Florio speaks of having seen Sidney's translation,[3] and others refer to its existence, but so far no scholar has found the key which might unlock the secret of that high place, in which, according to Sylvester, it was kept from common light.

In 1590 Joshua Sylvester, who was to become the acknow-

---

[1] Bk. IV, ll. 361–7.

[2] The editions of *La Sepmaine* and *La Seconde Sepmaine* are recorded in *Works*, vol. I, pp. 70–93.

[3] In the epistle addressed to the Countess of Rutland and Lady Penelope Rich prefixed to the second book of his translation of *The Essayes of Montaigne* (London, 1603).

ledged medium for Du Bartas to speak English, began the work by which he is known, publishing, only a few months after Du Bartas had presented the poem to the King of Navarre, *A Canticle of the Victorie Obtained by Henry the Fourth at Ivry*. In 1592 he published *The Triumph of Faith*, thus putting into English the third of the long poems of *La Chrestiene Muse*. In 1594, he published *Monodia*, ostensibly an elegy upon the death of a much elegized and eulogized lady, Dame Helen Branch, but in addition to her poetical biography and her meed of praise, he contributed to her volume the two translations from Du Bartas which had already been printed and also two sections from *The Second Week*, *The Sacrifice of Isaac* and *The Ship-wracke of Jonas*, here treated as independent narratives.[1]

In 1595, J. Jackson printed for G. Seaton *The First Day of the Worldes Creation*, the translation attributed to Sylvester in the *Short-Title Catalogue*, but the translator speaks of the work as undertaken 'in the nonage of my studies, before I was professed', it is not written in Sylvester's metre but in rhyme royal, and Professor William Jackson declares it is definitely not a Sylvester translation. Whoever he was, the author wrote modestly in dedicating his work to Anthony Bacon that he had hesitated to make known his work:

not in respect, either of the matter which is heavenly, nor the Author which is excellent, desired I to silence my infantlike penn from proceeding heerin: but bicause this most Christian Poet, and noble *Frenchman Lord of Bartas*, might have been naturalized amongst us, either by a generall act of a Poeticall Parliament: or have obtained a kingly translator for his weeke (as he did for his Furies): or rather a divine *Sidney*, a stately *Spencer*, or a sweet *Daniell* for an interpreter thereof. For so was I put in a false hope by some, that the living Pen of that worthie deceased knight, had amongst other his charitable legacies bequeathed a rich suit, after our best English fashion, unto this honorable Poet: and therefore suppressed my ragged weeds, till I perceived their promise shrunke, & my expectation still

---

[1] The *S.T.C.* lists *Epicedium: a funerall song upon Lady Helen Branch* published by T. Creede in 1594 as written by 'W. Har.'. The signature in the British Museum copy is W. Har., but I doubt whether that is the full name or even the name of the author. The Huntington Library, in offering a supplement to the *S.T.C.* Bulletin no. 4 (1933), presents two more commendatory volumes with no assigning of authorship.

naked. And yet if any of the fore-named Heroicall Spirits have undertaken the performance of that act, I would not have my seelie daies worke to prejudice their Weeke, nor my moat to flutter in the presence of their bright beames: wherefore though my rash quill hath tooke a further flight into this translation: yet have I pinioned up the rest of hir fethers, and suffered onely the first daies worke to passe abroad: till I may understand whether any of those sweete recording Swans have waded in the derivation of these streames or no.

Another edition of the work was published in 1596, still with no indication of the author.

In 1598 Sylvester published his version of *The Second Weeke, or Childhood of the World* dedicating the first book of the first day of the second week to the Earl of Essex, and it may be worth noting that the friendship between Essex and the King of Scotland had so far advanced that by 1598, according to the King's biographer, 'the French ambassador in London noticed how James entrusted to Essex all that he wished negotiated in the English court'.[1] However, Sylvester ventured to provide a new translation for the sections which the King had earlier translated—the opening invocation and *The Furies*. Further, he inserted in italics an addition to the invocation, speaking in his own person:

> And gracious guide, which doost all grace infuse,
> Since it hath pleas'd thee taske my tardy muse
> With these high theames, that through mine artles pen
> This holy Lampe may light my Countri-men:
> Ah teach my hand, tuch mine unlearned lips,
> Least, as the Earths grosse body doth eclipse
> Bright Cynthiaes beames, when it is interpos'd
> Twixt her and *Phoebus*: so mine ill-dispos'd
> Darke, gloomy, ignorance, obscure the rayes
> Of this divine Sunne of these learned dayes:
> O furnish me with an un-vulgar stile,
> That I by this may wean our wanton Ile
> From *Ovids* heires, and their unhallowed spell
> Heere charming sences, chaining soules in hell,
> Let this provoke our modern wits to sacre
> Their wondrous gifts to honor thee their Maker:

[1] Helen G. Stafford, *James VI of Scotland and the Throne of England* (N.Y. and London, 1940), p. 203.

That our mysterious ELFINE Oracle,
Deepe, morall, grave, inventions miracle:
My deere sweet DANIEL, sharpe-conceipted, breefe,
Civill, sententious, for pure accents chiefe:
And our new NASO, that so passionates
Th'heroik sighes of love sick Potentates,
May change their subject, and advance their wings
Up to these higher and more holy things;
And if (sufficient rich in selfe-invention)
They skorne (as I) to live of strangers pension,
Let them devise new Weekes, new works, new waies
To celebrate the supreme Prince of prayse.

Here is again the traditional message of Urania, the plea for the greatest of poets—Spenser, Daniel, and Drayton—to continue the work of Sidney, to dedicate their talents to Englishing this divine poetry of Du Bartas, or to create a new English divine poetry. Significantly, Sylvester opposes to this divine poetry that of Ovid's heirs who charm the senses and enchain the souls of men in hell.

Finally, when in 1605 Sylvester gathered together his translations in *Bartas his Divine Weekes and Workes*, he dedicated the whole to King James with an elaborate 'Corona Dedicatoria', prefacing his collection, however, by his supreme tribute to Sidney in a sonnet addressed to the readers but arranged in a pyramid of print, which I quote disregarding the idiosyncrasies of its printing:

England's Apelles (rather our Apollo) world's-wonder Sidney, that rare more-than-man, this lovely Venus first to limne beganne, with such a pencill as no penne dares followe: How then shold I, in wit & art so shalow, attempt the *Task* which yet none other can? Far be the thought that mine unlearned hand his heavenly labour shold so much unhallow, yet least (that holy-relique being shrin'd in some high-place, close lockt from common light) my country-men should bee debar'd the sight of these divine pure beauties of the minde; not daring to meddle with Apelles table; this have I muddled as my Muse was able.

In 1608 Sylvester added the translations of the *Third Day* and the *Fourth Day* which had been represented only by fragments in the 1605 edition. Du Bartas had gone no further himself. Meanwhile others had begun the translation of sections of Du Bartas's work, but when in 1621 the printer Lownes published a memorial edition of Sylvester's works, he had become, as I said before, the acknowledged medium for Du Bartas to speak English. Lownes, however, printed Hudson's translation of *Judit* as well as that of Sylvester (*Bethulians Rescue*) in this volume.

The long and complex bibliography of the works of Du Bartas in English has no place in this study, and I shall make no attempt to discuss in any adequate way his major work. *The First Week* has the unity prescribed by the theme, 'the WORLD'S renowned BIRTH', the creation of the world; and the invocation which opens it 'imploreth the gracious assistance of the true God of Heaven, Earth, Aire, and Sea', as the marginal notes indicate. It is divided into seven parts for the recounting of the week's story. *The Second Week* was divided into the inevitable seven sections for the seven days, but each *Day* was further divided into four parts. Four days (sixteen parts) were finished when death intervened. The *Fourth Day* concerns David and has, therefore, a certain unity, but the *Second Day* and the *Third Day* range over a great deal of Old Testament story. Moreover, Du Bartas did not let any of his vast reading in classical story, in natural and moral philosophy, and in theology go to waste in his writing.[1] He found opportunity to introduce references to contemporaries also. His epic similes were noted in the margins of Sylvester's translation, and the English reader would note also the elisions and the epithets which marked the heroic style.

Sylvester did other translations, but I shall mention only that of Fracastorius's *Joseph*, which he called *The Maiden's Blush*, and I mention it because I have already noted it as being written in Italy before Du Bartas began his Biblical poetry. In venturing into original poetry Sylvester was not so successful in winning applause, and Michael Drayton conveyed the general judgment when he wrote about the same time that Lownes was printing the memorial volume:

> And *Silvester* who from the French more weake,
> Made *Bartas* of his sixe dayes labour speake

[1] U. T. Holmes, in *Works*, vol. I, pp. 111–29.

In naturall *English*, who, had he there stayd,
He had done well, and never had bewraid,
His owne invention, to have bin so poore
Who still wrote lesse, in striving to write more.[1]

Drayton was, however, not uninfluenced by Du Bartas and Sylvester, as is apparent when we look at his last poems. He had begun his poetic career in translating the poetic part of the Bible, publishing *The Harmonie of the Church* in 1591. He ended it with the publication in 1630 of *The Muses Elizium* in which a section was set off by a special dedication to Mary, Countess of Dorset, saying 'To her Fame and Memory I consecrate these my divine Poems'.[2] One of the divine poems now called *Moses his Birth and Miracles* had been published earlier, in 1604, as *Moses in a Map of his Miracles*. The volume had been dedicated to Sir Walter Aston, and Drayton's friend, Beale Sapperton, had addressed a sonnet to him in this volume tracing the poet's progress in poetry:

> From humble Sheepcoates, to Loves bow and fires:
> Thence to the armes of Kings, and grieved Peeres:
> Now to the great *Jehovahs* acts aspires
> (Faire Sir) your Poets pen:...

Drayton himself had put his poem in the line of divine poetry when he addressed the reader, saying, 'Those that have accompanied us in this kinde, is that Reverende *Hierony: Vida* his *Christeis*, conteyning the life and miracles of *Christ*, that hath beene, and is, generally received through Christendome (and verie worthely). *Buchanan* his Tragedie of *Jephtha* in another kinde, and *Bartas* his *Judeth*. I could derive thee a Catalogue of their like, though I cite these onely for the varieties.' He explained that 'whatsoever we have from Historie, as from *Josephus, Lyra,* or others of lesse authoritie: we use rather as Jems and exteriour ornaments to beautifie our Subject, than any way to mix the same, with the solide bodie of that which is Canonicall and sacred'.[3]

It is *Judith* that is mentioned in this address, and it was

[1] Drayton, in his epistle to Henry Reynolds, *Works*, vol. III, p. 230.
[2] These poems are published in *Works*, vol. III, pp. 326–439.
[3] *Works*, vol. v, pp. 227–8.

apparently in *Judith* that he found a pattern for his *Moses in a Map of his Miracles*. It follows the epic formula as set by that poem, announcing first the theme or proposition as he proposes to sing of the man who had talked with God face to face. The following invocation carries something of Urania's message:

> *Muse* I invoke the utmost of thy might,...
> To shew how Poesie (simplie hath her praise)
> That from full *Jove* takes her celestiall birth,
> And quick as fire, her glorious self can raise
> Above this base abhominable earth.

Following the custom of French epics, the author then addresses Du Bartas and Sylvester in a dedicatory offering of his poem:

> And thou Translator of that faithfull Muse
> This ALLS creation that divinely song,
> From Courtly *French* (no travaile do'st refuse)
> To make him Master of thy *Genuin* tong,
> *Salust* to thess and *Silvester* thy friend,
> Comes my high Poem peaceably and chaste,
> Your hallow'd labours humbly to attend
> That wrackfull *Time* shall not have power to waste.

The poem is divided into books as *Judith* was divided, three rather than the six of Du Bartas's poem. Drayton does not begin his story *in medias res*, however, but with the birth of his hero, and he proceeds to recount his life and death as they are recorded in the Bible, beginning at the second chapter of Exodus. The first of the three books draws much from non-Biblical sources, and it humanizes and romanticizes the accounts of Moses's mother's grief in abandoning her child, of his sister's adroit handling of his rescue, and of his precocious childhood and youth and his relation to his princess saviour.

The second book is largely devoted to the miracles which Moses performed before the Egyptian king and the ten plagues brought upon his people when he refused to let the Israelites depart, and Drayton gives free rein to his imagination in describing the horrors of the time. Twice he interrupts the narrative to invoke divine aid anew, and once to compare the London plague of 1603 with the plight of Egypt.

In his last book, as Mrs Tillotson says, Drayton 'struggles through the rest of the Pentateuch', interrupting his narrative to apply the lesson of the Spanish Armada to England:

> Now then the Lord with a victorious hand
> In his high justice scourg'd th'*Iberian* pride.

There are a few epic similes in the poem and occasional striking epithets, but such ornaments are not outstanding.

The two other divine poems in this group were written by Drayton well beyond the sixteenth century and were published for the first time in 1630. *David and Goliah* announces its theme, 'Our sacred Muse, of *Israels* Singer sings', and proceeds logically to the invocation:

> Thou Lord of hosts be helping then to me,
> To sing of him who hath so sung of thee.

The story observes the order of events in time rather than plunging into the midst of things, but it is clearly a heroic poem, whether it be called legend or epic.

The third of Drayton's 'divine poems', *Noahs Floud*, is, like *David and Goliah*, not divided into books, but it approached closer to the epic as we conceive it in the tale of the flood which it unfolds. Mrs Tillotson, as I have said in the Introduction, decides that 'despite its noble invocation, it is not primarily a religious poem', and seemingly she cannot therefore recognize it as a divine poem. Anyone who has read thus far in this study will, I hope, see how it fits into the classification in which Drayton put these last three poems of his poetic life. It follows the epic pattern in introducing theme and invocation, but they are united in two verse paragraphs:

> My mighty Maker, O doe thou infuse
> Such life and spirit into my labouring Muse,
> That I may sing (what but from *Noah* thou hid'st)
> The gratest thing that ever yet thou didst
> Since the Creation; that the world may see
> The Muse is heavenly, and deriv'd from thee.
> O let thy glorious Angell which since kept
> That gorgeous *Eden*, where once *Adam* slept;
> When tempting *Eve* was taken from his side,
> Let him great God not onely be my guide,

But with his fiery Faucheon still be nie,
To keepe affliction farre from me, that I
With a free soule thy wondrous workes may show,
Then like that Deluge shall my numbers flow,
Telling the state wherein the earth then stood,
The Gyant race, the universall floud.

The description of the earth and its inhabitants existing at the time of the flood does not derive wholly from the Bible, as the marginal notes acknowledge. And the scholarship reflected in the dispute Noah carries on with the atheist Cham may echo Du Bartas as transmuted by Sylvester. That he knew and respected the great divine poet and his translator is in any case apparent.

Drayton's divine poems are beyond the prescribed limits of this account, but I have mentioned them because Drayton began as a divine poet, and because these poems carry over into English original poetry the divine heroic poetry which was introduced by the translation of *Judith*.

Another book, published in 1596, included a short divine epic, *The Old Worlds Tragedie*, but the whole work is interesting as a contribution to divine literature because it includes also a divine mirror, and a divine erotic epyllion which I shall consider in the following chapters. The author, Francis Sabie, was obviously desiring to offer poems which should set forth Biblical stories to compete with popular secular works. *The Old Worlds Tragedie* is the second poem in the volume. It follows the traditional epic formula, beginning with a statement of the proposition,

I sing of horrors sad and dreadful rage,

and advancing to the invocation,

Vouchsafe my muse, my dolefulst muse to tell
What made the King of heaven to be so fell:
Sole Architect of earth and earthly landes,
So furiously the fabricke of his handes
To bring to ruin.

Sabie begins his story of events which took place just 1656 years after the world's creation. Adam had been created as God's proto-plast, but after his sin, all kinds of awfulness came to the earth. God let Noah take just eight persons into the ark to make possible its re-inhabiting. The appearance of the rainbow to offer hope to mankind marks the close of the poem.

None of these heroic poems could presumably offer strong competition to those which chronicled the Trojan war or even the adventures of the knights of the Round Table, but the divine epic was to become one of the glories of English literature, and these initial offerings seem to me worthy of recognition.

CHAPTER XII

DIVINE MIRRORS AND
RELATED POEMS

T HE mirror, unlike the epic, was a distinctive sixteenth-century type, though it acknowledged its medieval ancestry. It came, indeed, to be one of the most popular and influential forms of narrative poetry—if not one of the most worthy. It began its sixteenth-century course with the publication of the *Mirror for Magistrates* in 1559, the attempt to publish it in 1555 having proved abortive. Conceived as a continuation of Lydgate's *Fall of Princes*, the English version of Boccaccio's work, it was planned with William Baldwin taking the place of Boccaccio as interlocutor to the ghosts of those persons in English history who might by reciting their complaints to him offer lessons from the past for the guidance of the present generation. The prose preface and the prose links between the recitals of misfortune offered opportunity for comment by the assembled group upon the appearance of the ghosts and upon their performances as literature. The metre of their pieces varied, but the lessons taught were regularly directed to political wisdom. One departure from the original plan is seen in regard to the tragedy of Richard Duke of York, whose ghost appeared to Baldwin in a dream vision rather than as a speaker to the assembled collaborators. In 1563 a new edition of the *Mirror* appeared with additional tragedies, among them that of the Duke of Buckingham with its own Induction, written by Thomas Sackville. The Induction was acclaimed as the best poetry of its age and was to have a profound influence upon Spenser and other later writers. It has, indeed, been deemed worthy to find a permanent place among the greater works of English literature collected in innumerable anthologies. Sackville represented himself as walking in the fields just as night was closing in, and seeing how the approach of winter had altered the scene about him, he was moved to think on the changing fortunes of men. In the mood of melancholy thus induced, he thought of the 'fall of piers' of the realm and wished that someone would describe them as a warning to others. Even as the thought came, Sorrow appeared to him and summoned him to follow her. The journey on which she led him took him past the personified figures of those dread experiences which are the lot of mankind. Having witnessed all the horrors of hell, he was led to Pluto on his throne, and Sorrow began to call before him the princes of renown who had fallen from the top of Fortune's wheel. Thus another device for introducing the ghostly tales was introduced into the *Mirror* literature, and many variants were to follow.

New editions of the original *Mirror* were published in 1571, 1574, 1575, and 1578. With the popularity of the work thus established imitations were bound to follow, and in 1574 the printer of the original Mirror published a new work by John Higgins, to which he gave the title of *The First Part of the Mirror for Magistrates*, and in which he undertook to extend the historical period covered in the work from the coming of Brute to the coming of Christ. Following the example set by Sackville's Induction, he introduced the ghosts of the fallen princes by a poetic Induction but represented Somnus as having called Morpheus to be his guide. Having led him through darkness to a great hall where he could perceive at its far end 'a darkish Ile', the guide summoned the Britons to tell him their story, but the lessons to which their stories pointed were no longer political. This work too became sufficiently popular to merit new editions in 1575 and 1578. In 1587 the 'first' and 'last' parts were printed together in a greatly enlarged edition. Meanwhile, in 1578, Thomas Blenerhasset had introduced a 'second part' to cover the period 'From the Conquest of Caesar, unto the commyng of Duke William the Conquerour'. Blenerhasset returned to the use of a prose induction and prose links but had his princes summoned by Inquisition to Memory. His work received no new edition, though some of his pieces were included in the 1610 work compiled by Richard Niccols and called *A Mirror for Magistrates*. The *Mirror* rearranged, enlarged, and largely rewritten by Niccols still bore testimony to the continued popularity of the type of poetical tragedy which it set forth (though the original authors would scarcely have found it recognizable), for it was republished in 1619 and 1620.

The appeal of the *Mirror* formula for poetic tragedy and the wide influence of Sackville's Induction can be seen in the appearance of a popular ballad based on Bible story which was registered in the Stationers' Register in 1564–5 as *A Pleasant Ballad of the Just Man Jobe*.[1] The unknown author takes upon himself Sackville's mood, briefly, as the ballad form demands:

> Walking alone not long agone,
>   I heard one weale and weep.
> 'Alas', he said, 'am now laid
>   in sorrowes strong and deepe'.
> To heare him cry, I did apply,
>   and privilie aboade;
> There did I find, in secret mind,
>   the just and patient *Jobe*.

In succeeding stanzas Jobe makes his complaint in specific terms:

> My kinsfolke walke, and by me talke
>   much wonderinge at my faule:
> They count my state unfortunate,
>   and thus forsake me all.
> My children five that were alive,
>   they be all cleane distroy'd;
> The like plague fell on my cattell,
>   and all that I injoy'd.

In the eighth and final stanza the author tells of staying on to hear of Jobe's final felicity, but of this part of Jobe's story he gives no account.

The year in which Higgins was extending the range of the *Mirror* by adding a 'first part' saw another work published which adopted the *Mirror* plan but used an independent title, *The Rewarde of Wickednesse*. The work has incidental interest in the fact that its author, Richard Robinson,[2] dedicated it to Gilbert Talbot, a son of the Earl of Shrewsbury, and wrote it

---

[1] No. 33 in Hyder Rollins, ed. *Old English Ballads 1553–1625* (Cambridge, 1920).

[2] An interesting account of Robinson is found in *The Old English Version of the Gesta Romanorum*, ed. Sir Frederic Madden for the Roxburghe Club (London, 1838), pp. xviii–xix.

during the times when he was serving his watch over 'the Scottishe Queene' while she was entrusted to the guardianship of the Earl. During such times, he explains, 'I collected this togeather, faining that in my sleepe MORPHEUS tooke me to PLUTOS kingdome in a Dreame'. Like Sackville and Higgins he uses a poetic induction to set the melancholy mood and to recount the journey on which he was led. 'Where Alecto had charge to rule and dispose' he sees in 'that stinking Stygian pitte' figures of the doomed, and in the decidedly mixed company of such characters as Helen of Troy, Pope Alexander the Sixth, Tarquin, Medea, and Heliogabalus, appear 'The two Judges for slaundering of Susanna: and bearing false witnesse against hir'. With Spenserian scorn he pictures slander:

> Before their faces with trumpet hoarse and dimme,
> To powting mouth a monster fell doth set,
> Whose voyce increaseth care that be the hearing in,
>> With foming jawe, his teeth beginnes to whet.
>> His glozing eyes with sparkes of fire fret.

We see him as the servant of Pluto letting the punishment fit the crime:

> (Quoth he) sith slaunder is committed to my charge,
> And it pleaseth *Pluto* my service to accept,
> Within this pitte mine office wide and large,
> His lawes and statutes streight shall be full truely kept.
> And therewithall aloft anon he lept,
>> From the gibbet cuts their tongues whereby they hange,
>> And like a madde man in a rage into a furnasse flange.

The heinousness of slander is expounded,

> But chiefly who be these (quod Morpheus) would I know
> That thus above the rest, so cruelly be used?

The two defamers of Susanna are thereupon presented by their keeper to make their own report.

The judges tell their often told tale of the virtuous Susanna, of their attempted rape, of their bearing false witness against her, and of the 'infant' Daniel's detecting their lies and securing their punishment. (Daniel's device for revealing their accusations as false is, however, not recited by the wicked judges.) 'The Auchtor to the two Judges' elucidates in couplets the moral that is to be drawn from their infamous conduct and their proper punishment.

In 1576 Robinson contributed another work to the divine literature of the period, a work having the rather misleading title *Certain Selected Histories for Christian Recreation with their severall Moralizations*, for it is a collection of Christian songs sung to popular tunes intended to be sung at Christmas 'or any other time', with varying emphasis on the narrative content.

In 1579 there was, however, published a Mirror that was announced as a Biblical Mirror. The author was Anthony Munday (or Mundy),[1] who after serving a brief period of his apprenticeship to the printer John Allde, had made a journey to Italy, apparently financed by Catholic gold and supported by Catholic hospitality on the continent. On his return he was enabled to find a patron in the Earl of Oxford, perhaps acting in the Earl's company of players. To that Italianate young lord he dedicated *The Mirrour of Mutabilitie, or Principall Part of the Mirrour for Magistrates*, which the title-page stated had been 'Selected out of the Sacred Scriptures'. Among the commendatory verses prefixed to the work was a sonnet by 'E.K.', identified as Ed. Knight, which has tantalized Spenser scholars who remember the 'E.K.' of the *Shepheardes Calendar* published in the same year. Another prefatory poem by 'T.N.' it is tempting to ascribe to Thomas Newton, who in 1581 published the English translations of *Seneca His Tenne Tragedies*, and who wrote a long poem to introduce the 1587 edition of the enlarged *Mirror for Magistrates*. At least the lines setting forth the common claim for the superiority of divine literature do not do that writer an injustice:

The woork it self no fables are but woven from holy Writ.
Whereto he hath in Tragick wise some pretty Stories knit.

Munday arranged his *Mirrour* in two parts. The first part contained seven tragedies concerned with the seven deadly sins. It is interesting to note that Munday found his authority for the seven deadly sins in a classical author rather than in the teaching of the church.

[1] The fullest account of Munday's life and works is in Celeste Turner [Wright], *Anthony Mundy: An Elizabethan Man of Letters* (Berkeley, Cal., 1928).

Marcus, Tullius, Cicero, that flourishing floure of all Eloquence, hath in divers and sundry places prescribed the direct rule of a verteous life, declaring many excellent exhortations to avoyd the vices which are incident to the weakned minde. As the Pride of life....

Whatever the source of his authority for the seven deadly sins, his examples are 'of divers personages forepassed, as the Scriptures by credible authoritie maketh deliberate mention'. Discarding all the usual machinery by which the ghosts are summoned for their appearance before him, Munday simply introduces each by a prose passage that gives opportunity for a description, such as that of Judas, who appeared 'with a currish countenance, his paunch torne out and round about beset with fearfull flames of fire'. First to utter his complaint was Nabuchodonozor, punished for his 'inordinate pride'; then Herod representing envy, Pharao wrath, David lechery, Dives gluttony, Judas avarice, and Jonas sloth. The complaints are written in various metres, and each is introduced by a poetic acrostic on the sin represented.

The second part of this 'principal part' of the *Mirrour for Magistrates* contains eleven histories, all written in the same stanza, the pentameter lines rhyming ababcc. Absalon here represents beauty which leads to vanity and vain aspiring, Sampson magnificence, Salomon sapience, Achab wickedness, though the other characters are used to demonstrate the fruits of more conventionally identified sins.

Munday's Christian zeal was to be further demonstrated in such works as his *Banquet of Dayntie Conceiptes* and his *Godly Exercise for Christian Families,* and his loyalty to his queen and his patrons was evidenced in his betrayal of the Catholics who had furthered his continental journey and in his attacks on the martyred Campion. Of his plays and his contribution to the attack on the stage made after the opening of the public theatres in 1576 I shall write later.

In the last decade of the sixteenth century ghosts appeared singly to aspiring writers to bemoan their sins and their melancholy fates. Whether a new *Mirror for Magistrates* of composite authorship was hoped for or projected I do not know, but the publication of Samuel Daniel's *Complaint of Rosamond* in 1592 seems to have popularized anew these ghostly repinings. In 1593 Thomas Churchyard was reaffirming his authorship of his most popular work by again republishing the tragedy of Jane Shore which had first appeared in the 1563 *Mirror*, Anthony Chute published his *Beawtie Dishonoured* in which the same lady rehearsed her misfortunes, and Michael Drayton entered on the Stationers' Register his *Piers Gaveston*, the first and best known of the many 'legends' which he was to compose. The flow of such tales—variously termed tragedies, complaints, and legends—continued for many years. Munday had already demonstrated that the Bible offered a storehouse of sinners who might be summoned to tell their melancholy stories.

In 1596 Francis Sabie contributed to divine literature three poems of different types in a single volume: *Adams Complaint*, *The Old Worldes Tragedie* (of which I have already written), and *David and Beersheba*. The author's purpose to mark it as divine literature was indicated by the mottoes on the title-page, 'A Jove Musa' and 'Heb. DDIM. HEB. DDIEV.' as well as by the dedication to Richard, Bishop of Peterborough. In the first poem the first of mankind's sinners came to rehearse his fall. Without any of the usual literary machinery to introduce him Adam appears:

> New formed *Adam* of the reddish earth,
> Exilde from *Eden*, Paradice of pleasure:
> By Gods decree cast down to woes from mirth,
> From lasting joyes to sorrowes out of measure:
>   Fetch'd many a sigh, comparing his estate
>   With happie blisse, which he forewent of late.

Interrupted only by the author's invocation to the 'great Jehovah, heavens great Architect' to direct his fainting Muse in this sad work, the description continues:

> With pensive heart he trac'd the earth new founded,
> Wringing his hands in lamentable wise:
> Earth never with ground-cleaving ploughshare wounded,
> Now to the starry globe he cast his eyes,
>   And now to *Eden* where he erst remained,
>   From which with fiery sword he was detained.

Sadly Adam speaks of God's mercies, of Evah's plucking the forbidden fruit, and of her tempting him. True to his role as the father of mankind, he calls Evah 'Sin-causing woman, bringer of mans woe', and prophesies:

> Henceforth therefore will womens words & beautie
> Seducers be of mankind from their dutie.

The poem is written in the *Mirror* tradition to present the fall, not of a temporary ruler but of the father of mankind, whose fall was of tragic importance to succeeding generations.

One of the several works of divine literature written by Nicholas Breton was *A Divine Poeme divided into two Partes: The Ravisht Soule, and the Blessed Weeper*, published in 1601. There are really two poems, and the second one is clearly written in the *Mirror* tradition. *The Blessed Weeper* introduces Mary Magdalen in a kind of dream vision:

> My thoughts amaz'd, I know not how, of late,
> Halfe in a slumber, and more halfe a sleepe,
> My troubled senses, at a strange debate,
> What kind of care should most my spirit keepe,
> Me thought, I sawe a silly woman weepe,
>   And with her weeping, as it seem'd, so pleas'd,
>   As if her heart had with her teares been eas'd.

Two angels and then Jesus himself had appeared to comfort her:

> But ere they came, how she in bitter teares
> Bewail'd the losse, or lacke of her deare love:
> As to her words my vision witnesse beares,
> And my remembrance, may for truth approove,
> The whole discourse, her passions seem'd to move:
>   In hearts deepe griefe, & soules high joy conceived,
>   Was as I write, were not my thoughts deceived.

She speaks of her sinful life, of Christ's gentle 'Much is forgiven her, for she loved much', of her bathing his feet with her tears, of his expelling the devils that possessed her, of his death and her grief as she saw the empty tomb. She concludes with the account of the appearance of the angels and of Jesus in the likeness of a gardener. Her lyrical outcries of repentance and of grief accompany her tears and interrupt the narrative at intervals. The story is ended:

> And with that word, she vanisht so away,
> As if that no such woman there had beene.

But the author cannot suppress his wish that all women might be such weepers.

These two poems are clearly intended as Mirrors in the tradition set by the *Mirror for Magistrates*, but there are other poems which bear the impress of this kind of narrative writing. In such poems the characters rehearse their own complaints somewhat as do the speakers in Browning's dramatic monologues rather than as ghosts invoked from the beyond, though they, of course, do not address a particular audience. The best known of such poems is probably *Saint Peters Complaint* by Robert Southwell, which 'with other poems' appeared in three editions in 1595, two printed by Wolfe and one by Roberts.[1] Three editions supposedly printed in London in the very year in which Southwell suffered martyrdom is a matter for wonder, but with the twelve other editions printed before 1620 they afford ample evidence of the appeal of the poetry. Perhaps because Southwell's name always brings to mind one of the most memorable of Elizabethan poems, his *Burning Babe*, or because his religious poems are haloed in our memory by his martyrdom, we feel in his writing the depth of sincerity that must move us. Though *Saint Peters Complaint* will scarcely be

---

[1] Mario Praz in 'Robert Southwell's "Saint Peter's Complaint" and its Italian Source', *Mod. Lang. Rev.* (1924), vol. XIX, pp. 273–90, traces Southwell's indebtedness to Luigi Tanzillo's *Le Lacrime di San Pietro*. Professor Praz concluded that Southwell's poem was probably written before he went to prison on 20 June 1592. The first edition would seem to be that printed by Wolfe. It ends on p. 56. The last poem is 'Loves Servile Lot'. The second edition would seem to be that printed by I. R[oberts]. for G. C[awood]., for the address to the reader speaks of the poem's having already been printed, but there are additional stanzas, and anyone who has not already bought the book ought not to be deprived of the poem of Saint Peter. The third edition, by Wolfe, has, like the first, marginal Biblical references and includes, as it does, the address to the 'Cosen'. For the last four stanzas of 'Loves Servile Lot' in the earlier edition, it substitutes seven new stanzas concerned with the disillusionment of love. Five new short poems on love are added. These changes correspond to those of the Roberts edition. See Louis L. Martz, *The Poetry of Meditation* (New Haven, 1954), Yale Studies in English, cxxv, pp. 12–13 (especially n. 19), 102–5, 184, 359–60. I have based my account on the Huntington Library copies.

ranked with *The Burning Babe* as poetry, it must have probed deep into the hearts of Englishmen who with the changes of religion in the reigns of Henry VIII and his children, whether Catholic or Protestant, had been called upon to deny the religion by which they had lived. The fact that it also contained passages reminiscent of his own suffering and of that of many others probably gave it added significance.

That Southwell was concerned that the great poetry of his time should not be devoted to the trivial affairs of men is made clear in a letter from 'the Author to his loving Cosen' which was printed by Wolfe with *Saint Peters Complaint*:

But the Divell as hee affecteth Deitie, and seeketh to have all the complements of Divine honor applied to his service, so hath he among the rest possessed also most Poets with his idle fansies. For in lieu of solemne and devout matter, to which in duety they owe their abilities, they now busy themselves in expressing such passions, as onely serve for testimonies to how unworthy affections they have wedded their wils. And because the best course to let them see the errour of their workes, is to weave a new webbe in their owne loome; I have heere layd a few course threds together, to invite some skillfuller wits to go forward in the same, or to begin some finer peece, wherein it may be seene, how well verse and vertue sute together.

His intention 'to weave a new webbe in their owne loome' was that of the divine poets in general, to use the same patterns for their poems that were used by the secular poets. It was to this task that Southwell devoted his poetic gift, for

> *Christes* Thorne is sharpe, no head his Garland weares:
> Still finest wits are stilling *Venus* Rose.
> In Paynim toyes the sweetest vaines are spent:
> To Christian workes, few have their tallents lent.[1]

Saint Peters Complaint presents Peter tortured in spirit as he looks back at his weakness and his failure to keep the faith. Three times Christ had found him with John and James asleep when he had bid them to watch, watch while he was praying his anguished prayer at Gethsemane. Three times he had denied his Lord before the cock crowed on that fateful dawn, fearful

---

[1] From 'The Author to the Reader'.

to confess himself a follower of his master, whom Judas had betrayed. But he remembers the blessed forgiveness of his Lord mirrored in the 'sacred eyes' even as he sees himself the most distressful of sinners. Many of the hundred and thirty-two stanzas are lyrical expressions of emotion, but Peter views himself in the tradition of the fall of princes:

> Can vertue, wisedome, strength by woemen spild
> In *Davids*, *Salomons*, and *Sampsons* fals,
> With semblance of excuse by errour guild,
> Or lend a marble glose to muddy walles?
> O no their fault had show of some pretense.
> No vayle can hide the shame of my offence.

Continuing to review the famous sinners of the Jewish past, he finds himself the basest among them, and grief and sorrow and troubled sleep are his punishment. Southwell here introduces for Peter an apostrophe to sleep, which is more reminiscent of Sackville's Induction than of Biblical lore:

> Sleepe, deathes allye: oblivion of teares:
> Silence of passions: balme of angry sore:
> Suspence of loves: securitie of feares:
> Wrathes lenitive: hartes ease: stormes calmest shore:
> Senses and soules reprivall from all cumbers:
> Benumming sence of ill, with quiet slumbers.

The poem closes with Peter's final plea to 'let grace forgive, let love forget my fall', a plea that all his debts for error and sin might be cancelled.

Mary Magdalens Complaint at Christs Death, which follows later in Southwell's volume is a lyrical lament of seven stanzas with none of the narrative content of the usual complaint and is not related except in its title to the progeny of the *Mirror for Magistrates*.[1]

Samuel Rowlands was another who in this period contributed several works to divine literature, condemning the employment of poetry for 'the fooleries of Love', but rejoicing that 'yet hath it a native divine off-spring and issue', which gains 'a quiet

---

[1] *Mary Magdalens Blush* likewise has little narrative content. Most of the additional poems are devoted to moralizing. *Mary Magdalens Funerall Tears*, previously printed in several editions, included in the 1616 edition of *Saint Peters Complaint*, is a prose work.

applause'. In 1598 a volume of his divine poems was published which bore on its title-page indication of their mixed genres: *The Betraying of Christ. Judas in Despaire. The Seven Words of Our Savior on the Crosse. With Other Poems on the Passion.*[1] Two of these poems resemble Southwell's complaints. *Judas in Despaire* represents Judas feeding his despair with memories of the details of his betrayal of his Lord until he can cry 'Let hangmans part performe thy des'prate mind'. *Peters Tears at the Cocks Crowing* offers a like picture of Peter's horror as he hears the crowing of the cock and realizes that he has thrice denied his fellowship with Christ, even as Christ had foretold. It is interesting to hear an echo of the *Spanish Tragedy* in the line, 'Let eies become the fountaines of my teares'. Other poems embroider Biblical passages in inadequate verse; none have the massive dignity of Southwell's poem on Peter.

In 1605 there was entered on the Stationers' Register as 'A theatre of divine recreation', a work which was to appear in that same year as *A Theater of Delightful Recreation*. The title under which it was entered gives a truer indication of its contents, for it is a collection of divine poems. One of the preliminary poems is addressed 'To all prophane Poets, wearing VENUS wanton liverie, with *Cupids* blind cognisance', whose poetic material Rowlands describes:

> One writes a Sonnet of his mistres fan,
> Blessing the bird that did the feathers beare:
> Another shewes himself as wise a man
> To rime upon the shoo-strings she doth weare
> And of her bodkin, scarfe, and paire of gloves,
> And little dog that she so kindly loves.

Another prefatory poem addressed to the muses but with no author indicated, invokes 'Calliope, divine and heavenly Muse' rather than Urania, as might be expected. 'Adams Passion upon His Fall' is a complaint written in pentameter couplets which do not enhance the Biblical account, but is interesting in its use of direct discourse when Adam recalls his conversations with God and with Eve. Cain's complaint follows the same

[1] The quotations in regard to poetry's use are from the dedication to Sir Nicholas Walsh.

method. Other poems summarily recount the sins of the characters, still others give only versified versions of their speeches. Even 'The Mirrour of Chastitie' consists merely of the speeches of Potiphar's wife in her attempt to seduce the favourite of the Lord, but the author intrudes on her poeticized allurements to assure the reader that Joseph did remain chaste.

Saint Peters Complaint is again brought to mind as we read Gervase Markam's *Tears of the Beloved*, published in 1600. John, the beloved disciple, shared with Peter and James the watch while Christ prayed at Gethsemane, and as with the others, sleep came upon him, so that the memory of his weakness must ever bring repentance and grief. The poem is a long poem, longer than Southwell's, for John describes the events that followed the anguish of Gethsemane. Much of the poem is, indeed, devoted to Judas, his betraying of Christ, his trial, all the sorrows that befell him. John thinks on others who have met disaster in their sleep, from Samson to Sisera, and he applies the lesson to all who sleep when religion is in danger. Yet he adds a note of consolation, 'For though we fell, yet God did us uphold', and he concludes that the victory will be Christ's at last, and he shall reign.

A work intended to offer hope to the sinner, showing as in a mirror the mercy granted one of the most miserable of offenders, was *Marie Magdalens Lamentations for the Losse of Her Master Jesus*. It was published anonymously in 1601 and again in 1604, having been registered in 1595. The final appeal from the unknown author is to the sinner who might be tempted to despair:

> Oh Christian soule take *Marie* to thy mirrour,
> And if thou wilt the like effects obtaine,
> Then follow her in like affections fervour,
> And so with her, like mercie shalt thou gaine:
> Learn sinfull man of this once sinfull woman,
> That sinners may find Christ, which sin abandon.

The poem consists for the most part of a series of lamentations, sub-titles indicating the occasions on which the laments were uttered: 'At the tombe of Jesus', 'For the losse of the bodie, which she came to annoint', 'Marie bewailes the losse of that part which Christ promised her: when he said, Marie hath chosen the better part, which shall not be taken from her', etc. Marie is apparently speaking of herself in the third person in 'The Conclusion', but it is difficult to tell whether the author is intruding in such passages. She speaks in the first person in the earlier laments. There is, unfortunately, more religious zeal than poetic inspiration in the poem.[1]

The Lamentation of the Lost Sheepe, in spite of its title, is not so much a lamentation as an invocation, spoken by one who has wandered from the fold, praying that the mercy may be bestowed on him which has been granted to other sinners whom he recalls as comfortable to his hopes. The poem was published in 1605, its author identified as G. E[llis]. That the author was consciously contributing to divine literature is indicated by the final stanza:

> I sing not I, of wanton-Love-sick laies,
> Or tickling toies, to feed fantastick eares:
> My MUSE respects no glozing tatling praise,
> A guiltie conscience thus sad passion bears:
> My straying from my Lord hath brought these tears
> My sinne-sick soule, with sorrow al besprent,
> Lamenting thus a wretched life misspent.

Poems in which Biblical sinners poured out the stories of their own sins in such poetry as their English mediums could command continued to come from the printing presses for many years,[2] a particularly great number appearing in the twenties and thirties of the new century, but that is not part of my story.

---

[1] In a poetic preface the author speaks of 'exciting Collin in his graver Muses, / To tell the manner of her hearts repent'. The author here assumes as do many others that Mary Magdalen was the sister of Lazarus and Martha. The relevant passages are found in Luke x. 38-42 and John xi. 2.

[2] Accounts of the publication of the Mirror and of its 'progeny' are found in William Farnham, The Medieval Heritage of Elizabethan Tragedy (Berkeley, 1936), pp. 271-339; Louis R. Zocca, Elizabethan Narrative Poetry (New Brunswick, N.J., 1950), pp. 3-93; Hallett Smith, Elizabethan Poetry (Cambridge, Mass., 1952); and in the prefaces to my editions of The Mirror for Magistrates (Cambridge, 1938) and Parts Added to The Mirror for Magistrates (Cambridge, 1946).

CHAPTER XIII

DIVINE EROTIC EPYLLIA

THE third divine poem in Sabie's 1596 volume was *David and Beersheba*,[1] written to form one of the goodly company about Shakespeare's *Venus and Adonis*. Lodge's *Scillaes Metamorphosis* or *Glaucus and Scilla* had appeared in 1589, *Venus and Adonis* in 1593, *Lucrece* in 1594, Barnfield's *Cassandra* and Drayton's *Endimion and Phoebe* in 1595. Marlowe's *Hero and Leander* had been registered in 1593 and was well known though it apparently remained unpublished until 1598. *David and Beersheba* was thus issued when this kind of poem was at the height of its popularity. C. S. Lewis is the first I think to identify the 'kind' by its classical name of *epyllion*,[2] Kathleen Tillotson having simply described it as 'a mythological-erotic poem, its action retarded with encrustations of description, simile, and "sentence"'.[3] The *Oxford Classical Dictionary* notes further that 'a distinctive feature is the digression'. Except that Bible story is substituted for that of pagan mythology Sabie's poem conforms to the characteristics of the type.

A description of the noon-tide heat in the first stanza is followed by the direct plunge into the narrative in the second:

> Such time as *Tytan* with his fiery beames
> In highest degree, made duskish *Leo* sweat:
> Field-tilling Swains drive home their toiling teams,
> Out-wearied with ardencie of heat:
> And country heards to seeke a shadie seate:
>   All mortall things from fervency of weather,
>   In sheltring shades doe shroud themselves together.

---

[1] The *S.T.C.* uses the spelling *Bathsheba*.

[2] C. S. Lewis, p. 323. A. M. Duff in the *Oxford Classical Dictionary* (Oxford, 1953) defines *Epyllion*: 'a literary type popular from Theocritus to Ovid, was a narrative poem of about 100 to 600 hexameters; the subject was usually taken from the life of a mythical hero or heroine, the love motif being prominent in later epyllia. Some dialogue and at least one speech generally appear. A distinctive feature is the digression.'

[3] Drayton, *Works*, vol. v, p. 19. See also Douglas Bush, *Mythology and the Renaissance Tradition in English Poetry* (1932), pp. 81–5, 136–8, and 156–163.

Beersheba wife unto *Urias* stout,
A captaine under *Joab* of renowne:
Whom princely *David* with a warring rout
Had sent to beat the pride of *Ammon* downe,
And to besiege and ransacke *Rabbah* towne,
   Betooke her selfe into a garden faire,
   Inricht with flowers, which sent a pleasant ayre.

After an extended description of the flowers in the garden, the sweetest of which she picks, Beersheba dips her fingers in the pool and decides to bathe in it:

Then nimbly castes she off her Damaske frocke,
Her Satten stole most curiously made:
Her Partlet needle-wrought, her Cambricke smocke,
And on a seat thereby them nicely laid,
And so to wash her in the well assay'd.
   O shut thine eies *Narcissus* come not neere,
   Least in the well a burning fire appeare.

David mounts his look-out tower, and the author again cries out a warning with a classical allusion:

Stop *Ishas* sonne thine eares, keep sayles on hie,
Lest Syrens songs doe drawe thy mind awry.

But David's heart which had never known evil now 'stroke with burning fever quaked'. The seduction is modestly described:

And now begins the combatant assault,
Betweene the willing flesh and nilling spirit,
The flesh alluring him unto the fault,
The spirit tels him of a dreadfull merit,
And in the end flesh conquered the spirit.
   He sends, she came, he wooes, she gave consent,
   And did the deed, not fearing to be shent.

The author again cries out 'What has thou done, O Psalmist, blush for shame', before he proceeds with the narrative. He dwells at greater length on David's treachery in sending for Urias, in trying to make him go home to Beersheba, on Urias's cunning in his refusal, and on David's final desperate sending of the husband back to Joab to be slain in battle. The author comments:

Thus evermore sinne leadeth unto sinne,
A lesser ends, and greater doth begin.

The judgment of the Lord is pronounced by the prophet Nathan, who comes as David and Beersheba weep for their dying child, the child born of their sinful love. Recounting the great things that God has done for the shepherd's boy in raising him to be King of Israel, Nathan tells the story which furnishes the digression for the epyllion. It is the story of the miserly rich man who, to feast the stranger who visited him, took and killed the 'one little sheep' belonging to the poor neighbour. David, possessed of many wives and concubines, had yet coveted the one wife that Urias had, and, as Nathan points the moral, David is moved to repentance, so that

> Rise up (quoth Nathan) God doth hear thy crie,
> Thy sin is pardon'd, but thy child shall die.

David then, as befits the poet of the Bible, 'warbled out this Ode', and the ode of thirteen stanzas is written with considerable poetic skill, as perhaps can be seen from this first stanza:

> O Great Creator of the starrie Pole,
>   and heavenly things:
> O mighty founder of the earthly mole,
>   chief king of Kings.
> Whose gentle pardon evermore is nere,
> To them which crie unfaynedly with feare,
>   Distrest with sin,
>   I now begin,
> To come to thee, O Lord give eare.

To a David sorrowing over his sins God grants mercy 'And all his sinnes did race out of his booke'.

The metre of the poem is that of *Lucrece*, and characteristics common to Shakespeare's companion poems are here: narrative interrupted by long descriptive passages, dialogue spoken as direct discourse, phrase epithets, moral comment by the author, and a digression. There are similes, too, but not in the epic manner.

Lucrece seems often to have called to mind the Biblical story of Susanna. Shakespeare's *Lucrece* was published in 1594, and ten years earlier, in 1584, there had been published a prose romance by Robert Greene, entitled *The Myrrour of Modestie*, embroidering the story of Susanna. G. Knox Pooler in the English Arden edition of *Shakespeare's Poems* called attention to the like method of telling and of embellishing the story in Shakespeare's two long poems and in Greene's romance, and he compared passages in *Lucrece* with passages in *The Myrrour of Modestie* which in their 'similarity of meaning and context' may have given hints to the later and greater writer. At any rate the similarity between the classical and the Biblical prototypes of chastity was apparently recognized by Robert Roche when in 1599 he published at Oxford his poem on *Eustathia or the Constancie of Susanna*. His Address to the Reader warned:

> Expect not heere, th'invention, or the vaine,
> Of *Lucrece rape-write*: or the curious scan,
> Of *Phillis* friend; or famous faery-*Swaine*;
> Or *Delias* prophet, or admired man.
>   My chicken fethered winges, no ympes enrich,
>   Pens not full sum'd, mount not so high a pitch.

The story of Susanna had been used by Robinson to teach the wages of slander in depicting the case of her judges; here it is used to tell the blessedness of chastity. The poem is written in rhyme royal as was *Lucrece*, though the prologue is written in the six-line stanza of *Venus and Adonis* and *Rosamond* and others of the type. There is a good deal of matter added to the Bible record before we reach the account of the attempted rape of Susanna. What the Bible does not provide is the long recital of her birth, education, courtship, and marriage, the most striking thing about the poem being the set of instructions and the advice offered the girl. Her mother 'With rod in hand, to keepe her babe in awe', early taught her good manners and good doctrine. Helchia instructs his 'sweete Suse' in the history of her race and in the precepts of grace and modesty. Whether the young poet with his 'chicken fethered winges' was striving to offer a digression to make his poem fit a pattern, I cannot tell, but there are two sections that may be so regarded. The one is the account of the institution of marriage, the other the debate between nature and conscience in Susanna's soul when she is past two times seven years old. But the many pages which embellish and embroider the simple Biblical statement that 'her parents also were righteous, and taught their daughter according to the law of Moses' are in themselves something of a digression in the ordinary meaning of the word.

Suitors come to woo Susanna, and epic similes are massed to describe her choice:

> But as the mounting Eagle, in the winde,
> Disdeines to stoope and check base flockes of flies,
> Or as a club-griping *Hercules*, by kind,
> Doth single combate, with a dwarfe dispise,...
>
> Yet as in gardens, whear all herbes do grow,
> Some fragrant are, whose sweetenesse doth excell,
> Though some eie-pleasing lilies trimlie shew,
> When as they yeeld the sent, a loathsome smell,...
>
> For as, while those bright globes of rare accoumpt,
> And splendant plannets, in their spheeres do ronne,
> One is superior, and doth all surmount,
> Without compare, aye gloryous shininge sonne,...

The similes are finally resolved in the choice of one who by his 'neate beehavior, grace, and bounty bright', dimmed all the others as the sun dims candlelight. The plethora of long-drawn-out comparisons gives evidence of the determination of the fledgling poet to write his divine poem in the manner of his models. So, too, does his use of phrase-epithets, such as club-gripping (quoted above), lust-breathed, hunger-starved,—epithets which are generally laborious and often inappropriate, never carrying that connotative aura with which Shakespeare often intrigues us.

Of more importance, though not more revealing, is the general structure of the poem with its narrative base, its descriptive passages, its dialogues carried on in direct discourse, its moral comments, its recital of other instances of lust and crime. 'What did prowd *Paris* gaine, to gad to *Greece*, | To fet that mynion, *Menelaus* wife?' he asks, and he recalls the history of Sardanapalus and of David.

The Biblical story, long postponed, is finally told, with amplification and additions. The lustful elders—here called seniors—hesitate a moment as they rush toward Susanna in her bath, and Satan appears to urge them to new fury, so that 'Good motions cannot enter, or come nigh them'. Her cries bring servants and husband. The seniors defame her with their lies, she is condemned, and Daniel frees her, cunningly detecting the falsity of their charges by finding they disagree as to under which kind of tree the outrage was committed. Two rather long lyrics are spoken by Susanna, one a prayer for divine help, the other a hymn of praise in which the author is able to express something of her exultation:

> The mightty Lord (saith shee)
> Is my defence and might.
> My king, my guide, my God;
> My champion, for to fight.
> The combate of my truth and conscience triall.

> He is my Anchor-hold,
> My refuge, rest, and port.
> My horne of saving health,
> And eke my strongest fort.
> Gainst whose command, there standeth no denial.

Susanna's progress through a cautious life to a virtuous old age is chronicled as is also her final advice to her children, and the author appends an epilogue to make the moral clear.

Saint Marie Magdalens Conversion is a love poem of a different kind. Instead of contrasting human love and lust, it deals with the victory of the love of the Lord over the base passions in the human soul. It was published with only 'IHS' and 'Printed with license' appearing on the title-page with the title of the poem. The 'Author to the Reader' is, however, signed 'I.C.' and is dated 'This last of January 1603'. The opening stanzas place it in opposition to the poems of human passion:

> Of Romes great conquest in the elder age,
> When she the world made subject to her thrall,
> Of lovers giddy fancies, and the rage,
> Wherewith that passion is possest withall,
> When jelousie with love doth share a part,
> And breedes a civill warre within the harte.

Of *Helens* rape, and *Troyes* beseiged Towne,
Of *Troylus* faith, and *Cressids* falsitie,
Of *Rychards* stratagems for the english crowne,
Of *Tarquins* lust, and Lucrece chastitie,
Of these, of none of these my muse now treates,
Of greater conquests, warres, and loves she speakes.

A womans conquest of her one affects,
A womans warre with her selfe-appetite,
A womans love, breeding such effects,
As th'age before nor since nere brought to light,
Of these; and such as these, my muse is prest,
To spend the idle houres of her rest.

Instead of an invocation to the Muses, there is a prayer to Saint
Marie, seeking her intercession with her Lord that he may give
such grace to these rhymes that readers may come to repentance.

It is a narrative poem in the frequently used six-line stanza,
written with the usual 'encrustation of description, simile, and
"sentence",' to use Mrs Tillotson's words again. It shows
Marie Magdalen as she perceives 'the errors of her life / Which
makes her with her selfe to be in strife'. But she does not see
what she can do. She cannot go to her good sister, or to her
kinsmen, and surely not to strangers, for her reputation bars
her from taking refuge with any of them. If she had sinned
only once, there might have been hope, but she had sinned
habitually. A simile of epic proportions is introduced as she
ponders:

Much like a crasie weather-beaten boate,
Who having all his syales and tacklinges loste,
Amid the surges of the seas doth floate,
And too and fro with everie guste is toste:
So waves my anxious soul mid'st stormy feares
No harbor can she finde, no calme appears.

As she considers seeking out Jesus, she is beset with doubts,
and her soul holds a parliament, where instead of the argument
between the characters featured in other erotic poems we hear
a debate between personified abstractions. Memory is heard,
and Hope, urging the mercy shown to other sinners. Strong
Opinion is heard too, and Distrust and Fear, while Will is
introduced as handmaid to the rest. Hope can argue Christ's

pity, but Distrust speaks of divine justice. At last Marie is
emboldened to go to Jesus, assured that Contrition will beg
Remission for her sins. 'Like to a Trav'ler in an unknowne
way', Marie's confusion is interpreted in another simile. Her
outward acts must show her inward love for her Lord, and
when she finds him, she pours precious oil upon his head, and
prostrating herself before him, wets his feet with her tears and
dries them with her hair. There is introduced an apostrophe to
silence, the four stanzas of which begin with words that suggest
the fundamental discipline of the nun:

> O silence; Companion of the wise,
> Thou surest note of spotless Chastitie.

The latter part of the poem is given over to showing the constancy of Marie's devotion, for 'When his Disciples fearfully
dismai'de / From persecutions angrie passions fled, / Shee
constantlie attendes him to his passion'. Mingling her tears
with his blood, she embraces the tree on which he is crucified,
taunting the Jews whose deeds have made the heavens black,
the sun to hide, the earth to tremble, the dead to arise, and the
rocks to break asunder. She speaks to his mother, and when
Joseph has taken his body away, she departs in sadness, 'Like
to a Turtle having lost her mate'. When Marie returns to the
'monument', unafraid of all the terrors of night, which the
poet describes,

> Love made her strong although herselfe were weake,
> Love gave swifte winges unto her quicke desire,
> Love added fire to her former heate:
> Of doubtes nor dangers Love doth not enquire,
> O powerful love, thou dost no perilles cast,
> The bitt'rest pilles seeme pleasant to thy taste.

As Marie finds the monument empty, she rails at the supposed
thieves who have stolen her Lord away. But the angels appear
to comfort her, and finally Jesus himself in the likeness of a
gardener. The author ends his poem with praise and prayer,
and in spite of the determined and inept similes, his sincere
devotion gives dignity to his offering.

CHAPTER XIV

DIVINE SONNETS

WYATT introduced to England the sonnet of fourteen lines of pentameter verse, and such sonnets continued to be written throughout the sixteenth century, though the term *sonnet* was very loosely applied for many years, as everyone knows who is familiar with the many collections of songs and sonnets. Sonnets were printed in miscellanies, they appeared among the dedicatory verses in numerous volumes, and Byrd provided music for two of Sidney's in a volume which I have already mentioned. In 1569 Spenser used unrhymed sonnets for his translations from the Book of Revelation, and the publication of Thomas Watson's *Hecatompathia, or Passionate Century of Love* in 1582 began the publication of collections of sonnets to be regarded as unified works (though Watson's were not orthodox sonnets). It was not, however, until Sidney's *Astrophel and Stella* appeared in 1591 that the sonnet sequence came to be one of the most popular forms of literature in England. Sidney's work was printed three times within a year. Then came Constable's *Diana* and Daniel's *Delia* in 1592; Lodge's *Phillis*, Barnabe Barnes's *Parthenophil and Parthenophe*, Giles Fletcher's *Licia*, and a second cycle by Thomas Watson, *The Tears of Fancy*, in 1593; William Percy's *Celia* and new editions of Constable's *Diana* and Daniel's *Delia* in 1594; Spenser's *Amoretti* and Barnfield's *Cynthia* in 1595. There were other collections of later date and a good many of lesser importance, but this list is enough to make clear why it seemed necessary that divine sonnets[1] should be written if Biblical story was to compete with the chronicles of love's agonies and ecstasies.

Henry Lok (or Locke) was one of those who contributed a sonnet of praise to King James's *Poeticall Exercises* in 1591. A letter of 18 May 1591, quoted by Westcott, says that Lok

---

[1] J. G. Scott in *Les Sonnets Élisabethains* (Paris, 1929) included a section, pp. 217–27, devoted to 'sonnets chrétiens'. On the possible indebtedness to continental sources of Constable and Barnes see pp. 217–21.

has been in Scotland more than a year and a half, and that 'his majesty and the queen have conceived no little opinion of his honest behavior, so that they would willingly employ him in their service'. According to Westcott he had been 'sent to Scotland to help carry out Elizabeth's ingenious and persistent policy of setting Scottish lords against their king', and his activities continued until 1602. His intrigues with Bothwell and Colville got him ultimately into trouble, and after 1603 he was addressing his appeals to Cecil from the Gatehouse and the Clink.[1] But when in 1593 his *Sundry Christian Passions Contained in two hundred Sonnets* was published by Richard Field, he was certainly engaged in literary work which would win favour with the Scottish King, who was probably engaged in a similar exercise himself. Lok dedicated his book to Queen Elizabeth and prefixed his work with an ingeniously devised square which, when analysed, contributed a votive offering to her. To the Christian Reader he explained that he had 'rather followed the force of mine owne inward feeling, then outward ornaments of Poeticall fictions or amplifications, as best beseeming the naked clothing of simple truth, & true Analogie of the nature of the Histories whereto they alude, and harmonie of scriptures whence they are borrowed'.[2] In spite, however, of his professed desire to look in his heart and write and his disavowal of poetical ornament, it is quite evident that Lok was not unacquainted with the 'conceited' sonnets of his time.

Lok divides his work into two sections, the first consisting of 'Meditations, Humiliations, and Praiers', the second expressing 'Comfort, Joy, and Thanksgiving'. Each, in addition to its hundred, had a sonnet as Preface, and another as Conclusion, so that altogether there were two hundred and four sonnets. I wonder whether he should not be given credit for

---

[1] Westcott, pp. xlii–xliii and n. 5 to p. xlii. For Lok's dealings with Bothwell and Colville, see Helen G. Stafford, *James VI of Scotland and the Throne of England* (New York, 1940), ch. III.

[2] I have used a photostat facsimile reproduced from the copy of the 1593 edition in the Huntington Library. Grosart printed the edition which had been published with *Ecclesiastes* in 1597, *Miscellanies of the Fuller Worthies' Library* (Printed for Private Circulation, 1871) vol. II, pp. 137–449.

writing the longest sonnet sequence of them all. The first
hundred are generally written with three linked quatrains and
a final couplet. The second hundred are written in varied
patterns for the quatrains, but all retain the closing couplet.
One method by which Lok used Bible story as his frame of
reference can be seen in the way in which he uses the story of
Jonah. I quote the first quatrain:

> Fro out the darkness of this sea of feare,
>> Where I in whale remaine devourde of sin,
>> With true remorse of former life I reare
>> My heart to heaven, in hope some help to win. (Son. II.)

Parables, too, can be given new interpretation, as can be seen
in the sonnet dealing with the five foolish virgins:

> Five foolish virgins in my senses dwell,
>> And seeke to make me slumber over long,
>> They dreame, that all my deeds do fall out well,
>> Whereas indeed I headlong run to wrong:
> To vanities their humours do belong,
>> And sin who doth their fancie chiefly feed,
>> They cheined are to linkes of lust so strong,
>> That their best soile, brings forth but bitter weed.
> They lacke the oyle which should be usde in deed,
>> To lead them to the everlasting light:
>> It growes not Lord in frute of humane seed,
>> Man sleepes all day and gropes his way at night.
>>> Unlesse thou lend thy hand and fill our lampes,
>>> Our light goes forth with smothering sinful damps.
>>>> (Son. XVII.)

From the second section I quote one sonnet to show how in
some of the sonnets Bible story is almost incidental, though
the spiritual theme remains constant. I have chosen this particular sonnet because of the 'Dolfins did Aryons musicke
beare' passage which might indicate that Lok as well as Shakespeare watched the pageantry at Kenilworth in 1575. It serves
to illustrate too the way in which Lok used in many of the later
sonnets an internal rhyme in the first line of the couplet, em-
phasizing its presence by beginning the next word with a
capital letter:

Who so of perfect temprature is framde,
  Must needs delight in heavenly harmony,
  His sences so shall be renude thereby,
  As savage beasts by Orpheus harpe were tamde,
Young Davids harpe Sauls furious spirit shamde,
  And Dolfins did Aryons musicke beare,
  Such sympathie in all things doth appeare,
  That never musicke was by wisedome blamde,
But he that could conceive with judgment cleare,
  The sweet records that heavenly motions cry,
  Their constant course that never swarves awry,
  But by discords, whose concords after cheare,
    Would hold so deare, The mover of the same,
  That love of him should base affections tame.

(Son. LXIIII.)

In 1597, Field published Lok's *Ecclesiastes abridged and dilated in English poesie*, which I have written about in discussing the translations of the Bible into English verse. To this volume were appended the *Sundry Christian Passions* and also a whole flock of dedicatory sonnets addressed to almost everyone of influence. Presumably these sonnets accompanied hopeful presentation copies of the author's works. Among those addressed are the Countess of Pembroke (Sidney's sister), the Countess of Essex (formerly Sidney's wife), and Lady Rich (Sidney's Stella and Essex's sister); Archbishop Whitgift and Bishop Toby Matthew; Lord Burleigh, the Earl of Essex, Sir Walter Raleigh, Fulke Greville, and Edward Dyer. It is a comprehensive list, but Lok's claim upon the people he addressed is unknown. We do know, however, that he must have been writing his divine sonnets when he was seeking the favour of the Scottish King and would-be poet, comparing himself to the fly that would perish in the flame if he attempted to imitate that royal quill.[1]

Another English poet to address a laudatory sonnet to King James in his *Poeticall Exercises* was Henry Constable, whose fame as a sonneteer was to be established by his *Diana* a year later. Constable was a zealous Catholic, and 'from 1584 on', he had been as Westcott says, 'an active Catholic messenger both

---

[1] The comparison is made in the sonnet addressed to King James in the *Poeticall Exercises*.

at home and abroad'. It is curious to see him and Lok both as members of the King's literary circle, both political agents but on quite conflicting missions, both authors of divine sonnet sequences. Constable came in the interest of Arabella Stuart, and a letter of 20 October 1589, quoted by Westcott reports that he was having secret conferences with the King, and that he had a commission from Essex and Lord and Lady Rich. His activities forced him into exile, but I need not follow his career there. He came home after the death of Elizabeth, but we find him in the Tower, from which he was released in 1604. He remained largely unnoticed until his death in 1613. He addressed sonnets to, among others, Queen Elizabeth, Arabella Stuart, Lady Rich, the Countess of Essex, the Countesses of Cumberland and Warwick,[1] and the Countess of Shrewsbury, in whose custody 'his dear Mistresse' (Mary Queen of Scots) was then living. He addressed, in all, four sonnets to King James. Of most interest to this study are, however, the four sonnets prefixed to Sidney's *Apologie for Poetrie* printed by Henry Olney in 1595, 'written by Henrie Constable to Sir Phillip Sidney's soule'.[2]

Though his sonnets to Delia were published in two editions, though Olney dared to print the sonnets to Sidney's soul, and though Constable's poems might appear in a collection of miscellaneous poems, his *Spirituall Sonnettes to the Honour of God and His Sayntes* remained unprinted until the nineteenth century, presumably because of their definitely Catholic orientation. Not only the Bible but the lives of the saints furnish the background story, and one sonnet is addressed 'To the blessed sacrament'. Of the seventeen printed by W. C. Hazlitt four are offered 'To our blessed Lady', four 'To St Mary Magdalen', one 'To God the Father', one 'To God the Sonne', and one 'To God the Holy Ghost', while St Michael, St John the

---

[1] It was to these two ladies that Spenser dedicated his *Fowre Hymnes*.

[2] Concerning Constable see Westcott, pp. xxxvi–xxxviii, and W. C. Hazlitt's *Diana: The Sonnets and Other Poems of Henry Constable, B.A. of St John's College, Cambridge*, with notes and illustration by Thomas Park (London, 1859). *The Poems & Sonnets of Henry Constable*, ed. by John Gray and ornamented by Charles Picketts, published by the Ballantyne Press in 1897, provides a text without introduction or notes. My references are to the Hazlitt text.

Baptist, St Peter and St Paul, St Katherine and St Margaret
are hailed in the other five. I quote the first sonnet, 'To God
the Father', because it illustrates the mystical and devotional
side of his divine poetry:

Greate God! within whose symple essence wee
　　Nothyng but that which ys thy self can fynde:
　　When on thy self thou dyddst reflect thy mynde,
　　Thy thought was God, which tooke the forme of Thee;
And when this God, thus borne, thou lov'st, and Hee
　　Lov'd thee agayne with passion of lyke kynde,
　　(As lovers syghes which meete, become one mynde,)
　　Both breath'd one spryght of aequall Deitye.
Æternal Father! whence theis twoe doe come
　　And wil'st the tytle of my father have,
　　A heavenly knowledge in my mynde engrave,
That yt thy Sonne's true image may become,
　　And sente my hart with syghes of holy love,
　　That yt the temple of thy Spryght may prove. (Son. 1.)

The sonnet 'To St Peter and St Paul' lets his classical education
shine through as well as his Catholic predilection:

He that for feare hys mayster dyd denye,
　　And at a mayden's voyce amazed stoode,
　　The myghtyest monarche of the earth withstoode,
　　And on his mayster's crosse rejoyc'd to dye.
He whose blynde zeale dyd rage with crueltye,
　　And helpt to shedd the fyrst of martyr's bloode,
　　By lyght from heaven hys blyndenesse understoode,
　　And with the cheife apostle slayne doth lye.
O three tymes happy twoe! O golden payre!
　　Who with your bloode dyd lay the churches grounde
　　Within the fatall towne, which twynnes dyd founde,
And setled there the Hebrew fisher's chayre,
　　Where fyrst the Latyn sheepehyrd rais'd his throne,
　　And synce the world and church were rul'd by one. (Son. 8.)

He can address St Margaret as 'Fayre Amazon of heaven' and
hope that Cupid 'May gett his syght, and lyke an angell prove',
but he can use Biblical story figuratively also, as when he speaks
of repentance:

So shall my sowle no foolysh vyrgyn bee
　　With empty lampe: but, lyke a Magdalen, beare
　　For oyntment boxe a breast with oyle of grace:

And so the zeale, which then shall burne in mee,
May make my hart lyke to a lampe appere,
And in my spouse's pallace gyve me place. (Son. 15.)

The variation in the rhyming pattern of the sestet in this sonnet
is also characteristic of Constable's sonnets, though it is the
choice of Biblical allusions that is of interest here.

When Judicio in the Second Part of the *Returne from Parnassus*
was passing judgment upon the poets of England before the
students of Constable's own Cambridge college in 1601, he
had kind words for him:

Sweete *Constable* doth take the wondring eare,
And layes it up in willing prisonment.

But when he was asked about the two others we have seen as
members of King James's literary coterie, Lok and Hudson,
he spoke scornfully and in prose:

Locke and *Hudson*, sleepe, you quiet shavers, among the shavings
of the presse, and let your bookes lye in some old nookes amongst
old bootes and shooes, so you may avoide my censure.[1]

Barnabe Barnes dedicated his *Foure Bookes of Offices* to
King James, but the dedication came in 1606, when James was
King of England. Even Mark Eccles, who has made the most
diligent search for material concerning his life, can find little
about it after 1598 and can only say that his friend William
Percy in his commendation in this book 'permits us to hope,
if not to believe, that he had really become a changed spirit'.[2]
The son of a father who had been in turn Bishop of Nottingham, Bishop of Carlisle, and Bishop of Durham, he justified all
taunts regularly hurled at clergymen's children. He matriculated at Brasenose College in 1586, but did not stay to get an
Oxford degree. He went on Essex's expedition to Normandy
in 1591. In 1593 he published his *Parthenophil and Parthenophe*,

---

[1] G. G. Smith, vol. II, pp. 401–2.
[2] Mark Eccles, 'Barnabe Barnes' in C. J. Sisson, *Thomas Lodge and Other
Elizabethans* (Cambridge, Mass., Harvard Press, 1933), pp. 165–241. My facts
are taken from this account. See also Thomas Campion's Epigrams in G. G.
Smith, vol. II, p. 346, and John Harington's Epigrams on *Lynus*, p. 52 and index.
I have used A. B. Grosart's reprint in *Occasional Issues of Very Rare Books* (privately
printed, 1871), vol. I.

which Eccles calls 'a more extensive collection of love poetry than an English author had ever before published'. It contained a great variety of lyric poetry written in many metres in addition to the sonnets. He entered the lists on the side of Harvey in the Harvey–Nashe quarrel, and Nashe ridiculed his braggart bravery and his literary ventures, asserting that he and Chute could not know how to knock at a printing-house door until they consorted with Gabriel Harvey.

About this time he seems to have become aware of the popularity of Du Bartas and divine poetry, for in a letter of June 1593 to Harvey he recommends that Harvey turn his endeavours to 'the highest treasury of heavenly Muses', and he takes his leave with a sonnet of that 'Muse, that honoreth the Urany of du Bartas, and yourself'. It is not surprising, there-fore, that in 1595 he published *A Divine Centurie of Spirituall Sonnets* with a dedication to Bishop Toby Matthew, his father's successor as Bishop of Durham, the dedication copy 'bound in vellum with a gold border and each page ornamented'. Addressing the Christian Reader he acknowledges the primacy of the great French divine poet:

if any man feels in himself (by the secret fire of immortall Enthu-siasme) the learned motions of strange and divine passions of spirite, let him refine and illuminate his numerous Muses with the most sacred splendour of the Holy Ghost, and then he shall (with divine Salust the true learned frenche Poet) finde that as humane furie maketh a man lesse then a man...so divine rage and sacred instinct of a man maketh more then man.

The first sonnet indicates that, like all followers of Du Bartas and Urania, he is turning from his earliest profane verse to divine poetry:

> No more lewde laies of Lighter loves I sing,
> Nor teach my lustfull Muse abus'de to flie,
> With Sparrowes plumes and for compassion crie,
> To mortall beauties which no succour bring.
> But my Muse fethered with an Angels wing,
> Divinely mounts aloft unto the skie,
> Where her loves subjects with my hopes do lie:
> For Cupids darts prefigurate hell's sting.

His quenchlesse Torch foreshadowes hell's quenchles fire,
Kindling mens wits with lustful laies of sinne:
   Thy wounds my Cure, deare Saviour I desire
To pearce my thoughts thy fierie Cherubinnes
   (By kindling my desires) true zeale t'infuse,
   Thy love my theame, and holy Ghost my Muse!

A great number of these sonnets are in the nature of prayers offered to his 'Sweete Saviour', 'Sacred Redeemer', 'Deare Comforter', 'Lovely Samaritane', 'Great God of Abraham', and to Divinity under similar aspects. The Bible stories are implicit for the most part rather than woven in figurative language into the texture of the poems.

Barnes's divine interlude does not seem to have been more than that, for Eccles has traced his picaresque career through the time of his adventures in the Border feuds which culminated in his arrest in 1598 for having poisoned John Browne, the Recorder of Berwick.

It is possible that he became a clergyman but, as Eccles says, we can rather hope than believe that he was a reformed character under King James. What his divine poems show is that he was following in the Du Bartas tradition rather than that he was a spiritual leader.

PART II

DIVINE DRAMA IN SIXTEENTH-CENTURY ENGLAND

CHAPTER I

THE DIVINE DRAMA AND
THE MIRACLE PLAY

WHEN in the eighteenth century the resourceful Hannah More undertook to provide suitable intellectual food for the young scholars in her charge and compiled her *Sacred Dramas*, they elicited the scornful description of Peter Pindar as dramas 'Where all the Nine and little Moses snore'.[1] The 'divine' dramas[2] written in the sixteenth century originated in the same laudable desire that prompted Miss Hannah More to her task and sometimes produce the same effect, but they constitute an important and much neglected part of the history of the drama. In the general movement to create a divine literature to compete with or to supplant the pagan literature and its secular offspring which the Revival of Learning had produced, the drama played a substantial part on the continent of Europe. The continental precedent was inevitably influential in England, though there the movement culminated in no dramatic Milton and never reached the proportions that it did in some parts of Europe, particularly in the Jesuit schools of the seventeenth and eighteenth centuries. Yet there was in England, as part of this general movement, a very considerable body of divine plays, the significance of which has been passed over by the historians of English drama.

The principal reason for the neglect of the divine dramas has been that they have been considered merely an aftermath of the miracle play, whereas they are really a new crop and must,

---

[1] [John Wolcot], *The Lousiad* in *The Works of Peter Pindar* (London, 1816), vol. I, p. 145.

[2] John M. Manly, 'The Miracle Play in Mediaeval England', *Essays by Divers Hands*, new series, vol. VII (London, 1927), pp. 134–53, distinguished the miracle plays from the scriptural cycles as 'plays of the lives and sufferings and miracles of saints and martyrs'. I have, however, ventured to depart from the teaching of my teacher in referring to the cycle plays as miracles, as the 'Wyclifite' and other writers, including E. K. Chambers, have done. I have used the term *divine plays* alternately with *Scriptural* or *Biblical plays*. They were called *sacred plays* by George Buchanan and by Hannah More.

I think, be considered independently. They differ from the miracles in content, in form, and in purpose, though that purpose became obscured to some of their later writers.

Like the miracles, the divine plays which I shall discuss were derived from Biblical story, but there the likeness ceases. The writers of the miracle plays chose for the most part stories of the wonders chronicled in the Bible or in the lives of the martyrs, much as the universities which today stage scientific exhibitions for the multitude demonstrate the wonders of science, from the making of artificial snowflakes to the workings of the mechanical brain or the cyclotron. When they presented the ministry of Christ, they were more often concerned with the miracles he performed than with his sermons. In the great English cycles they attempted to show the whole Christian story from the Creation to the Last Judgment as the Church analysed it and to picture the plan of salvation as the Church conceived it.[1]

The authors of the new Scriptural drama generally chose stories from the Old Testament, very often from the Apocrypha, frequently supplementing their accounts from the works of Josephus. When they turned to the New Testament, it was the sermons and particularly the parables that most often seemed to suit their purpose. Their concern was with the special problems of their own time: whether faith or good works assured eternal salvation, whether a vow once made should be kept even though it had been foolishly made, how to train a child according to Biblical precept. They sometimes also used Biblical history as secular history was being used to furnish a political mirror to their contemporaries.

The new Scriptural dramas were not written in a single form, for they followed whatever structural pattern was being used by the secular plays they were rivalling. When the schoolmasters wanted to use them to teach classical Latin as well as assurance and deportment in public speaking, they wrote Latin plays based on Biblical stories as substitutes for classical plays of pagan origin. They imitated Terence and Plautus and Euri-

[1] Father Harold C. Gardiner, *Mysteries' End: An Investigation of the Last Days of the Medieval Religious Stage* (New Haven, 1946), *Yale Studies in English*, vol. 103, argues that it was political anti-Catholicism that caused the cycle plays to be put down within the period 1569–80. See particularly p. 72 for his thesis.

pides and Seneca as they understood them. When other writers experimented with Biblical interludes in English, they wrote them in the fashion current in secular interludes. When professional dramatists later wrote Biblical plays for the public theatres, they shaped them for the stages on which they were to be produced and gave the audience what they would pay for in the way of spectacle or rhetoric. It is this changing pattern of the Scriptural plays which needs to be specially noted, for they met the competition of secular offerings by pouring Biblical story into the currently accepted forms.

These differences in subject-matter and in form were at least in part the result of the purpose which motivated their original creators. The miracle play is recognized as a descendant of the drama which originated in the Church. In its most characteristic English form, the cycle play, it furnished a living picture of God's plan for man's redemption after his fall from innocence and bliss.[1] The divine play of the sixteenth century, on the other hand, was a part of the opposition movement to glorify the God of the Christians instead of the pagan gods; to use Bible stories because they were true, as opposed to the lies of fiction; and to offer Christian modes of conduct instead of the depravity shown in secular works. However much they departed from these ideals set forth by their promoters and defenders, it must be borne in mind that their origin in opposition to a great extent determined their content as well as their form.

In giving an account of the English divine drama published or produced before the end of the Tudor reigns I have perforce found it necessary to give some account of the origins of the movement to create this new kind of drama. I have, however, not attempted to give a history of the divine drama on the continent, a task for which I am unfitted even if it were possible in a single book. I have, therefore, attempted only to give a brief account of the origins of the movement which lent the

---

[1] Since I wrote this chapter, I have seen Hardin Craig's *English Religious Drama of the Middle Ages* (Oxford, 1955) in which he says (p. 355): 'The mystery plays were not primarily doctrinal and did not derive their popularity from the systematic support of the Catholic Church, since they were religious in their origin and nature rather than ecclesiastical.' Though *primarily* is a safety word, I should point out that religion was not divorced from the Church's teaching at this period.

initial impetus to the writing of similar plays in England and to notice particularly those continental plays which were produced or published in England.

The theological drama of polemic has been generally disregarded in this study, for it was directed to different purposes. It adopted many of the devices of the old morality and is often classed as a morality because of its personification of abstractions and its allegorical plots. Just as the morality elements were sometimes found in miracle plays, so the elements of the theological drama impinged on some of the Biblical plays, but where Biblical story entered prominently into a play I have considered the play here.

CHAPTER II

CONTINENTAL ORIGINS OF THE DIVINE DRAMA IN LATIN

THE use of the drama in the grammar schools of the sixteenth century as an effective method for teaching Latin as a living language has been recorded in our histories of education. Since it was the language of church and diplomacy and the language of learning, it was essential that all who were to be considered educated should speak as well as read and write Latin, and to this end the dialogue and the drama were particularly useful. During the Middle Ages the classical dramatists were largely forgotten, but as Chambers says:

> The marked exception is Terence who, as Dr Ward puts it, led 'a charmed life in the darkest ages of learning.' This he owed, doubtless, to his unrivalled gift of packing up the most impeccable sentiments in the neatest of phrases. His vogue as a school author was early and enduring, and the whole of mediaevalism, a few of the stricter moralists alone dissenting, hailed him as a master of the wisdom of life.[1]

It is not to be wondered at, then, that Terence was the first of the classical dramatists to be printed on the continent (in 1470 at Strasbourg), the first to be printed in England (in 1495–7 by Pynson), and the first to find a translator in England. Indeed, Lathrop calls the *Andria*, published probably by John Rastell in 1520 under the title *Terens in englysh*, 'the only complete poetical or imaginative work' translated in the period between 1517 and 1557, and he notes that it was apparently arranged for schoolboys to act.[2]

The popularity of Terence was, however, largely attributable to the authority he exercised as a model of diction. The concern of those who were fearful of the revival of paganism and the degradation of morals through the rebirth of the old classical

---

[1] E. K. Chambers, *The Mediaeval Stage* (Oxford, 1903), vol. ii, p. 207.
[2] J. E. Sandys, *A History of Classical Scholarship* (Cambridge, 1908), vol. ii, p. 103; *Short-Title Catalogue*, no. 23885; H. B. Lathrop, *Translations from the Classics into English* (Madison, 1933), p. 31. W. W. Greg dates the play 'about 1530'.

literature was augmented by the swift rise of the drama acted on the stage. The search for manuscripts on the part of the new humanists was resulting in the gradual restoration of the European heritage of Latin and Greek drama. Among the academies to foster the new learning, the Roman Academy, with Julius Pomponius Laetus at its head, gained pre-eminence in reviving the presentation of plays as one of its important activities. Just how early it took up the acting of plays is not known, but before 1468, when the academy was suppressed by Pope Paul II 'on the ground of its political aims and pagan spirit'. It was revived in 1571 under Sixtus II, and under the patronage of the two cardinals Riario, whom he appointed successively, the presentation of plays attained new grandeur.[1] It is not my purpose here to recapitulate the often told story of the revival of classical drama, but it is essential to remember that the drama became one of the great preoccupations of the humanists. The rediscovery of Vitruvius established a basis for reviving the arts of the theatre. Princes of the church as well as princes of the state delighted in the revivals which the research of scholars and artists made possible.

With the influx of classical plays and new secular plays into the schools, the schoolmasters became increasingly concerned about the manners and morals as well as the pagan theogony to which the boys in their charge were being exposed. Even Terence did not escape censure. And they undertook to do something to offset the danger. Thomas Becon most clearly, it seems to me, expressed the spirit of their approach when he later wrote that 'to teach them nothing but the doctrine of heathen and prophane writers is not to defye, but to destroy, not to correct, but to corrupt, the youthe of the Christians'. Heathen writers, he said, should be taught 'not that they should be mates with Gods word, but rather handmaids unto it, and serve to set forth the honour and glory thereof'.[2] It was in this spirit of making drama serve the purposes of Christian education

---

[1] I reviewed these revivals in *Scenes and Machines on the English Stage during the Renaissance* (Cambridge, 1923), pp. 10–16.

[2] Thomas Becon, *A New Catechism* in *Works of Thomas Becon*, Parker Society, vol. XIII (Cambridge, 1844), p. 382.

that these schoolmasters and their followers undertook to create a Christian drama.

The classical drama, when it was accepted as handmaid to the new divine drama, served to offer form for new content. The desire to return to the Bible as the fount of all truth which characterized the whole movement determined the story material. There was, however, no attempt to fashion plays after the Hebrew model as exemplified in the Book of Job, but rather unquestioning acceptance of Latin and Greek models and classical theory. The first distinguishing characteristic which they seem to have noted was that of dramatic genre, and they accordingly wrote tragedies and comedies and tragicomedies. Horace and the plays of Plautus and Terence gave them authority for act and scene division of their plays. They labelled their dramatis personae with generic names according to classical precedent whenever possible. They introduced prologues and epilogues and sometimes a formal 'argument' into their plays. With the devices used in classical drama they experimented without uniform success: the chorus in tragedy, the description of a character followed by something equivalent to the pointing finger and a 'there he comes' identification,[1] the rehearsal of actions taking place off-stage, the summons of a character from indoors to come out in the open to speak, the liaison of the scenes, the eavesdropping of one character on the conversation of others, the soliloquy and the aside, the announcement of a character that he is departing, the recognition scene which resolves the action. Of course not all plays show all these devices, but in general when they occur they appear to indicate that the handmaid of classical precedent is serving to set forth God's word acceptably.

The development of Christian drama to offset the evils incident to the spread of the 'heathen' drama was necessarily the work of the humanist scholars, for they were the ones who

---

[1] W. W. Greg in editing *Respublica* (Early English Text Society, 1952), ccvi, xi–xii, argues for Udall's authorship largely on the basis of the use of these devices as they are used in *Ralph Roister Doister*. He notes particularly the *lupus in fabula*. M. P. Tilley, *Proverbs in England in the Sixteenth and Seventeenth Centuries* (Ann Arbor, 1950), W. 607, quotes Elyot's 1538 definition: 'a proverbe, when he cometh, which is spoken of.'

had both the knowledge of the ancient languages and the familiarity with classical dramatic techniques. The history of this development was traced by C. H. Herford, and his account has been the basis of practically all accounts in English. It still has unquestioned authority in many matters, but much new material has come to light since the eighteen-eighties to supplement and correct his findings, and his conclusions, therefore, need to be re-examined. According to Herford, the effort of Hrostvitha, the Nun of Gandersheim, 'to create an immaculate Terence out of Biblical and legendary history, was far too congenial to the religious Humanism of Germany to be wholly neglected; and her newly discovered writings, edited in 1501 by the discoverer Conrad Celtes, soon found a disciple at one of the centres of religious Humanism, the young university of Wittenberg', and he notes the *Dorothea* of Chilianus which was produced there in 1507. Yet it is to Reuchlin that he would give the credit for making a new Latin drama possible, and he continues his account with the statement which has been the basis for most of the misunderstanding of the history of the Biblical drama:

It was in the north, in Holland, still as ever to the forefront of Teutonic civilization, that the work of Reuchlin was first worthily taken up and directed into a fruitful channel. His mantle fell directly upon a man of great eminence,...George Macropedius, master of Utrecht school.

With Macropedius Herford would associate the names of William Gnapheus (William de Volder, generally known as Fullonius) of The Hague and Cornelius Crocus of Amsterdam, saying of the three men that they 'appear to have arrived independently at the same solution for a practical problem which as schoolmasters they all had to meet: how, namely, to steep a boy's mind in the admirable colloquial Latin of Terence and Plautus without introducing him prematurely to a world of *lenones* and *meretrices*. All three found the solution in what may be generally called the Biblical drama, or, as the strange phrase went, the *comedia sacra*'. To the plays of this school Herford applies the name of the 'Christian Terence'. Later he chronicles the advent of a 'Christian Seneca', initiated by

148

George Buchanan at Bordeaux with his *Jephthes*, which he calls 'the earliest tragedy composed north of the Alps in decidedly Senecan form'.[1]

E. K. Chambers recorded the movement in such a way as to lead to further misunderstanding, for, in writing of the development of the interlude in the time of Henry VIII, he noted the effect of a fresh wave of humanist influence:

> This came from the wing of the movement which had occupied itself, not only with erudition, but also with the spiritual stirrings that issued in the Reformation.... The Lutheran reformers were humanists as well as theologians, and it was natural to them to shape a literary weapon to their own purposes, rather than to cast it aside as unfit for furbishing. About 1530 a new school of neo-Latin drama arose in Holland, which stood in much closer relations to mediaevalism than that which had its origin in Italy. It aimed at applying the structure and the style of Terence to an edifying subject-matter drawn from the tradition of the religious drama.

He then noted the plays of Gnapheus and Macropedius as of the 'Christian Terence', and the beginnings of a 'Christian Seneca' with the plays of Buchanan. He did say that 'The movement began uncontroversially, but developed Protestant tendencies'.[2]

The result of Herford's acount and Chambers's modification of it has been that it has been popularly believed that the Biblical drama of the sixteenth century was inaugurated in the Netherlands as a by-product of the Reformation; that the Christian Terence originated by these Dutch schoolmasters was followed by a Christian Seneca initiated by George Buchanan at Bordeaux; the plays used 'edifying subject-matter drawn from the tradition of the religious drama', and the Bible plays produced in England from time to time were in fact neo-miracles, as Chambers regularly classifies them.

This view of the Christian drama as a recrudescence of an outworn type seems to me to ignore the existence of a whole new movement toward establishing a Christian literature and to treat drama as though it existed in isolation. Certain assumptions as

[1] C. H. Herford, *Studies in the Literary Relations of England and Germany in the Sixteenth Century* (Cambridge, 1886), pp. 79–80, 84–6, and 98.

[2] Chambers, *Med. Stage*, vol. II, pp. 216–17.

to its origin and development need also to be reconsidered. First, the three Dutch schoolmasters were not the first to publish Biblical dramas. Second, this drama was not a product of the Reformation, though the men who were its originators and promoters had a reforming spirit. Both in its initial stages and in its later development it was written by Catholics and Protestants with a common aim, and though it was later used for theological controversy, it continued to show the effects of its being a rival of the secular drama. Third, the Biblical drama did not come into existence as a Christian Terence succeeded by a Christian Seneca introduced by Buchanan, for the classical genres were recognized from the beginning, and Buchanan himself accepted Euripides as his model. Fourth, it did not draw its subject-matter 'from the tradition of the religious drama' but from the Bible, often reinforced by the works of Josephus. In its development saints' lives were naturally a corollary source, but for obvious reasons they did not contribute much to the English drama of this period. It is the facts that lead to these conclusions that I purpose to review briefly.

The idea of a Christian drama came to many different people in widely scattered places, as Herford recognizes, though he insists that this innovation of the Dutch schoolmasters was 'nevertheless essentially a new departure'.[1] One instance suffices in itself, however, to challenge his account and to offer proof, it seems to me, for the conclusions arrived at here. It was in 1508 that Francisco Conti, generally known as Quintianus Stoa, an Italian by birth and a Catholic, published in Milan a Latin tragedy on Christ's death to which he pedantically gave the Greek title *Theoandrothanatos*. In 1514 a second tragedy *Theocrisis* (this on the Last Judgment) was included in a volume of his *Christiana Opera* published in Paris. Lebègue calls these the first modern pieces published in France to be named tragedies and Stoa the first imitator of Seneca. That Stoa was writing his Christian works to oppose the profane literature which was absorbing current interest even in the Vatican is made evident in his letter to Spolète published in his *Christiana Opera*. The letter cited the example set by Prudentius, Sedulius, Juvencus, and

[1] Herford, p. 89 n.

Proba Falconia, and certainly, as Lebègue says, here 'Stoa révèle son dessein d'obtenir la gloire en créant un théâtre chrétienne, comme Juvencus et ses pareils ont jadis créé une poesie épique chrétienne'. Whether the plays were read, recited, or acted has been the subject of discussion among authorities without final decision, but that Stoa hoped that they would be acted and that he expected them to be useful in the instruction of youth seems clear.[1] An Italian Catholic writing Christian tragedy long before Buchanan and before the plays of the Netherlands group were published offers sufficient evidence to disprove the popular idea of the Christian Terence and the Christian Seneca. There was a definite recognition of genre, for Stoa called his plays tragedies. Not Hrostvitha, but Prudentius, Sedulius, and Juvencus had given him precedents if not models. And Savonarola in Florence had a decade earlier conceived the idea of turning the forms used in the heathen works to Christian uses. The first divine plays of the Dutch group mentioned by Herford were not published until much later: the *Acolastus* of Gnapheus in 1529; the *Asotus* of Macropedius in 1537, though it may have been written much earlier;[2] the *Joseph* of Crocus in 1536.

The list of original neo-Latin plays published on the continent before 1650, compiled by Leicester Bradner,[3] makes apparent at once the popularity of Bible plays during the sixteenth century. A good sampling may be had by examining the two great collections published at Basel.[4] The first of these

[1] The facts concerning Stoa are summarized by Raymond Lebègue, *La Tragédie Religieuse en France* (Paris, 1929), pp. 129–42.

[2] Herford thought it was written about 1510 (p. 153 marginal n.); Lebègue would date it about 1507 (p. 160), but it was not published until eight years after *Acolastus*.

[3] Leicester Bradner printed a list of authors and dates in 'A Check-List of Original Neo-Latin Dramas by Continental Writers before 1650', *P.M.L.A.*, LVIII (1943), 621–33. Conti was there identified by his pseudonym as a French writer rather than an Italian. In 1957 Bradner published a more complete 'List of Neo-Latin Plays Printed before 1650' in *Studies in the Renaissance*, IV, 55–70. Conti is there listed under his Latin name with no nationality indicated. See also Alfred Harbage, 'A Census of Anglo-Latin Plays', *P.M.L.A.* LIII (1938), 624–8.

[4] Lebègue lists the contents of the two collections, pp. xvii–xviii. Craig (pp. 363–77) notes these volumes, but follows Herford and Chambers in saying that the 'model of these biblical dramas was usually Terentian and that the word "comedy" is very loosely used, apparently referring to Terentian technique'. This statement is not in accord with the record, for these volumes do *not* use the word *comedy* loosely.

collected by the printer Brylinger in 1541 as *Comoediae ac Tragoediae aliquot ex Novo et Vetere Testamento Desumptae* was prefaced by an address of the printer to the reader which praised the new comedies and tragedies as worthy to find a place in the public theatres, in Christian schools, and in the libraries of the great, not only because of the purity of their language, but also because of their sacred argument. They would offer, the printer said, an opportunity for innocent boys to imbibe the rudiments of the Latin language by exercising themselves, not in profane and base matters, but in sacred and divine writings.

Among the ten plays contained in the Brylinger volume were several that were to be famous: *Acolastus*, the most influential of the prodigal-son dramas, by Gnapheus; *Pammachius*, 'the Protestant version of the Antichrist', by Naogeorgus (Thomas Kirchmeyer); *Christus Xilonicus* by Bartholomaeus (Nicholas Bartélémy); *Susanna* by Xystus Betuleius (Sixt Birck); and *Joseph* by Cornelius Crocus. *Pammachius*, first published in 1538, was dedicated to Thomas Cranmer, Archbishop of Canterbury. Crocus is said to have received orders at the hands of Bishop John Fisher and is presumed to have been in England at some time. Certain of the plays were well known in England as we shall see, and it is probable that the whole volume was familiar to many there. Each play was identified as *comoedia*, *tragoedia*, *comoedia tragica*, or *historia*. And it should be noted that along with the Protestant Naogeorgus and Betuleius, the Catholic Macropedius, Crocus, and Bartholomaeus were among the contributors, as well as Gnapheus, whom Herford calls a Crypto-Protestant, one who finally renounced his Catholicism.

The plays of Stoa were not included in this collection, and Lebègue suggests that it may have been for this reason that another printer in Basel, Oporinus, inserted the *Theoandrothanatos* in the volume of *Christianae Poeseos Opuscula*, where it was the only drama to be included. In 1547 Oporinus published a still more inclusive collection of divine plays than that of Brylinger, a two-volume work, *Dramata Sacra, Comoediae atque Tragoediae aliquot e Vetere Testamento Desumptae*. Sixteen plays were to be found in this work, but neither of Stoa's was there, though the *Susanna* of Betuleius and the *Joseph* of Crocus were again printed. Of possible interest in this study of English drama were certain others: *Eva, Judith,* and *Sapientia Solomonis* by Betuleius, *Hamanus* by Naogeorgus, and *Heli* by Hieronymus Ziegler (one of the five he contributed). Oporinus is known as the friend of Bale and Foxe and the publisher of many works important to the Reformation, but Catholic and Protestant authors were alike represented. Also it must again be pointed out that the genre of each play was indicated.

As I have said, George Buchanan has been given undeserved credit for having originated the 'Christian Seneca', but if he was not the first to write Biblical tragedy in classical form, he was probably the most famous. Educated at St Andrews in his native Scotland and at the University of Paris, he became a dramatist while he was teaching in the Collège de Guyenne at Bordeaux. The founder of the college had prescribed certain exercises to enable the scholars to compose and speak Latin, plays being regarded as necessary parts of these exercises. In fulfilment of this requirement, Buchanan wrote two Biblical tragedies, *Jephthes, sive Votum* and *Baptistes sive Calumnia,* and translated the *Medea* and the *Alcestis* of Euripides for the boys to produce. One of the pupils was Michael Montaigne who later wrote in his essay on education:

> Mettray-je en compte cette faculté de mon enfance: une asseurance de visage, et soupplesse de voix et de gest, à m'appliquer aux rolles que j'entreprenois? Car avent l'aage,
>
> > Alter ab undecimo tum me vix ceperat annus,
>
> j'ai soustenu les premieres personnages ès tragedies latines de Buchanan, de Guerente et de Muret, qui se representairent en nostre college de Guienne avec dignité. En cela Andreas Goveanus, nostre principal, come en toutes autres parties de sa charge, fut sans comparison le plus grand principal de France; et m'en tenoit-on maistre ouvrier.[1]

The four plays were certainly written before Buchanan left Bordeaux in 1544. According to his autobiography the *Baptistes* was the first to be written. Then followed the *Medea* translation, and afterwards the *Jephthes* and the *Alcestis,* with which

---

[1] Quoted from *Essais,* vol. I, p. xxvi, by H. de la Ville de Mirmont, 'Buchanan à Bordeaux' in *George Buchanan: A Memorial 1506–1906,* ed. D. A. Millar (St Andrews and London, 1907), p. 38.

he took greater pains in view of the prospects for their wider audience. The *Jephthes* was first published in Paris in 1554, and the list of editions and translations which followed attests its wide and long-continued importance. The *Baptistes* was not published until 1577, when its dedication to the young King James, then the author's pupil, explained his purpose in having thus dramatized the Bible story, 'adolescentes a vulgari fabularum scenicarum consuetudine ad imitationem antiquitatis provocet: & ad pietatis studium'. Two editions were published in London, in 1577 and 1578, and one in Edinburgh in 1578, but it did not have the wide publication of the *Jephthes*.[1] However, it is significant that in an edition of Buchanan's poetical works in 1597 all four tragedies were published, the two Biblical tragedies labelled *Tragoediae Sacrae*, the translations from Euripides *Tragoediae Externae*, thus placing the divine and the secular dramas in opposition.

In making the translations from Euripides, Buchanan seems to have desired to imitate and to rival Erasmus, who translated the *Iphigenia* and the *Hecuba*, and Lebègue notes that in *Jephthes* he imitates these particular plays. In each of the two Bible plays there is a long informative prologue, that in *Jephthes* being spoken by an angel, but there is no act and scene division. A chorus participates in the dialogue and also offers lyrical comment upon the action. In each play a messenger is used to relate the action, most of which takes place off-stage, but there is in his account no realistic description of horrors in the Senecan fashion. Because Buchanan has generally been considered the initiator of the Senecan drama, it is necessary to stress the fact that he translated Euripides and used Euripides as his model. It will be remembered too that when all four plays were published in 1597 the *tragoediae externae* juxtaposed to the *tragoediae sacrae* were those of Euripides. It was Euripides, not Seneca, whom Ascham later used as a touchstone by which to evaluate him.

The sub-titles plays must also be recognized as important in any consideration of the two divine plays. When Buchanan

---

[1] *S.T.C.* nos. 3969–71, where the Edinburgh copy is listed as an issue rather than a new edition, Lebègue, p. xviii.

was called before the Inquisition in Lisbon to answer charges of heresy, charges which were not unconnected with his attacks on the Franciscans, he testified in regard to the *Baptistes*:

> I used to disagree with the English [particularly in recognizing the King as head of the church]. Other issues on which we disagreed were purgatory, free-will, the Pope's authority, vows and the Church. ...Accordingly, as soon as possible when I escaped thence, I recorded my opinion of the English in that tragedy which deals with John the Baptist, wherein, so far as the likeness of the material would permit, I represented the death and accusation of Thomas More and set before the eyes an image of the tyranny of that time.

Commentators have long recognized the *Baptistes* as a mirror of tyranny, for the dialogue as well as the plot exhibited a preponderant theme. In 1642 it was translated, possibly by Milton, and published at the order of the House of Commons as *Tyrannical-Government Anatomized or A Discourse concerning Evil-Councillors* and was 'Presented to the Kings most Excellent Majesty by the Author'. However, the attempt to fit the story of Herod and Herodias and John to mirror Henry VIII, Anne Boleyn, and More has perplexed modern authorities when the other characters in the play are considered.

At the time Buchanan was writing, a pamphlet war between the Protestant Bucer and the Catholic Latomus on the subject of vows was being waged. Buchanan testified before the Inquisition:

> On vows, I revealed my opinion by a passage in my tragedy on the vow of Jephthah. The sum of the discussion was as follows:—vows which were lawfully made should always be kept, and moreover many know that at Coimbra it was my custom gladly to read and always to commend the speech of Barthélémy Latomus on this subject against Bucer.[1]

Lebègue has shown that the arguments between the priest and Jephthes in the play bear a marked resemblance to the arguments between the current opponents. On the strength of his own testimony, then, Buchanan used Biblical history to mirror contemporary situations. It must be remembered that it was

[1] See James M. Atkin, *The Trial of George Buchanan before the Lisbon Inquisition* (Edinburgh and London, 1939). The quotations are from Atkin's translation, pp. 23 and 13 respectively. See also pp. 55–6.

only when he returned to Scotland in 1561 that he formally renounced Catholicism and joined the Church of Scotland.

It was not until the plays of Cornelius Schonaeus were published in Cologne in 1592 that the *Terentius Christianus* of Hrostvitha was again used as a title for a collection of Biblical plays. Descent by pupilship can apparently be traced in Cornelius Schonaeus, for he is said to have had his interest in poetry roused as a student under Cornelius Valerius (Wauters) who had been a pupil of Macropedius in Utrecht. During his school years Schonaeus composed certain elegies and epigrams, but it would seem that the fact of the existence of two societies for the promotion of the Latin drama at the time of his residence at Louvain was of primary importance for his future work. I have found no record of his contributions to these societies, however. After leaving the university Schonaeus held various positions as a private tutor until in 1575 he was made rector of the Haarlem school, and there he remained until 1610, the last Catholic rector of the institution. In writing school plays from Bible story he announced the same desires that had motivated the earlier schoolmasters. His *Tobaeus*, written in 1568, was published in 1570 with a book of elegies, *Nehemias* in 1569, *Saul* in 1570, and these with plays on Naaman, Judith, and Joseph made up the 1592 volume. In 1599 a second part of the *Christian Terence* contained six additional plays. In 1603 a third part was published which contained a book of epigrams and the earlier printed elegies as well as the new plays, some of this matter non-Biblical.[1] The *Christian Terence* was used in many countries for many years as a text-book. Of its use in England I shall write later.

I have tried to show that Catholic and Protestant authors, moved by a common impulse to offset the dangers of an exclusive classical education, turned to the Bible for more healthful fare for their pupils. It was the Jesuit schools, however, that turned the Biblical drama and its corollary drama

[1] The fullest account is in the *Allgemeine Deutsche Biographie*, vol. xxxiv, pp. 731–2. R. B. Hepple started a discussion on '*Terentius Christianus*: A School-Book of 330 Years Ago', in *Notes and Queries*, vol. clxix, pp. 273–4. Others added comment in later numbers, but the German work would have made their conjectures unnecessary.

based on the lives of the saints to their special purpose and produced the greatest number of such dramas. 'From its foundation, in 1540, to its temporary suppression, in 1773', Henry Schnitzler writes, 'the Order carried on a vast theatrical program. During nearly two and a half centuries, Jesuit priests and their students devoted a large part of their time and energy to work in every conceivable area related to the stage.' It was a propaganda theatre, and there was printed 'at the end of every synopsis and at the bottom of every program, the letters "O.A.M.D.G.", an abbreviation of the motto *Omnia Ad Majorem Dei Gloriam* i.e. "All to the Greater Glory of God".'[1] The official programme for the Jesuit schools, their *Ratio Studiorum*, ultimately prescribed the conditions under which the drama was to be produced. Their tragedies and comedies were required to be written in Latin and were to be infrequent. The subject-matter must be sacred and pious. Nothing might be inserted between the acts which was not Latin and seemly. No women or women's dress might be introduced in the plays.[2]

The regulations seem to have been enforced without undue severity, and every form of theatrical entertainment, even ballet, was offered. Though some of the plays seem to have found their way into England in manuscript, I have seen no indication that they were produced there, however much they may have done to create a spirit of emulation. The College of St Omers should, nevertheless, be specially noted, for W. H. McCabe has demonstrated that 'The College was thoroughly British, though placed on the Continent', and 'it was host to a steady stream of travellers between England and the Continent, Protestants as well as Catholics, whom its theatre often entertained'.[3] Like the Jesuit theatre in general however, it attained greater importance in the seventeenth than in the sixteenth century.

[1] 'The Jesuit Contribution to the Theatre', *Educational Theatre Journal*, vol. IV, pp. 283–92.
[2] Ernest Boysse, *Le Théâtre des Jésuits* (Paris, 1880), p. 18 and n. Professor Edna Purdie has given an account of its history on the continent in her article 'Jesuit Drama' in the *Oxford Companion to the Theatre* (London, 1951), pp. 415–22.
[3] 'The Play-List of the English College of St Omers, 1592–1762', *Revue de Littérature Comparée* (1937), pp. 355–75. 'Notes on the St Omers College Theatre', *Philological Quarterly* (1938), XV, pp. 225–39.

CHAPTER III

CONTINENTAL SCHOOL DRAMA
IN THE VERNACULAR

ACCORDING to Lebègue,[1] *The Abraham Sacrifiant* of Theodore de Bèze was the first tragedy in France which was not a translation and, so far as our knowledge goes, it was the only one of the continental divine dramas composed in the vernacular which found its way to England. It is, therefore, the only one with which we are concerned.[2]

Bèze's play was written and performed at Lausanne in 1550 and printed at Geneva in the same year. It was translated into English by Arthur Golding in 1575 and published in London in 1577 with illustrations which cannot represent accurately a practicable stage setting. It would be expected to find an audience in England, where the writings of both Golding and Bèze were familiar; yet there is no evidence for its ever having been given an English production. Its influence, however, demands that it be considered here in some detail.

Golding was one of the great translators of the Tudor period. His later fame rests for the most part on his translations of Caesar and Ovid, and Lathrop judged his version of the *Metamorphoses* to stand out 'above all the verse translations of the period'.[3] In his own day, however, he was also known as the translator of the Psalms and of the works of contemporary Frenchmen, particularly of various works of Calvin. It was fitting, therefore, that he should also translate Bèze's drama, for Bèze was Calvin's successor at Geneva.

---

[1] For most of the facts here recorded I am indebted to Lebègue, pp. 293–318. A list of editions of the play before 1928 is given, pp. 507–13. I have used the Bèze text and Golding's translation edited by Malcolm W. Wallace (Toronto, 1906). A list of Golding's work is given, pp. xxxii–xxxvii.

[2] Probably the most prolific writer of Bible plays in the period was Hans Sachs, but I have found no evidence of their being brought to England. Joseph E. Gilbert, 'The German Dramatist of the Sixteenth Century and His Bible', *P.M.L.A.* vol. XXXIV (1919), gives a good summary of the German movement to substitute Biblical for secular plays.

[3] Lathrop, p. 126. See pp. 126–9, 168–72 for a full acount of his work.

Bèze had written poems characteristic of a young man's fancy before he was twenty and had published them in Paris in 1548 as *Juvenilia*. Later in that year he went secretly to Switzerland and in 1549 settled in Lausanne as professor of Greek at the academy there. He was, of course, to become head of Calvin's school at Geneva and one of the most influential and prominent of the post-Calvin Calvinists. According to Lebègue he took the opportunity offered by the request of the academy authorities at Lausanne for a play that students of the academy could perform to efface the memory of his *Juvenilia* by writing *Abraham Sacrifiant*. His conscience bothered him over his youthful folly, as he wrote in the preface to his play, for having always delighted in poetry, 'it greveth me right sore, that the little grace which God gave me in that behalfe, was imployed by me in such things, as the very remembrance of them irketh me now at the hart'. He was then working on the translation of the Psalms, wishing the good wits of Frenchmen could be exercised likewise in holy matters, rather 'to sing a song of God, then to counterfet a ballet of Petrarks, & to make amorous ditties, worthy to have the garlande of sonnetts, or to counterfet the furies of the auncient Poets, to blase abroad the glory of this world, or to consecrate this man or that woman to immortalitie'. Abraham, Moses, and David seemed to him those in whom God had shown forth his greatest wonders.

Bèze's choice for his drama was, consequently, the story of Abraham and Isaac as told in the twenty-second chapter of Genesis. It is possible that he drew upon *Le Mistere du Viel Testament* and the *Isaaci Immolatio* of the Catholic Ziegler (in the Oporinus collection), but he himself carefully indicated his great debts. On the title-page of the 1550 edition with references to the fifteenth chapter of Genesis and the fourth of Romans there stood the quotation '*Abraham a creu à Dieu, & il luy a esté reputé à justice*'. These are the chapters which treat of God's promise to Abraham and its fulfilment, chapters fundamental to the Calvinist doctrine that we are justified by faith rather than works. This is the theme of the play, and the story of Abraham and Isaac exemplified its truth. The twenty-second chapter of Genesis was, therefore, printed as the 'argument' of the play after the classical fashion. Bèze's own account gives his reasons for the variations and additions to the Bible story to be found in the play: 'I have altered some small circumstances of the storie, to apply myselfe to the companye. Moreover I have followed the ground as neare the text as I could, according to such conjectures as I thought most convenient for the matter and persons.'

Bèze was writing a school play to be produced for the young scholars in their native language, and he says he refused to use technical terms like *strophe* and *antistrophe*, as obsolete and serving only 'to amase simple folke' (so Golding renders his words). In keeping with this determination he divided his play by *pawses* and identified the company of shepherds in his play as a *troupe*. He also called attention to the fact that he introduced a song without a chorus, presumably a reference to the morning hymn of praise sung by Abraham and Sara near the beginning of the play, since a song by the *troupe* is sung in each of the first two parts of the play. In other ways too Bèze departed from the classical formula generally observed in the academic drama. The pauses divide the play into three parts, the action of the first part taking place outside Abraham's house, that of the second at the base of the mountain, that of the third on the summit of the mountain where the sacrifice was to be performed. An unusual interpolation of an interior scene comes in the third part when we are given a glimpse of Sara at home worrying over her husband and child. Unity of time is disregarded also, for three days elapse between the first and second parts of the play. As to why he called it a tragedy he explains:

it is partly tragical and partly comicall: & therefore I have separated the prologue, & divided the whole into pawses, after the maner of actes in comedies, howbeit without binding of my selfe thereto. And because it holdeth more of the one then of the other: I thought best to name it a tragedie.

It would seem much simpler to have called it a tragi-comedy.[1]

---

[1] F. H. Ristine, *English Tragicomedy* (Columbia Studies in English, New York, 1910), discusses Grimald's definition (p. 23) and Gascoigne's (pp. 63–6), but does not mention Bèze's play as translated by Golding.

The prologue begins with the usual greeting and the request for silence, but an extra admonitory note is introduced:

> Would God we might eache weeke through all the yeare
> See such resort in Churches as is here.

The word to the imaginary traveller is, however, a more interesting departure from the usual, recalling as it does Shakespeare's use of the same device in *Henry V*:

> You thinke your selves perchaunce to be in place,
> Where as you be not, now as standes the case.
> For Lausan is not here, it is far hence.
> But yit when neede requires, I will dispence
> With all of you, that hence within an hower
> Eche one may safely be within his bowre.

Shakespeare comes to mind also as Satan speaks a series of soliloquies in the play after the manner of Richard III and Iago when they plot their villainy.

Perhaps the most significant feature of Bèze's play, after the fact that it is written in the vernacular, however, is the psychological conflict that is given external reality (1) by introducing Satan 'in the habit of a Monke' to argue against obedience to the Lord's command; (2) by adding Sara to the dramatis personae to take a mother's part against her husband; and (3) by having the *troupe* or company of shepherds 'divided in two partes'. Isaac's natural appeal to pity, emphasized by his thought of his mother's concern, is, I think, not quite the same thing as the conflict represented by these arguments; it touches rather the springs of pathos that have made many critics call the old miracle of *Abraham and Isaac* a tragedy.

Abraham Sacrifiant was Bèze's only play and Golding's too. Chambers has pointed out its significance in indicating something of the Calvinist attitude toward drama in general. The fact that it was printed in Geneva and that in 1560 it was approved by the consistory for reprinting offers important evidence in the matter.[1] That its moving story has long continued to make

---

[1] E. K. Chambers, *The Elizabethan Stage* (Oxford, 1923), vol. 1, pp. 245–9. See also Lebègue, pp. 314–17; Kosta Loukovitch, *La Tragédie Religieuse Classique en France* (Paris, 1932), pp. 17–19 and 239.

an appeal is apparent in the thirty-six editions listed by Lebègue between its first appearance and 1923.[1] It seems strange that apparently it never reached production in England, as indeed it seems strange that none but this of all the Biblical plays written in the vernacular of the various continental countries was produced or translated in England during this period, as far as we know.

[1] Pp. 507–13.

CHAPTER IV

LATIN DIVINE DRAMAS IN ENGLISH SCHOOLS

THE use of Biblical plays for the teaching of facility in translation is of subordinate interest in this study to their production as theatre, but that such use was proposed is a fact to be recorded. Actually the first of the continental plays of this kind to be printed in England for this purpose was the prodigal-son play *Acolastus*, originally published in Antwerp in 1529 and now published in London in 1540 with an English translation intended to illustrate how translation should be taught. Written by the schoolmaster Gnaphaeus (Fullonius), it was translated by the schoolmaster John Palsgrave.[1] Palsgrave had been schoolmaster to the children of royal and noble persons, he was the friend of Erasmus and Thomas More, he held degrees from both universities, and he was chaplain to the King. He had written *Lesclarcissement de la Langue Francoyse*.

In 1540 the King issued his proclamation commanding the use in English schools of the grammar generally known as Lily's grammar. Palsgrave seems to have decided to further the good work and published in that year his *Ecphrasis Anglica in Comoediam Acolasti* with a dedication to the King in which he explained:

I wyshed, that unto this moch expedient reformation of your schole maisters unstayd libertie, which hytherto have taught such grammers, and of the same so dyvers and sondry sortes, as to every of theym semed best (and was to their fantasies mooste approved) myght thereto also folowe and succede one stedy and unyforme maner of interpretation of the latyn authors into our tonge, after that the latyn principles were by your graces youth ones surely conned and perceyved.

---

[1] P. L. Carver in his edition of *The Comedy of Acolastus* for the Early English Text Society (Original Series, vol. 202, London, 1937) has given an account of Palsgrave's life, the facts concerning his relation to Mary, the younger sister of Henry VIII, and concerning his opposition to Wolsey being of special interest. Quotations are from Carver's edition. For a discussion of the date of the King's proclamation see pp. 183–4.

He hoped to establish thus a uniform method by which English youth might be able to write and speak both idiomatic Latin and idiomatic English, turning Latin expressions into their equivalent as well as their literal English expressions. He chose *Acolastus* to exhibit his method, he said, because he considered it 'to be a very curiouse and artificiall compacted nosegay, gathered out of the moche excellent and odoriferouse swete smellynge gardeynes of the moste pure latyne auctors', and also because he hoped through making English writers envious of such good Latin composition to stir them to emulation.

Palsgrave's method was to indicate every possible variant translation for each phrase. He included and expanded Gnapheus's notation of the metres used. In spite of all the scholarly apparatus thus provided, there is no record of the King's having commanded uniformity in the use of Palsgrave's method, and only the one edition of the work was needed. I shall describe the play as it was acted a little later.[1]

A different fate met the work of another schoolmaster, however, for the *Terentius Christianus* of Schonaeus, which was first printed in England in 1595, was reprinted frequently in the seventeenth century. Brinsley in his *Ludus Literarius* in 1612 recommended it as an alternative to Terence, following the study of Corderius's dialogues.[2] Foster Watson calls it the most famous collection of foreign plays used in English schools.[3] However, the English edition contained only *Tobaeus* and *Juditha* from the first edition and *Pseudostratiotes*, which had been newly printed separately. The English edition contained an address to the reader which is of interest for its citing of Lily's authority and for its comment concerning the use of Bible story in plays, as well as for its inclusion of the usual reasons for creating a Christian drama:

For boys (as the grammarian Lily, not unknown in England, said), only pure things are suitable. In Terence there is pure language, but the subject-matter for the most part is not pure, nor is that strange. What can you expect from a poor ethnic, ignorant of the true God, the source of true purity? Therefore Schonaeus, a very

---

[1] The English prodigal-son plays are described later in ch. VI.   [2] P. 221.

[3] Foster Watson, *The English Grammar Schools to 1660* (Cambridge, 1908), p. 322.

learned man, did something worth while: for the benefit of Christian boys he has clothed more chaste subject-matter in the pure language of Terence, in order that along with elegance of style boys may imbibe holiness and uprightness of character.

As his reason for selecting plays from the Apocrypha, the English editor said he chose them, not because they were truer or more sacred than others, but because they seemed more suitable for plays, a learned theologian [Luther] having considered them rather poems than histories. He added significantly:

> There is an old familiar proverb, *It is not good to play with sacred things*. And what is holier and more sacred than the divinely inspired canonical scriptures? Therefore to add, to subtract, to omit anything from them, to insert speeches and characters, as poetic license permits, becomes a scruple in the eyes of some whom we do not want to offend needlessly.[1]

Schonaeus, like Gnapheus and the other schoolmasters, prepared his plays as exercises for his scholars, patterning them after classical authority with five acts and many scenes, prologue, argument, and epilogue. The prologues stress the fact that they were taken from the Bible, making what is taught in the pulpit more moving when it is presented on the stage. The epilogues regularly explain the moral or the mystical significance of the story and seek to apply it to the present time.

A manuscript in the National Library of Wales discovered by Gwen Jones offers evidence as to how these divine plays were used in British schools, for the manuscript includes 'Cato construed by Corderius' together with the Latin text of *Juditha Constantia* with the not very facile translation into English of the prologue, the argument, and a section of the first scene of the first act.[2] Among the Bodleian manuscripts there are four volumes described as 'Translations into English prose of the plays written for the use of the scholars of the school at Haarlem by the master Cornelius Schonaeus'. The first two volumes contain Schonaeus's *Naaman, Tobit, Nehemiah, Saul, Joseph*, and *Judith*.[3] (It will be noticed that Schonaeus did not confine

---

[1] The translation was made by Frederick M. Carey, Professor of Classics in the University of California, Los Angeles.

[2] *Modern Language Notes* (1917), vol. XXXII, pp. 1-6.

[3] Bodleian MSS. Rawlinson, nos. 1388-91.

himself to the apocryphal books of the Bible in searching for play material.) The third volume is made up of the four Buchanan plays, and the fourth has six plays of Plautus with a fragment of another on the last leaf. Why these plays were translated or by whom must be a matter for conjecture, but they were clearly not adapted for production in England since the prologues continue to refer to 'our Master Schonaeus' as they carry the good wishes of 'the whole Quire of boyes' to the 'Honour'd Srs. and most courteous Cittizens' in the audience. To find Schonaeus and Buchanan and Plautus linked together as obviously proper material for practice in translation is interesting. Submitting the plays for translation would certainly create in schoolboys little enthusiasm, no matter how excellent the moral instruction, but the plays of Gnapheus and Schonaeus as well as those of Plautus were intended by their authors for production.

English schoolboys, like those on the continent, were acting plays in the sixteenth century, as well as being confronted by them as textbooks. Just how early these productions began remains uncertain, but William Lily, the first headmaster of Saint Paul's grammar school as it was re-established by Dean Colet, came to his duties after a sojourn in Rome, where he had studied under Pomponius Laetus. Whether he carried home to his school the enthusiasm of his Roman teacher for the acted drama is not known, but under the mastership of his son-in-law John Ritwise, who succeeded him, the boys of the school acted before both Henry VIII and Cardinal Wolsey as early as 1527 and 1528. Eton records offer evidence of productions in 1525.[1] Exactly a hundred years later, in 1625, Ben Jonson made his Censure, one of the gossips in *The Staple of News*, complain of the schoolmasters of England:

They make all their scholars playboys! Is't not a fine sight, to see all our children made interluders? Do we pay our money for this? We send them to learn their grammar and their Terence, and they learn their playbooks![2]

[1] Chambers, *Med. Stage*, vol. II, pp. 196, and *Eliz. Stage*, vol. II, pp. 11 and 12 n.
[2] Act III, sc. ii.

The records of the schoolboys' offerings are disappointing, for they rarely give the titles of plays produced or any indication of their identity. Our scattered knowledge does, however, offer grounds for concluding that the movement to dramatize Bible stories for schoolboy production had reached England. The most specific account that has been preserved is that of John Bale, who in 1552 visited the school conducted by Ralph Radcliffe at Hitchin in Hertfordshire. There a building of the old Carmelite monastery after its dissolution in 1538 had been turned into a school, and Bale wrote that what had pleased him most about it was the beautiful large theatre in the lower part of the house. The scholars could there see and hear plays 'simul jocunda & honesta', and in performing them they could learn to speak clearly and eloquently with assurance. He listed ten of their plays, six of the ten being built on the Bible stories of Jonah, Lazarus and the rich man, Judith, Job, Susanna, and the destruction of Jerusalem. Bale's habit of turning all titles into Latin leads to uncertainty, but at least some of the plays he listed were evidently written in Latin since he gives the Latin first lines of two. Some of the Hitchin plays, were, however, produced before the townspeople, and it is unlikely that they suffered Latin gladly. Both Herford and Chambers accepted the loss of these plays as apparently final, but in 1937 W. R. Hughes wrote in *Blackwood's Magazine* that Reginald Hine, the historian of Hitchin, had discovered three of them in manuscript in the Welsh library of Lord Harlech,[1] and some day we may learn more about them, for they are now in the National Library of Wales.

Shrewsbury School was also producing plays, and the Ordinances formulated by its headmaster, Thomas Ashton, prescribed that the highest form was to declaim and play one act of a comedy once a week. Thomas Ashton had been summoned to Shrewsbury in 1560 from St John's College, Cambridge, to produce *The Passion of Christ* in the Quarry where, according to the historians of the school, the performance of a 'mystery' play had been an annual event. After producing the *Passion of*

---

[1] Chambers, *Med. Stage*, vol. II, p. 197 and n. 1; W. R. Hughes, 'They All Wrote Plays', *Blackwood's*, vol. CII, pp. 70–84. According to the *Dictionary of National Biography* Radcliffe disputed with Sir John Cheke the pronunciation of Greek.

Christ in 1560, Ashton was appointed headmaster in 1561.
Under him Philip Sidney and Fulke Greville began their school-
days. Under his direction the plays in the Quarry continued to
be produced, and to them came great numbers of noblemen
and others according to an early account. It is assumed by the
historians of the school that the boys of the school were the
actors in the plays, and they note that when Legge's *Richard
Tertius* was performed at St John's College, Cambridge, in
1579, five of the actors were from the Shrewsbury School.
Thomas Ashton had been a fellow of St John's when the *Absalon*
of Thomas Watson was performed, the play which Ascham felt
worthy to be compared with the plays of Euripides. Though
I doubt whether he was summoned to Shrewsbury to produce
a 'mystery', he was certainly summoned to produce a Bible
play. Thomas Churchyard calls Ashton 'a good and godly
preacher', the plays produced in the Quarry were evidently
religious plays, and he was their producer, perhaps also their
author as the old account calls him. There the evidence ends,
but Churchyard has given an account of the amphitheatre 'in
goodly auncient guise' constructed in the Quarry which is of
special interest:[1]

> There is a ground, newe made Theator wise,
> Both deepe and hye, in goodly auncient guise:
> Where well may sit, ten thousand men at ease,
> And yet the one, the other not displease.

> A space belowe, to bayt both Bull and Beare,
> For Players too, great roume and place at will.
> And in the same, A Cocke pit wondrous feare,
> Besides where men, may wrastle in their fill.
> A ground most apt, and they that sits above,
> At once in vewe, all this may see for love:
> At Astons play, who had beheld this then,
> Might well have seene, there twentie thousand men.

---

[1] J. Basil Oldham, *A History of Shrewsbury School 1552–1592* (Oxford, 1952),
pp. 5–7, 9–13. See also George W. Fisher, *Annals of Shrewsbury School* (London,
1899), pp. 5, 17–20. Oldham asserts that Ashton was a member of St John's
College, not Trinity, as Fisher said. The quotation found in part in these authorities is from *The Worthiness of Wales* (London, 1587), sigs. K^v–L^r.

Whatever doubts we must feel as to the numbers of play-goers as computed by Churchyard, there can be little question of the widespread popularity of Ashton's plays. At the end of Pals-grave's translation of *Acolastus* it is stated that 'William Fullonius the maker of this presente Comedy, did set it forthe before the bourgeses of Hagen in Holand. Anno. M.D. XXIX', and the plays of Schonaeus were clearly performed before a citizen audience. It is evident that both the Hitchin school of Ralph Radcliffe and the Shrewsbury school of Thomas Ashton were following the continental example in thus offering enter-tainment to their fellow citizens who were not of the academic world.

How often the English schoolmasters drew their plays from the continent we cannot tell. *Acolastus* was performed in Trinity College, Cambridge, in 1560–1, but Thomas Nashe was not born until 1567, and the performance which he described in two different works was evidently put on by schoolboys. In *The Unfortunate Traveller* he has Jack Wilton report that the Duke of Saxony 'was bidden to one of the chiefe schooles [of Wittenberg] to a Comedie handled by schollers':

Acolastus, the prodigal child, was the name of it, which was so filthily acted, so leathernly set forth, as would have moved laughter in *Heraclitus*. One as if he had ben playning a clay floore, stampingly trode the stage so harde with his feete that I thought verily he had resolved to do the Carpenter that set it up some utter shame. Another flong his armes lyke cudgels at a peare tree, insomuch as it was mightily dreaded that he wold strike the candles that hung above their heades out of their socketts, and leave them all darke. Another did nothing but winke and make faces. There was a parasite, and he with clapping his handes and thripping his fingers seemed to dance an antike to and fro. The onely thing they did well, was the prodigall childs hunger, most of their schollers being hungerly kept; & surely you would have sayd they had bin brought up in the hogs academie to learne to eate acornes, if you had seene how sedulously they fell to them.[1]

[1] *The Works of Thomas Nashe*, ed. R. B. McKerrow (London, 1904–9), vol. II, p. 249, and vol IV, p. 274, where a note mentions a performance of *Acolastus* at Wittenberg in 1572. Such references as 'n'er a penny in his purse' seem to indicate an English version.

Again in *Summers Last Will and Testament* Will Summer is made to decry the entertainment offered him, describing the prodigal child 'in his dublet and hose all greasy, his shirt hanging forth, and ne'r a penny in his purse, and talke what a fine thing it is to walke summerly, or sit whistling under a hedge and keepe hogges'.[1]

As to where and when Nashe may have seen a performance we have no information, but that the play was widely known there can be little doubt. The phrase-stuttering translation of the Palsgrave text certainly would not have offered the basis for a production, but the Brylinger volume of Bible plays in which it had been reprinted was apparently familiar to many, and later prodigal-son plays written in English bear the marks of its influence, though no other translations into English have come down to us. As a school play, therefore, it may not inappropriately be described here as it appeared in the Brylinger volume.

Gnapheus in his prologue praises Terence and Plautus as the best of poets and patterns his comedy after theirs, indicating that there is a hidden meaning in the story, though the hidden meaning is not explored until the epilogue. The prologue closes with an appeal for applause as payment for the pleasure received from the play and introduces the argument, which simply rehearses the Bible story. The elder son is not among the dramatis personae, but a number of characters are added: a good counsellor for the father, a bad counsellor for the prodigal and—straight out of Latin comedy—two parasites, an ingenious and intriguing servant, a courtesan, a confidential maid, a procurer. The main characters are given symbolic names, the minor characters names from Terence and Plautus. It is of some interest that the wise counsellor is called Eubulus and the bad counsellor Philautus.

The five acts are divided into scenes, the most fully realized scenes being those which exhibit the riotous living and the wanton adventures of Acolastus with the 'common woman' Lais. Perhaps these were the scenes that would induce the scholars to search more diligently for equivalent English idiom,

[1] *Ibid.* vol. III, p. 247.

but it is difficult to see how less harm would come to them in this than in a Terentian comedy.

Acolastus on his departure from home is presented with a Bible by his father, but Philautus induces him to discard it at once. Incidental references are to classical authors and classical precedents, and oaths are commonly sworn by Hercules or by the temple of Pollux. The epilogue brings the hidden meaning which the prologue foretold: that though a man sin, yet God, like a loving father, welcomes home again his repentant child. Christ himself spoke this parable to explain the mercy of God.

The *Sapientia Solomonis* of Sixt Birck (Betuleius) was published in the second great collection of sacred plays, that of Oporinus. It had already been performed at Cambridge in 1559–60 when it was offered by the boys of the Westminster School for the entertainment of Queen Elizabeth and her royal guest, Princess Cecilia of Sweden, on 17 January 1565–6. The manuscript of the play in the British Museum (now edited by Elizabeth Rogers Payne)[1] gives us our only exact knowledge of the text of a continental Biblical play as it was altered for an English production, and also something of the way in which it was set forth. Who wrote the adaptation for the Westminster performance, or whether it was the same version that had been used at Cambridge is not known, but quite evidently the play had been made a little more 'jocunda' when it was presented to the royal visitors and the privy council.

The list of 'expenses for the furniture and setting forthe' of the play shows that the Office of the Revels contributed 'apparel', and that Thomas Browne, the headmaster, was reimbursed by Dean Goodman for the fifty-two shillings and tenpence he had spent on it. The title of the play as well as the names of the houses were done in red and black ink. Colours and gold foil were needed 'in coloring the childrens faces, & in gylting the garlandes for the prologes'. A painter was paid for 'Drawing the cytee & temple of Jerusalem, & for paynting

---

[1] *Yale Studies in English* (New Haven, 1938), vol. 89. Ed. from B.M. Add. MS. 20061 and collated with the original play. All quotations are from this edition.

towres'. But perhaps the most intriguing item is that which indicates that a real baby had a part in the production, for five shillings was paid to 'A woman that brawght hir childe to the stadge & there attended uppon itt'.[1]

These items of expense help us to get the picture of the stage which was set in the great room known as the College Hall, for the action of the play clearly takes place in a street scene. Characters are hailed as they approach, and they speak of withdrawing into the hall or the palace or the citadel. Even the judgment of the King between the two women quarrelling over the dead child and the living one is delivered in the street. The King goes to meet the Queen of Sheba in the street, and they sit together in the portico for their sweet discourses. The 'houses' were evidently arranged about the street (probably in a blunted triangle after the manner prescribed by Serlio) with the city and temple painted on the scene which blocked the apex of the triangle. The houses were practicable, permitting exits and entrances, and the 'house' of the palace evidently had a portico large enough for regal splendour to be displayed.[2]

Birck's play covered the accounts of Solomon's reputation for wisdom, the dream, the judgment between the two mothers, his negotiations for the building of the temple, and his reception of the Queen of Sheba. It was based upon the Vulgate and the Greek editions of Josephus, as the editor has proved. The adapter made much of the character of the non-Biblical fool Marcolphus, traditionally associated with Solomon, and he introduced three characters to speak—or sing—what Birck gave to a chorus: Sapientia, Justicia, and Pax.

The play, called a tragi-comedy, as presented at Westminster School was set in contrast to the *Miles Gloriosus* of Plautus which had been presented the year before. The new prologue (in the Payne translation) stresses the contrast:

It is not a comic poet that we bring this time, but a serious history, drawn from the sacred fount of truth. Blessed Solomon will see

---

[1] The expense account is inserted opposite p. 40.

[2] My interpretation of the stage setting differs from that of the editor (p. 43), for the 'houses' seem to me clearly to have been practicable and built as I have described them from Serlio's instructions and pictures in my *Scenes and Machines* (Cambridge, 1923), pp. 34-5.

presently another ruler greatly blessed by the same tokens and the same good omens and likewise administering justice and the law to the people whom God gave her to rule over.

The classical pattern is kept: prologue, argument, five acts divided into scenes, the scenes marked by change of speakers and with the liaison of the scenes generally observed. The unity of place is inevitable with the street scene. The time is compressed, but more than one day is involved. Such familiar devices as 'there he comes' and the announced withdrawal into a house, the concealed observers of what takes place on the stage, the recital of events happening off-stage, and the soliloquy are used. The personified characters appear instead of the chorus in scenes at the end of all acts except Act II. The two mothers are called *meretrices*, their language is Plautine, and I am afraid that they must be reckoned the most interesting of the characters to the modern reader. The Biblical characters, however, preserve decorum in their speech.

No doubt the Queen of England was pleased to hear the Queen of Sheba affirm that though a woman, she ruled justly, and that in her country girls as well as boys were to be educated and learn useful arts. And no doubt she recognized the tribute of Solomon to the Queen of Sheba, 'Because you bear learning and power instead of a distaff, and are experienced in the virtues, you transcend your sex'. The epilogue makes the application specific, the Swedish princess serving as the Queen of Sheba who had come to enjoy the light-giving of Elizabeth. And an anti-Catholic twist is given to the detailed comparison:

Solomon was just; our Queen is unjust to no man. Solomon was merciful; our Queen is mercy itself. The King, exceedingly skillful, gave the living offspring to the true parent and assigned the dead child to the wicked mother. Our Queen restored her sons to the true Church,...Solomon built a holy temple to God; our Queen has done nothing more important than to renew quickly the ritual of holy worship which had been overthrown.

CHAPTER V

DIVINE DRAMAS IN ENGLISH
UNIVERSITIES

OXFORD men contributed certain original scriptural
plays to the general movement for a Biblical drama,
but so far as our present knowledge goes, it was only
Cambridge that gave hospitality to importations from the
continent. Though mentions of payments for windows broken
during the performance of plays are much more numerous than
those of the titles of the plays that were being produced, it
is from the expense accounts of the Cambridge colleges that
our list of plays is chiefly derived. When Boas assembled the
calendar of all plays of all kinds produced in English universities, it is not surprising, therefore, that he had to state that the
plays represented by these titles 'form only a fraction of the
tragedies, comedies, and miscellaneous "shows" produced on
College stages during the Tudor period'.[1] He added, however, that these may be taken as representative of the types
performed there. Biblical plays constitute a considerable
fraction of the total list compiled, and by this reckoning
Cambridge at least for about twenty-five years found receptive
audiences for the dramas that had already become well known
in Europe.

Queens' College, Cambridge, would seem to have been in
the forefront of those participating in the revival of classical
drama, for in 1522–3 a play of Plautus was produced there,[2]
but few of their plays are named in their records. In 1543 a

---

[1] Frederick S. Boas, *University Drama in the Tudor Age* (Oxford, 1914), pp. 385–
90. See also George B. Churchill and Wolfgang Keller, 'Die lateinischen Uni-
versitäts-Dramen Englands in der Zeit der Königin Elizabeth', *Jahrbuch der
Deutschen Shakespeare-Gesellschaft*, vol. XXXIV, pp. 224–32; G. C. Moore Smith,
College Plays Performed in the University of Cambridge (Cambridge, 1923), and 'The
Academic Drama in Cambridge', Malone Society *Collections*, vol. II, pt. ii,
pp. 150–230.
[2] On the play and its possible actors see Leicester Bradner, 'The First Cambridge Production of *Miles Gloriosus*', *Mod. Lang. Notes*, vol. LXX (1955),
pp. 400–3.

dialogue of Textor was performed, probably *Thersites*,[1] but it should be noted that a fragment conjectured by Greg to have been printed between 1530 and 1534 and identified as a translation of Textor's *Juventus Pater et Uxor* indicates the early knowledge in England of that seminal drama found in Textor's dialogues.[2] In 1547–8 charcoal was provided at Queens' when 'adelphes et Heli erant recitatae', offering evidence that the *Adelphi* of Terence and the *Heli* of Hieronymus Ziegler were produced companionably.

At Christ's College during the Lenten season of 1545 the *Pammachius* of Kirchmeyer (Naogeorgus) was presented, to the great annoyance of the chancellor of the university, Stephen Gardiner. The vice-chancellor, Matthew Parker, was called upon to defend it, which he did in a letter dated on Good Friday. Gardiner was not satisfied with the expurgated version of the play as performed which was sent to him, and the matter, reached the privy council. With one of the leading performers bound over to appear before that body when called for, the matter apparently became quiescent.[3] The play is not a dramatization of Bible story, but it was included in the Brylinger volume, and it had been dedicated to the Archbishop of Canterbury (Thomas Cranmer). It presented what Mullinger calls a 'rude caricature of papal history, as seen through Calvinist spectacles', and, though the action should culminate in the second coming of Christ, that event had perforce to be left for an unwritten fifth act. The play seems to have been much to the taste of John Bale, who lists it among his works as a translation.

At Trinity College the continental Bible play found its greatest acceptance. The *Sapientia Solomonis* of Sixt Birck was presented in 1559–60. In 1560–1 the *Acolastus* of Gnapheus, which should have been anathema to every schoolboy if Palsgrave had had his way, was among the offerings. The 'John

---

[1] The Textor dialogue is entered on 15 January. On 22 February an entry occurs 'pro picto clipeo quo miles gloriosus usus est in comoedia', Mal. Soc. *Coll.* II, ii, 184, which may indicate a performance of the play of Plautus, or as Boas thinks (pp. 20–1), it may identify the Textor dialogue as *Thersites*.

[2] No. 19 in W. W. Greg, *Bibliography of the English Printed Drama to the Restoration* (London, 1939). The fragment is printed in Mal. Soc. *Coll.* I, i, 26–30.

[3] J. B. Mullinger, *The University of Cambridge* (Cambridge, 1884), vol. II, pp. 74–6.

babtiste' acted in 1562–3 was presumably Buchanan's *Baptistes*. In 1565–6 the *Asotus* of Macropedius was performed. In 1566–7 a play of *Jephthes* was acted, but whether it was Buchanan's is a matter to be discussed later.

Though Oxford did not, so far as I have discovered, import Biblical plays from the continent, it imported from Cambridge one of the first English humanists to turn to the writing of such plays. Today Nicholas Grimald[1] is known as, after Wyatt and Surrey, the most extensive contributor to the *Songes and Sonnetes* published by Tottel in 1557, but the long list of his writings accredited to him by his friend John Bale gives good reason for the reputation he had in his own day.[2] Barnaby Googe wrote an epitaph on his death, affirming

> A thousand doltysh
> Geese we myght have sparde,
> A thousand wytles
> heads, death might have found
> And taken them,
> for whom no man had carde,
> And layde them lowe,
> in deepe oblivious grounde,
> But fortune fa-
> vours Fooles—as old men saye
> And lets them lyve,
> and take the wyse away.[3]

Googe credited him with wit, eloquence, and deep learning. Bale called him 'scholasticorum sui temporis non infimum decus', and praised him for his writing, his knowledge of languages, his eloquence, but most of all for his Christian teaching and his seeking divine glory rather than his own. He

[1] Boas devotes his entire chapter on 'Biblical Plays at Oxford' to Grimald, pp. 26–42. The fullest account is given by L. R. Merrill, *The Life and Poems of Nicholas Grimald, Yale Studies in English* (New Haven, 1925). Criticism of Merrill's conclusions especially to be noted are by Charles R. Baskervill, *Modern Philology*, vol. XXIII (1926), pp. 377–8, and A. W. Reed, *Review of English Studies*, vol. II (1926), pp. 483–5.

[2] Merrill, pp. 15–17, quotes Bale's list from his *Index Britanniae Scriptorum* (Oxford, 1902), pp. 302–4.

[3] Merrill, p. 52, with one minor change from Googe, *Eglogs, Epytaphes, and Sonettes* (London, 1563), ff. 4–5. All quotations of Grimald are from Merrill's translation.

translated Cicero and Hesiod and Xenophon and Plato, wrote paraphrases of Virgil and other Latin authors and commentaries on them. He translated portions of the Psalms and wrote on disputed passages of the Scripture. He wrote, indeed, as a Christian humanist. That he wrote both secular and Biblical plays, therefore, is in keeping with his role among men of learning. What other role he played in events of his time is uncertain. The documents printed by his biographer, L. R. Merrill, in 1925 seemed to point to him as a double-dealer, who betrayed the martyred Protestant bishop, Ridley, while professing loyalty to him. Such eminent scholars as A. W. Reed and Charles R. Baskervill refused, however, to accept Merrill's conclusions from the evidence. Certainly Bale gave no hint of suspicion concerning his friend.

Grimald left Cambridge, where he had been a member of Christ's College, after taking his B.A. degree in the year 1539–40. He then went to Oxford, on the advice of Gilbert Smith, Archdeacon of Peterborough, who helped him with money as well as advice. For a time he stayed at Brasenose College, where the principal was a relative of his patron. Since his books did not reach him there for several weeks, he decided to occupy his time in writing a play, and it was performed in 1540. He was urged to publish it, and accordingly *Christus Redivivus* was printed in 1543 at Cologne as a *comoedia tragica, sacra et nova*. Grimald dedicated his drama to his patron, as was fitting, explaining that his tutor had approved what he had done:

I had incorporated in the play no frivolous epigrams, no jokes about love, no silly talk, no mimes, no dialogue of the lowest type of men, no Atellan comedy, no tavern-plays, none of the strange tales of heathen dramas, which contribute nothing of profit toward the formation of character, to sound learning, or to the extension of divine praise.

Instead of such offerings, Grimald had presented what was valuable:

I had taken for the subject of my poem a Creator, instead of creatures; instead of lost and deplorable human beings, a Saviour and Redeemer; instead of human display, the furtherance of divine glory; in short, the very author of song, Jesus Christ:...Therefore my teacher constantly asserted that my labor in this task was praiseworthy, because the doctrine, for faith in which Christ so earnestly builded, and on which all hope of human power ought to be founded, was not only audible, but even visible in my work.[1]

The structure of his play had also been approved by his tutor because the events proceeded in chronological order, and as a tragi-comedy the first act dealt with real sorrow while 'the fifth and last adapts itself to delight and joy', and in 'all the other intermediate acts sad and cheerful incidents are inserted in turn'. The metre was 'almost that of Terence', the tutor said, and decorum was observed as to 'character, theme, time, and place'. The action was arranged for one stage setting, and the author had the *Captivi* of Plautus as authority for his failure to observe the unity of time and for the sad opening and the happy conclusion of the play. With his verses he had been as strictly correct as if he had been writing in a spirit not of Christian liberty but of pagan exactness. Apparently Grimald saw nothing incongruous in justifying his drama about the death of Christ by a precedent from Plautus or making Christian liberty apply to the too free verse.

The effect of classical precedent is evidenced in other matters too. Sometimes the play exceeds its models, for there are not only a prologue and an epilogue but also five arguments, one prefixed to each of the five acts. A chorus of Galilean women, a chorus of disciples, and a group of spirits of the dead take part in the dialogue though they do not mark the division between the acts. The classical metres are carefully marked. The most notable additions to the Biblical characters are Alecto, the fury, and Dromo, Dorus, Sangax, and Brumax, the four comic soldiers who certainly derive from the *miles gloriosus* even though they guard the tomb of Christ. Merrill has shown also that much of the dialogue between the others was taken from Virgil, sometimes by the line-full, and oaths are sworn by Hector and by Apollo.

Not only classical elements are to be considered in Grimald's

---

[1] Merrill, p. 52, with one minor change from Googe, *Eglogs, Epytaphes, and Sonettes* (London, 1563), ff. 4–5. All quotations of Grimald are from Merrill's translation.

play, however, for as Boas has pointed out, the *Christus Xylonicus* of Barthélémy must have been in Grimald's mind as he wrote his play. It was printed in the Brylinger volume, but it had been previously printed at Paris in 1529, and several continental editions had followed. Boas writes:

Alecto would not have tempted Caiaphas in *Christus Redivivus* (IV, v) had she not already tempted Judas in *Christus Xylonicus*. The Roman soldiers who guard the tomb in the Brasenose drama are called Dromo, Dorus, Brumax, and Sangax; Grimald took these names (the last wih an 'x' added) from those of the minor characters in the continental play. He even makes Caiaphas speak of 'Christus xylonicus' (IV, iii) after the Resurrection, though the phrase, as devised by Bartholomaeus, applies to the Saviour triumphant on the Cross itself.[1]

The second of Grimald's Biblical plays that have come down to us, *Archipropheta*,[2] was produced at Christ Church, Oxford, probably in 1546, and with some emendations was printed in 1548, at Cologne, as his *Christus Redivivus* had been. In the dedication to Doctor Richard Cox, Dean of Christ Church, Grimald explained the quality which caused the Greeks to accord the name of poet to a writer, as Sidney and Ben Jonson were to do later.

Such a thing happens when a deed is portrayed in adequate language, and characters are introduced as though living and breathing; when time, place, words, and deeds are vividly depicted; when the whole action is brought before your eyes and ears, so that it seems not so much to be told, to be narrated, as to be done, to be enacted.

He pointed out also the spiritual and ethical lessons to be learned from this portrayal of John the Baptist.

Grimald's theory of the poet as maker or creator acquires significance as we study his play, for, while Jehovah and John's

---

[1] Boas, pp. 28–9.
[2] Merrill, pp. 222–5, finds the source of the play in Josephus. To me the Bible narrative as it is given in Matt. xiv. 3–12, Mark vi. 17–29, and Luke iii. 19–20 seems its basic source. Boas, pp. 34–5, discusses its probable indebtedness to Jacob Schoepper's *Ectrachelistis sive Jonannes Decollatus*. Alfred Harbage, *Annals of the English Drama* (Philadelphia, 1940), classes it as an adaptation of Schoepper's play, but the careful comparison made by Boas could not lead to this conclusion. G. C. Taylor, 'The *Christus Redivivus* of Nicholas Grimald and the Hegge Resurrection Plays', *P.M.L.A.* vol. XLI (1926), pp. 84–9, suggested another possible source.

followers give recitals of preceding events, the greater part of
the dialogue and of the action is realistically presented. Herod
and Herodias speak with passion of their love. When, in the
fourth act, Herodias adorns her daughter Tryphera for conquest, she takes care to place every jewel in its most seductive
place; she arranges her robe and teaches her her steps and her
body movements, shows her how to be effective. Every fish,
fowl, and red meat that is set before the banqueters is listed by
a chorus of Herod's men. The revelry is presented with song
and wine and dance and varied music. As the daughter of
Herodias leads the dance, Herod comments with gusto on her
performance. At her demand that he fulfil his vow to give her
whatever she may desire, he commands the beheading of the
prophet, the severed head is actually brought on the stage and
after being offered to Herodias is placed on the king's table.
The fifth act includes a recital by the Syrian girl to John's disciples of the events that have taken place, describing them with
Senecan relish. John's disciples and a chorus of plebeians take
farewell of the prophet, apparently standing about the bloody
ground on which rests his headless body. Herod passes by,
repenting his reckless vow and his having fulfilled it even though
it had been given. He gives permission for them to bury their
leader, and they seemingly cover the still headless body with a
mound of earth.

Archipropheta has no prologue or epilogue, though the
speech of Jehovah which makes up the first scene functions well
as a prologue. There are five acts with many scenes, determined
by a change of speakers. A chorus marks the end of the first
four acts, but there are directions for other choruses of
plebeians, of Herod's followers, of banqueters, and of Idu-
maeans as well as a group of John's disciples, who function as
a chorus. Minor characters are multiplied,—the Syrian man,
the Syrian slave girl, and the court fool furnishing common
sense, and sometimes comic, foils for the impassioned and tragic
principals. The lyrics introduced in the banqueting scene give
charm and variety to the episode which ends in horror:
beginning with a Sapphic ode saluting the feast, and ranging
through lyrics in varied metres (all carefully identified), they

reach a climax in a great drinking song and a song praising the fruit and nuts being offered as the final course.

The staging of the play would seem to present many problems, but there are no stage directions to indicate how they were solved. Jehovah speaks in the first and fifth acts. The place changes. There are interior and exterior scenes. The number of actors required seems formidable, since all the choruses must apparently be present for the banqueting scene.

The *Christus Redivivus* and the *Archievropheta* are the only two of Grimald's plays which are known to have survived, but Bale has recorded four others which Boas has assumed were also acted. Two are Biblical plays: *Christus Nascens*, a comedy according to Bale, and *Protomartyr*, a tragedy, presumably concerning the stoning of Stephen as the first Christian martyr. The other two must have been written as studies in contrast: *Fama* and *Athanasius sive Infamia*. It is of interest that he wrote also two non-Biblical plays in English: *Troilus*, based on Chaucer's poem, and *De Puerorum in Musicis Institutione*, the Latin title of which was probably contributed by Bale in line with his habitual and confusing practice. Altogether Grimald must have been reckoned a considerable dramatist in academic circles.

John Foxe at Magdalen College wrote Latin plays on religious subjects at the same time that Grimald was writing,[1] according to his son, and there were probably others at Oxford whose plays have disappeared; but today we know only the two plays of Grimald—who came from Cambridge.

Judging from surviving records and surviving plays we can only assume, therefore, that Cambridge was more hospitable to the dramatization of Bible story than was Oxford. At about the time when Grimald went from Cambridge to Oxford and there busied himself with *Christus Redivivus* while waiting for his books to follow, a young man in St John's College, Cambridge, was writing a play which has become famous because of what

---

[1] J. F. Mozley, *John Foxe and His Book* (London, 1940), p. 20. A footnote refers to Lans. MS. 388, 11, 112–46. This manuscript offers a challenge in its bad penmanship and cross-writing, but it is a challenge I have refused, as apparently the biographer did also.

Roger Ascham wrote about it in his *Scholemaster*. The passage is one of the most frequently quoted in all histories of dramatic literature, but it needs to be considered against the background of Ascham's general maxim that 'preceptes in all Authors, and namelie in *Aristotle*, without applying unto them the Imitation of examples, be hard, drie, and cold, and therefore barrayn, unfruitfull, and unpleasant'. It is this comment that must be remembered as we read further:

Whan *M. Watson* in S. Johns College at Cambridge wrote his ex-cellent Tragedie of *Absalon*, *M. Cheke*, he, and I for that part of trew Imitation, had many pleasant talkes togither, in comparing the preceptes of *Aristotle* and *Horace de Arte Poetica* with the examples of *Euripides*, *Sophocles*, and *Seneca*. Few men, in writyng of Tragedies in our dayes, have shot at this marke. Some in *England*, more in *France*, *Germanie*, and *Italie* also have written Tragedies in our tyme: of the which not one I am sure is able to abyde the trew touch of *Aristotles* preceptes and *Euripides* examples, savè onely two that ever I saw, *M. Watsons Absalon* and *Georgius Buckananus Jephthe*.

Ascham wrote further of Watson's meticulous care in composi-tion. He commented on Watson's criticism of a fellow drama-tist for his deviation from approved metrical usage, noting that Watson himself 'would never suffer yet his *Absalon* to go abroad, and that onelie bicause, *in locis paribus*, *Anapestus* is twise or thrise used in stede of *Iambus*: A smal faulte, and such one as perchance would never be marked, no neither in *Italie* nor *France*'.[1] It would seem that Watson as well as Grimald was writing in the spirit of pagan exactness rather than Christian liberty. At any rate, though his praises were sounded by Gabriel Harvey, William Webbe, Thomas Nashe, Francis Meres, and others of his time, his metrical scruples have seemingly lost his play to posterity. An avowed and aggressive Catholic, he was one of Gardiner's chaplains. In difficulties during the reign of Edward VI, he became after Mary's accession master of St John's College, Cambridge, Dean of Durham, and Bishop of Lincoln, only to lose his dignities when Elizabeth came to the throne and to live for the most part in custody. So far as is known, *Absalon* was his only dramatic production.

[1] G. Gregory Smith, *Elizabethan Critical Essays* (London, 1904 and 1937), vol. 1, pp. 21 and 23–4.

A play with Absalon as its tragic hero exists in manuscript in the British Museum. It is without title-page or title, no record of author or production has been found, and Boas, who gave a full summary of its plot, decided that it probably was not Watson's much-discussed play.[1] The manuscript is much corrected, and its provenance is far outside the concern of this study, but with its five acts, each closed by a chorus, its many scenes in a variety of carefully labelled metres, the play by any author offers an instance of Bible story poured into a classical mould.

In 1544 or thereabouts John Christopherson, another outspoken young Catholic, was writing another play on Jephthah, and it cannot be without significance that the writers who used Jephthah and Herod as the archetypes of those who reap the whirlwind of disaster from thoughtlessly made vows were dealing with a subject on which violent controversy was raging. Christopherson, however, was not compelled to justify the theological orthodoxy of his play as was Buchanan before the Inquisition.[2] His play has interested modern students of dramatic history chiefly because, as Boas says, it is 'the only English academic play in Greek to have survived'.[3] A Latin version, credibly reported to have existed, is now lost. The Greek play was dedicated (in Latin) to William Parr, Earl of

---

[1] Boas, pp. 352–65. See also Churchill and Keller, n. on p. 174 above.

[2] *A Briefe Treatise concerning the Burnynge of Bucer and Phagius at Cambrydge, in the Time of Queene Mary, with Their Restitution in the Time of Our Most Gracious Soverayne Lady That Now Is*, transl. by Arthur Golding (London, 1562), gives a gruesome account of the burning and mal-treating of the corpses of the two, their bodies having been exhumed as not worthy of Christian burial. Watson and Christopherson were prominent in the affair. See ch. II, p. 155, above for Buchanan's testimony on vows and its relation to the Bucer–Latomus controversy. Christopherson's play is edited and translated by F. H. Forbes with an introduction by W. O. Sypherd (Newark, Delaware, 1928). The Chorus (in Forbes's translation) comments on vows (p. 135):

> Before he sware,
> The wise man should debate.
> Be sure fulfilment must ensue,
> For God demands the promised price.
> Ere swearing meditate.
> 'Pay sans regret. On foolish vow
> 'Reproach attends; on vow discreet
> 'Abundant honors wait.'

[3] Boas, pp. 43–62. For an account of the founding of Trinity College see Mullinger, vol. II, pp. 80–5.

Essex; the lost Latin version was dedicated to King Henry VIII; and another dedication to Bishop Tunstall exists presumably intended for a copy of either the Greek or the Latin version. The dedications are indicative at least of ambition for access to the great.

Christopherson's fortunes, like those of his friend Watson, changed with the changing fortunes of his religion. He had received his B.A. degree in 1540–1 and his M.A. in 1543. He had been a fellow of Pembroke and St John's and was one of the original fellows of Trinity College when it was formally established by the royal letters of 19 December 1546. Thomas Nashe praised St John's as a university in itself that had 'sent from her fruitefull wombe sufficient Schollers, both to support her own weale as also to supplie all other inferiour foundations defects, and namelie the royall erection of Trinitie Colledge'.[1] While Edward VI was on the throne, Christopherson went into exile. When Mary became Queen he was appointed Master of Trinity, as Watson was made Master of St John's, both being given authority in the revision of their colleges' statutes. An opportune pamphlet on rebellion by Christopherson at the time of Wyatt's rebellion was pleasing to the authorities. His advancement to Dean of Norwich and Bishop of Chichester was obliterated, however, when on the second Sunday after Elizabeth's accession he preached a controversial sermon that led to his arrest. He died soon after.

Whether Christopherson's play was ever performed is not clear. Boas tentatively assigns it to Trinity in 1544, but Trinity as Trinity was not established until 1546, and the records of the college begin then. In the Steward's Book of Trinity for 1566–7 there is listed a payment 'to Mr Legge in regard to his playe' and in that year the Junior Bursar's Accounts record a payment 'To Mr Legge ffor the charges offe Jephthes as appearith by his bille'.[2] Boas lists the play as Christopherson's but notes that it may have been Buchanan's. It is even possible that it may have been still another play by Thomas Legge, praised by Meres for his *Richardus Tertius* and *The Destruction of Jerusalem*.

[1] G. G. Smith, vol. 1, p. 313.
[2] Moore Smith, Mal. Soc. *Coll.* ii, ii, 165–6.

Whoever was the author of the play produced at Trinity in 1566–7, the 1544 Greek play of Christopherson exists, and we have the various dedications which are of interest in proving the motive of his writing. To Essex he noted his progress from philosophy to religion as his chosen study. To Bishop Tunstall he said that he had chanced upon the story of Jephthah and his daughter in the eleventh chapter of the book of Judges, and seeing in it a pattern similar to that familiar to him in the *Iphigenia in Aulis* of Euripides, he recognized that it was an appropriate subject for tragedy. It is a greater story than that told by the Greek poet, he thought, because this in the Bible is true. Christopherson, therefore, proceeded to write a Greek tragedy in Greek, and in order to make it conform more nearly to the classical prototype he added certain characters: the wife of Jephthah, modelled after Clytemnestra in *Iphigenia*, and Hecuba in the play of that title; two messengers to report affairs of war; the manservant who acts as the messenger to give an eye-witness report of the sacrifice; and a chorus to function as in Greek tragedy. The stages of the action are marked by the intervention of the chorus which serves to emphasize the psychological struggles involved as well as the moral problem focused on the Jephthah vow. Jephthah's opening speech furnished a prologue, and in the absence of an epilogue the chorus ends the play with a final admonition that 'A vow made cannot be set aside', and a warning that 'a vow at random made / Oft ends in ruin'. It is an argument that has no appeal to the mother of the doomed girl. There is pathos and horror, tenderness and tragedy in the play, and a creative imagination is evident in the new meaning given to the old story.

In 1562–3 two scriptural dramas were performed at Trinity College. The 'John babtiste' was probably the play of Buchanan produced earlier on the continent. *Christus Triumphans* was quite certainly the play by John Foxe which had been printed at Basel in 1556 as a 'comoedia apocalyptica', thus setting up a new dramatic genre. Appended was a prose panegyric to Christ. So far as I have been able to find out, the play has never been translated into English, though a French translation was made in 1562, but in 1579 Richard Day published *Christ Jesus*

Triumphant as 'translated from the Latin',[1] and it has been assumed by Herford and others that he translated Foxe's play, whereas he translated only the prose panegyric and the closing prayers. He did, however, in dedicating the translation to William, Lord Howard of Effingham, the son of Charles, Earl of Nottingham, give many facts concerning Foxe which formed the texture of later biographies. Foxe had his B.A. degree from Oxford in 1537 and his M.A. in 1543. He became a fellow of Magdalen in 1539 and remained there for seven years, leaving when it became necessary to take priest's orders if he remained. Some time during his university career he had come to a change of religion. After a brief stay at Charlecote as tutor in the Lucy household he knew a distressing poverty from which he was rescued by being appointed tutor to the children of the Earl of Surrey, the unfortunate children who after the execution of their father had been put in the charge of his sister, the Duchess of Richmond. Another Howard nephew, Charles (later to lead the English fleet against the Armada), joined them at Reigate, the house of the Duke of Norfolk. From that time on Foxe owed much to the Howards. Day himself referred to the sixth chapter of Revelation in his account of Foxe:

When Sathans red Horse and bloudy sword marched forth against the Gospel of Christ his kingdome, newly planted in England: Wily Winchester (Bishop Gardiner) fastened his fiery eyes upon this good man. First gladly woulde hee have brought him to the field for the bluddy and fierie battaile: but the speedier favor of that most princely Duke, sent him away safely into Germany, where in the Cittie of Basill hee became a most painefull traveller at his pen in the house of Oporinus that learned, and famous Printer: Among many other woorkes this little Treatise was there penned in Latine: Likewise there he compiled in Latine his first Martyrologe, which he exhibited to the same Princely Lord and Duke.

The *Christus Triumphans* was printed by Oporinus in 1556, as I have said, and the 1559 edition of Foxe's martyrology in Latin was printed by Nicholas Brylinger and John Oporinus, the two printers responsible for the great collections of Bible plays. When Elizabeth became Queen, and it was possible for Foxe

---

[1] Another edition was printed in 1607.

to return to England, it was his former pupil who took him in, the young Duke of Norfolk, marked in history because of his fatal plan to marry Mary of Scotland. Richard Day recounts the facts of Foxe's residence in the Duke's manor house:

From that his house he travailed weekly every Monday to the most worthy Printing-house of John Day: In that my fathers house many dayes and yeares, and infinite summes of mony were spent to accomplish and consummate his English Monumentes, and other many excellent Workes.

Editions of Foxe's Latin play were published in London in 1672 and 1676, the editor 'T.C.' [Thomas Combes], M.A., of Sidney Sussex College, dedicating it to 'Doctis, Scholarchis, & Ludi Literarii Ducibus' in words that demonstrate the persistence of the ideals which from the first had motivated the writers of the academic Biblical drama. 'Why, when you imprint in the minds of boys history, rhetoric, poetic, comic and tragic matters, do you not also train them in Christian writings seasoned with rhetorical and poetic wit?' he asks. And he argues that pagan tragedies and comedies plunge the lips and the mind into the use of pagan oaths and teach what faith teaches must be untaught. Such oaths as *by Pollux, by the temple of Pollux, by Castor, by Hercules*, are not fit for Christian tongues, he said, and it will be evident in the succeeding pages that 'T.C.' was commenting on the oaths too often found in the Biblical plays of Foxe's own century. His play, at any rate, was free of them. And the editor also praises the play for having no 'ware from the lewd workshop of Ovid' and no Plautine slaves teaching tricks to ne'er-do-wells.

Foxe lived with John Bale at Reigate and in Basel and worked with him in the printing-house of Oporinus. He refers to *Asotus* in the preface of his play and uses Barthélémy's word *xylonicus*. Brylinger and Oporinus printed his great work. Thus he was inevitably familiar with the aims of the men who were writing and promoting the attempt to create a new literature based on the Bible. Even in his Oxford days he was writing religious plays. His *Christus Triumphans* is not strictly a Biblical play, being directed primarily to pointing out the perils of the time, chiefly as they were seen in the Catholic church of his day.

Like *Pammachius* it does not come strictly within the class of plays which I have undertaken to review, but Foxe's participation in the whole movement is important. Herford gives an exhaustive account of the play, tracing perhaps overzealously its indebtedness to *Pammachius*, indications of which he finds in some unlikely places.

Foxe professed to dramatize those parts of the Apocalypse that applied to the history of the church, but he incorporated much extraneous matter into the Biblical patchwork of his plot and wandered far from Biblical authority in the number and range of his characters. Constructing his drama on the accepted classical pattern, he began with a prologue asking silence as

> Poeta novus, (spectatores novi) novam
> Rem dum spectandum profert in proscenium.

Then came a 'periocha' which outlines the plot and concludes with a demand for applause. The five acts are divided into scenes. Opening with Eva talking with Maria and mourning her children Psyche (identified by Foxe as *anima humana*) and Soma, the play closes with Africus and Europus reunited to their mother Ecclesia attended by a chorus of five virgins. An epithalamium is sung. Herford thought the drama should rather be divided into three parts 'corresponding to the three times of trial through which the ideal Church had passed': the periods represented by the Jewish law, the Roman persecution, and the tyranny of the papal Antichrist.[1] Such a division would, however, disregard the five-act formula set for those plays written to substitute Biblical material for that of the pagans. The production must have presented difficulties in staging for Messrs Browne and Wilkynson in Cambridge in 1562–3,[2] for Satan falls from above, Christ leads Psyche from Orcus, and diverse scenes crowd the stage. The members of Trinity College who sat through a performance of Foxe's apocalyptic drama would, it seems to a modern reader, be worthy of inclusion in his most famous work.

[1] Herford, pp. 138–48. Boas does not discuss the play but lists it as performed. The 1556 Latin text carefully notes the varied metres of the play. The French translation omits the panegyric and the metrical notes, but it gives the music for the nuptial song. It was made by Jaques Bienvenu and printed in Geneva.
[2] Moore Smith, Mal. Soc. *Coll.* II, ii, 163.

A far better dramatist than Foxe wrote at least one Bible play, but unfortunately the only original academic scriptural play written in English about which there is sufficient evidence to be included here is lost. We know, however, that the *Ezechias* written by Nicholas Udall and produced on 8 August 1564, in the King's College chapel, was among those offered at Cambridge for the entertainment of Elizabeth during her progress that year. Udall died in 1556, but his plays seem to have lived after him. *Ralph Roister Doister* was entered on the Stationers' Register in 1566 and was probably printed soon after that date. Bale said that Udall had written many plays, as seems probable, for he was in charge of the production of plays while he was schoolmaster at Eton, and the Loseley Manuscripts contain a copy of the warrant issued by Queen Mary on 13 December 1554, to the master and yeoman of the Revels which may once more be quoted in part:

Wher as our welbelovid Nicholas udall haith at sondry seasons convenient hertofore shewid and myndeth herafter to shewe his diligence in settinge forthe of dialogwes and Entreludes before us four our Regall disport and recreacion to thentent that he may be in the better redynes at all tymes when it shalbe our pleasure to call. wee will and comaunde you and every of you that at all & every soche tyme and tymes so ofte and when so ever he shall neade & requier it for shewing of any thinge before us ye delyver or cause to be delyvered to the said udall or the bringer herof in his name out of our office of Revelles soche apperell for his Auctors as he shall thinke necessarye....And that ye faile not thus to doe from tyme to tyme as ye tender our pleasure till ye shall receve expresse comaundement from us to the contrary herof.

There are also records of the payments made between 13 December and the following 7 January in connection with 'certen plaies made by Nicholas udall & their incydentes'.[1] It is clear that before and after this date Udall set forth interludes for Mary. Various plays still extant have been attributed to him, only *Ralph Roister Doister* with complete assurance. It is, therefore, tantalizing to have a record of *Ezechias* without the play itself.

Ezechias has a special interest for another reason in connection

---

[1] 'The Loseley Manuscripts', *Documents Relating to the Revels at Court in the Time of King Edward VI and Queen Mary*, ed. Albert Feuillerat (Louvain, 1914); *Materialen zur Kunde des älteren englischen Dramas*, vol. XLIV, pp. 159 and 166.

with its author, for it will be remembered that Udall had translated Erasmus's paraphrase of the gospel of Luke in 1545, and
that in his preface to his translation he had called Henry VIII
'a new Ezechias to confound al idols, to destroy all hillalters
of supersticion, to roote up all counterfait religions, and to
restore...the true religion and worship of god, the syncere
prechyng of gods word, and the booke of the lawe, that is to
say of Christes holy testament to be read of the people in their
vulgare toung'. It must be recalled also that, when in 1547 the
Privy Council ordered the paraphrase of the gospels to be set
up in all the churches, Udall was made responsible for the
editing of the first volume, and he included the paraphrase of
John done by the then Princess Mary. The editor of *Ralph
Roister Doister* has suggested that this collaboration with Mary
may account for the special favour she showed him as Queen.
Of course, she may have just recognized in him the ability to
write entertaining plays. In any case the puzzle remains as to
why Udall as a known adherent of the Reformation was in
Queen Mary's good grace unless he had tempered his religious
enthusiasm by the time she was on the throne.[1] The accounts
of *Ezechias* indicate that it was a Protestant play more fitted
to be played before Elizabeth in 1564.

Ironically the two accounts of the lone academic Biblical play
written in English were written in Latin, one by Abraham
Hartwell, the other by Nicholas Robinson. Boas has given a
summary of the drama as he has attempted to reconstruct it
from these accounts.[2] Based on chapters eighteen and nineteen
of the second book of Kings it began he thinks with Hezekiah's destruction of the 'idolatrous images and the brazen
serpent'. The subsequent rebellion and destruction of the altars
of the God of Israel by the supporters of the heathen worship
were followed by the appearance of a prophet (Isaiah probably)
who warned them of the punishment to come. A messenger

[1] The fullest account of Udall is given by G. Scheurwegh as editor of *Roister
Doister, Materialen*, n.s. XVI (Louvain, 1939). See xxxv–xlviii on *Ezechias* and
Udall's religion.

[2] Boas, pp. 94–7. The Latin account of Hartwell, *Regina Literata* (London,
1565), is reprinted in Nichols, *Progresses of Elizabeth*, 1788 ed. vol. I, and that of
Robinson in the 1805 ed. vol. III. They are found in Scheurwegh, pp. xxv–
xxxviii also.

announced the approach of the invading Assyrians, the Israelites were called upon to surrender, Hezekiah prayed for their deliverance, and according to the Bible story the angel of the Lord smote the Assyrians in the night so that 'an hundred four-score and five thousand' were dead when morning came. Boas thinks this catastrophic conclusion of the Assyrian invasion must have been recited by a messenger and, indeed even though the audience could 'Into a thousand parts divide one man', the stage would have been overcrowded with corpses if the Assyrians were actually on the stage. Apparently there was some admixture of facetiae in the play, but the destruction of Israel's enemies may have constituted a happy ending and helped to justify Robinson in calling it a comedy.

Though these are the only university plays which can with any certainty be identified as Bible plays so far as I have been able to discover, the number is sufficient to indicate first that the continental scriptural drama was known and was being heard in England, and second that English writers too were contributing to the movement for a literature based on the Bible. The very list of these English writers is impressive. Grimald, Watson, Christopherson, Foxe, and Udall were all men of consequence in the sixteenth century. Though there were some who decried plays in general and some who decried Biblical plays in particular, as I shall indicate later, even they were inclined to make exception of university plays, especially such plays as I have been describing. Geoffrey Fenton was not speaking with a lone voice when he said:

Heare I reproove not the Plaies of scollers in actions of comedies & tragedies, common and Christian, wherein is exercise of morral doctrines, & much lesse of the historye of the Bible, exhibited for good instructions and exhortacions to vertue, and by the which they are prepared to a boldnes of speache in all honorable assemblies, enhabling their tongues to readye and well disposed eloquence. Such plaies are far from merit of blame specially, if they hold no commixture with the superstitions of the Gentiles, not othes by the Gods and Goddesses, which often times is peformed in the name of Jupiter, & pertake nothing with the lascivious jestuures and mirth of the *Pagans*.[1]

[1] Geoffrey Fenton, *A Forme of Christian Pollicie* (London, 1574), pp. 146–7.

CHAPTER VI

BIBLICAL PLAYS FOR SPECIAL AUDIENCES: PRODIGAL-SON PLAYS

Two movements need to be taken into account in considering the Biblical drama written in English. The first is the rise of a new English secular drama as part of the general movement to create an English literature. So far as has been discovered this drama found its first enthusiasts in the group usually identified as the Sir Thomas More circle.[1] This circle was fortunate in including printers who gave their work permanency, the most notable of those who were both authors and printers being More's brother-in-law and nephew, John and William Rastell. John Rastell's son-in-law, John Heywood, is reckoned generally as the most important in the development of the drama. The earliest play of the new type now known was *Fulgens and Lucrece*, written before 1500 and published by John Rastell some time between 1512 and 1516. The title-page describes it as a 'godely interlude' and names the author as Henry Medwall, chaplain to John Morton, Cardinal and Archbishop of Canterbury. It will be remembered that More as a young member of Cardinal Morton's household was said to have acted in plays there.

This earliest of the new secular plays was derived from a *débat* by Bonaccorso, *De Vera Nobilitate*,[2] and the fact is significant, for the dialogue was a formative influence in shaping the drama of the period. Not only in the training of schoolboys but in the literature of the period it held a conspicuous place, and the More circle contributed to its popularity. More's most important works were put in dialogue form, and both John

---

[1] The history of the group and a record of their individual activities is given by A. W. Reed, *Early Tudor Drama* (London, 1926).

[2] That Medwall and Sixt Birck (Betuleius) wrote independently plays based on Bonaccorso's treatise, *De Vera Nobilitate*, is demonstrated by A. W. Reed, 'Sixt Birck and Henry Medwall', *R.E.S.* vol. II (1926), pp. 411–15. A fuller account is given by Reed, *Early Tudor Drama*, pp. 96–100, where Medwall's immediate source was stated to be a translation of the *débat* by John Tiptoft, Earl of Worcester, from a French version. It was printed by Caxton in 1481.

Rastell and John Heywood wrote dialogues. It is not to be wondered at, then, that their plays were in fact little more than dramatized dialogues. They called their plays *interludes*, for what reason is not clear. Some critics have thought the term implied a performance put on between the courses of a banquet or during an interval between other activities; others have followed Chambers in thinking it referred to an action or a dialogue between two or more people. Whatever the meaning attached to it, the term distinguished the dramas in the vernacular for a good many years to come, though sometimes an indication of classical genre was added, as it was in John Rastell's play *Calisto and Melebea*, described as 'A new commodye in englysh in maner of an interlude'. The Biblical dramas followed the course of the secular dramas, consisting at first largely of dialogue not organized into acts and scenes and called interludes.

The second movement contributing to the evolving of a Biblical drama in English to which I have referred was the movement which resulted in the translation of the Bible into English and the authorization of the English prayer-books. Throughout Protestant Christendom it was becoming possible to think of religion as not being served exclusively in the Latin language. The Genevan acceptance of *Abraham Sacrifiant* demonstrated most conspicuously the more flexible attitude of the Protestants toward the use of the vernacular in Scriptural plays, but they were coming to be produced in considerable numbers by such writers as Hans Sachs[1] elsewhere than in this Calvinist city.

Of the Biblical dramas written in English in the sixteenth century, a rather surprisingly large number have survived; but the time and place of their composition or of their production can be inferred only from internal evidence in most cases. Other than that afforded by surviving copies and the entries in the Stationers' Register after 1557, there is little external evidence available. I have, nevertheless, ventured to group separately those which seem to be directed to limited groups and those

[1] See, for instance, the account of Sachs in William Creizenach, *Geschichte des Neueren Dramas* (Halle, 1923), vol. III, pp. 338–52.

clearly intended for all who would listen, though any such separation can at best be only tentative.

Stories from the Old Testament and the sermons and particularly the parables of the New Testament were most often chosen for dramatization on the continent, as I have already pointed out, and the story of the prodigal son in the fifteenth chapter of Luke was the most popular of all. It seems to have offered a specially tempting opportunity to the pedagogical mind, and the pattern of the prodigal-son play as it was established by continental schoolmasters influenced directly the writers of such plays in England. Because there was a pattern established, I have chosen to isolate these plays and describe them in this chapter separately.

Ravisius Textor,[1] professor in the College of Navarre in the University of Paris and later rector of the university, included among his dramatic dialogues *Juvenis Pater et Uxor*, which is generally regarded as the forerunner of the prodigal-son play. The earliest version to be printed in England, known only by a single leaf of text in which Pater, Filius, Uxor, and Servus speak,[2] evidently is related to the Textor dialogue and is thought by Greg to have been printed by William Rastell between 1530 and 1534.[3] It is written in English, and it suggests a lively picture of a young man who refused the education his father wanted him to have, chose 'a shrewde queane to his wyfe', and is forced to sell faggots. His wife beats him, the servant anticipates the famous Jeeves in correcting his pronunciation, and his wife sings a song marking him a cuckold. *The Disobedient Child*, it will be seen, seems but to amplify this story.

Of the many continental dramatizations of the parable Herford considered the *Acolastus* of Gnaphaeus, the *Rebelles* of

[1] Jean Tissier de Ravisy is generally known by the Latin form of his name. He is entered as Ravisius in the index to Chambers's *Med. Stage* and as Textor in his *Eliz. Stage*. A full account is given by Creizenach (Halle, 1918), vol. II, pp. 56–62. See also vol. III, 468–9, and Boas, p. 19.

[2] The leaf is reprinted in Mal. Soc. *Coll.* I, i (1907), 27–30.

[3] No. 19 in Greg, *Bibliography of the English Printed Drama to the Restoration* (Oxford, 1939), vol. I. The number of each English play will be given as in that work. Titles of plays will be transcribed as they are there recorded except that I shall normalize *i* and *j*, *u* and *v* according to modern usage. Bibliographical information will be given only when it seems relevant to this particular study.

Macropedius, and the *Studentes* of Stymmelius to have been the most influential. I have already written of Palsgrave's English 'ecphrasis' of *Acolastus* and also of the knowledge of it in England as a performed play, and it will be remembered that both *Acolastus* and *Asotus* were performed in Trinity College, Cambridge. *Rebelles* and *Studentes* are not known to have been translated into English or produced for English audiences, but they seemingly set the precedent for certain English plays in presenting the reluctant scholar. As Herford says, 'From the "prodigal son" to the dissolute student or the truant schoolboy, is not a very difficult step', and it is a step frequently taken in the English plays.[1]

One of the earliest if not the earliest of the prodigal-son plays written originally in English is *An Enterlude called lusty Juventus Lyvely describing the frailtie of youth: of natur, prone to vyce: by grace and good counsayll traynable to vertue* by R. Wever[2] (still unidentified). It is closely akin to the morality, its characters being personified abstractions though actually resembling rather real people who exhibit the qualities they represent. It is linked to the Biblical story directly when Good Counsaill offers Juventus hope for God's mercy:

> The prodigal son, as in Luke we read,
> Which in vicious living his good doth waste,
> As soon as his living he hath remembered,
> To confess his wretchednesse he was not aghast;
> Wherefore his father lovingly him embrac'd;
> And was right joyful, the text saith plain,
> Because his son was returnen again.

The quotation comes near the end of the play, however, and as we turn to the beginning, the prologue is citing a more rigorous pronouncement from Ecclesiasticus:

> An untamed horse will be hard, saith he,
> And a wanton child wilful will be.

---

[1] Herford, pp. 152–5.

[2] No. 41 (*b*). Text from John S. Farmer, *Early English Dramatists* (London, 1905), vol. VIII, pp. 1–42. There are three undated eds., this printed by Copland and one by Veale have the prayer for the king, that by Awdely has the prayer for the queen. I have not considered *Thenterlude of Youth* (no. 20), sometimes called a prodigal-son play, since it is a simple morality unconnected with the Bible story.

Juventus, a wanton 'prone to vice', enters singing his simple ditty, one familiar to us in the slightly altered form in which it appears in the play of *Sir Thomas More*:[1]

> In a herber green, asleep where as I lay,
> The birds sang sweet in the middes of the day;
> I dreamed fast of mirth and play:
>   In youth is pleasure, in youth is pleasure.

To the youth who would like to follow the minstrels and dance, Good Counsaill gives guidance for a more sober life, finding his authority in Saint Paul to the Ephesians and Moses in the book of Deuteronomy. Juventus starts on a programme of continual prayer, aided by Knowledge, who, citing texts lavishly, grounds him in good Protestant doctrine.

At this point 'Sathan the devyll' enters in a discouraged mood, which is dissipated by Hypocrisie who boasts of what he has done by introducing superstition as religion:

> As holy cardinals, holy popes
> .   .   .   .   .   .
> Holy fire, holy palm,
> Holy oil, holy cream,
> And holy ashes also;
> Holy brooches, holy rings,
> Holy kneeling, holy censings,
> And a hundred trim-trams mo.

Disguised as Friendship, he dissuades Juventus from going to a preaching and introduces him to Fellowship and Abhominable Living (called Bess for the occasion). His inexperience in whoredom is cleverly suggested as Bess leads him to swearing and blasphemy and bawdry. From his degradation he is rescued by Good Counsaill and is saved from his consequent despair by the entrance of God's Promises and the tale of the prodigal son. Thus set on the narrow way which leads to eternal life, he offers a lengthy homily to 'All Christian people which be here present'. The play closes with the usual call to pray for those

---

[1] C. F. Tucker Brooke, *The Shakespeare Apocrypha* (Oxford, 1939), in a footnote to *The Booke of Sir Thomas More*, IV. i. 174, noted that the interlude, *The Marriage of Wit and Science*, there introduced is up to l. 243 an adaptation of part of *Lusty Juventus*.

in authority, but it must be noted that here it is the *king* who is mentioned in the prayer, a fact which suggests that the play was written during the reign of Edward VI though it was entered on the Stationers' Register in 1560, and though the undated editions which we have clearly date from the reign of Elizabeth.

A Preaty Interlude called, Nice wanton,[1] probably dating also from the earlier reign, though the first edition now known is of 1560, shows a writer taking greater liberties with the prodigal-son story and writing a more realistic play. Chambers calls it an adaptation of the *Rebelles* of Macropedius,[2] but the marked differences which it shows from that play would indicate only a very tenuous connection. There is a prodigal son but also a prodigal daughter as well as a good boy who admonishes the fatuous mother, here substituted for the father in the Bible story.

The title-page contains a poem, the second stanza of which embodies the proverb which forms the theme of the play and should be remembered particularly because it is again given prominence in *Jacob and Esau*:[3]

> Early sharpe, that wyll be thorne,
> Soone yll, that wyll be naught:
> To be naught, better unborne,
> Better unfed, then naughtely taught.

The Messenger speaks the prologue which embroiders the saying of the 'prudent Prince Solomon', 'He that spareth the rod, the child doth hate',[4] and summarizes the plot to demonstrate its truth:

> By two children brought up wantonly in play.
> Whom the mother doth excuse, when she should chastise;
> They delight in dalliance and mischief alway,
> At last they end their lives in miserable wise.

---

[1] No. 31. Text from Farmer, *Early Eng. Dr.* vol. VIII, pp. 93–115. In the closing speech *things* is made to rhyme with *queens*, indicating that *kings* was the original word used.

[2] *Med. Stage*, vol. II, pp. 223 and 460.   [3] See ch. VII, p. 213.

[4] It is to be noted that this reference to Prov. xiii. 24 is present in almost every prodigal-son play.

The mother persuaded by worldly shame,
That she was the cause of their wretched life,
So pensive, so sorrowful, for their death she became,
That in despair she would sle herself with a knife.
    Then her son Barnabas (by interpretation[1]
The son of comfort), her ill-purpose do[th] stay,
By the scriptures he giveth her godly consolation,
And so concludeth; All these parts will we play.

The classics intrude in the curiously misnamed mother, Xantippe, who beats the good Barnabas when Ismael and Dalilah, her 'tender tidlings', complain. They will not go to school and just want to have fun. Iniquity leads them into bawdry and dice-playing. Xantippe will not heed the warning of her neighbour about the manner in which she is bringing up her children even when the neighbour quotes Solomon on the subject, and the wayward children continue their evil habits.

With no time interval indicated Dalilah comes in 'ragged, her face hid, or disfigured, halting on a staff'. Barnabas comforts her with hope for God's grace if she will confess and repent. Ismael is brought before Daniel the judge, the Quest pronounces him guilty, and Daniel sentences Iniquity with him as his partner in crime. The news is brought to Xantippe of Dalilah dead of the pox and Ismael hanged in chains, but she is prevented from doing away with herself by the pious Barnabas. Both children repented, and Dalilah died thinking she would be saved, he says, and he advises his mother to have faith and to comfort her husband. He then turns to warn parents to chastise their children 'before they be sore infect', and to advise children to apply themselves to learning and to obey their parents.

The play is adorned with a song sung by the children in their gay interval and by a song printed at the end without any indication where it should be sung.

'An enterlude for boyes to handle and to passe tyme at Christinmas' was entered on the Stationers' Register in 1569, and with considerable uncertainty this interlude has been identi-

---

[1] Acts iv. 36.

fied as *A pretie and Mery new Enterlude: called the Disobedient Child*.[1] The title-page establishes the author as 'Thomas Ingeland late Student in Cambridge', a young man apparently bent on exhibiting his classical learning. Only one edition is known, probably that published soon after the entry and, though various critics have found evidence for its having been written earlier,[2] it is written with more skill than the other interludes I have so far discussed.

As I have said, the fragment with the characters Pater, Filius, Uxor, and Servus indicates a dialogue or interlude stemming from a Textor dialogue, and the *Disobedient Child* evidently is an amplification of the Textor dialogue or its earlier English adaptation. This later interlude is also interestingly related to the play *Sir Thomas More*, for the prologue opens with the eight lines which introduce *The Marriage of Wit and Wisdom* played before More and his guests. Since Witt in that play entered with the song 'In youth is pleasure' with which Lusty Juventus made his initial appearance, it seems probable that these earlier interludes were still current when *Sir Thomas More* was written.

The Disobedient Child marks an advance in that its characters have a local habitation, and they are made distinct individuals, so that we feel they ought to have names. However, all of them are given generic names with the single exception of the woman-cook, Blanche. She addresses the man-cook as Longtongue, a soubriquet apparently equivalent to the modern loudmouth. The prologue sets the residence of Rich Man, the father of the prodigal, in London.

The Rich Man and his 'wanton son' enter as the prologue speaker announces their coming. The father is urging his son to go to school, but Son has heard that school is an unpleasant place, that masters beat their charges, one boy having died from such a beating. Demosthenes and Tully together could not persuade him to go to school. Father suggests soldiering,

---

[1] No. 54. Text from Farmer, *Early Eng. Dr.* vol. VIII, pp. 43–92. See Chambers, *Eliz. Stage*, vol. III, pp. 350–1.

[2] The discussion is based on the line (p. 90), 'Look that ye truly serve the king', but as *king* is used here, it may mean simply *ruler*. See Farmer, p. 122, under the play's title.

but Son refuses to subject himself to the 'wounds and strokes' of that life. In fact, the only thing that interests him is having a wife. Father realizes that 'we parents must have a regard / Our children in time for to subdue', that parents must 'thrust them alway to school' if they are to be brought 'to honesty, virtue and nurture'. Son is obstinate, and Father finally agrees to help him if he will just choose his wife wisely.

As Rich Man goes out, two cooks come in discussing Son's wedding, which is to take place on the morrow, he having travelled forty miles in the meantime. The bride, so we hear, comes from Saint Albans and is a shrew. But then we see the lovers. Son's greeting is to 'My darling, my coney, my bird so bright of ble', and their billing and cooing is climaxed by his song of many stanzas with the refrain,

> Wherefore let my father spite and spurn,
> My fantasy will never turn!

Time goes unaccounted for as we hear a priest railing at his absent clerk who has not appeared for the wedding, and Rich Man explaining his refusal to pay his son's debts and discoursing at length on the miseries of marriage, with Ovid as his chief authority. Then the young couple enter rejoicing in the pleasures of their marriage state, some of which are distinctly non-Ovidian, such as going to plays and church together. The young man who would not go to school is able to comment on Aristotle's Ethics and to instance the example of Pythagoras, Socrates, and Crates as married men. His servant announces a visitor and as hosts and visitor go out, he remains to give an account of their riotous and extravagant living.

Again there is no accounting for the necessary lapse of time as we see the inevitable aftermath with the wife demanding that her husband go to work and get some money. She forces him out to sell faggots, she makes him carry water and wash clothes, she strikes him and knocks him down. She bids him stay indoors as she goes off visiting, and he wishes the devil to go with her. And then, as he too leaves the scene, Satan the Devil comes on to claim credit for all the evil in the world. He is a curious intrusion in this realistic action.

The play does not follow the Bible story in its ending, for as the repentant prodigal returns to his home, his father reminds him of what Socrates had to endure from Xantippe and bids him go back to his wife and stay there. Only a little help for his penury will he get. The fatted calf is not even mentioned, but the Perorator comes on to enforce the lesson to both fathers and sons that as the twig is bent, so will the bough incline. After the usual prayer said with all the players kneeling, there comes a song on the *Where is now?* pattern, Solomon, Samson, Absalom, Jonathan, Caesar, Dives, Tully, and Aristotle being listed among those who exemplify the transitoriness of all glory and the inevitable end of all as 'meat of worms' and heaps of dust.

Misogonus survives only as an imperfect manuscript,[1] but it is of particular interest because it develops the prodigal-son story into a five-act comedy with considerable dramatic skill. It is constructed quite consciously on the accepted classical model, its setting Laurentum, its main characters traditional types given classical names. But England breaks through with the minor characters, with the rustic dialect, with references to English story and English customs. It is a strange blend that results.

The prologue opens with an invocation to the Muses and bears the impress of classical lore in references to 'Pernassus' sacred mount', 'Aganippe fount', 'Sir Phoebus', Apollo, and 'Dame Luna'. It recites adequately the argument of the play, the scene Laurentum, and the fortunes of Philogonus:

In lusty youth a wife he took, a dame of flourishing green,
Who soon after conceived and brought him forth at once two twins.
Th'eldest she sent away, whereof her husband did not ween.
Forthwith she died: at th'other son our comedy begins.
Through wanton education he began to be contemptuous,
And sticked not with taunting terms his father to miscall;
And straightway, in lascivious lust, he waxed so licentious
That's father he did often vex, and brought him to great thrall.

[1] Text from Farmer, *Early Eng. Dr.* (1906), vol. x, pp. 135–243. Concerning the author see Chambers, *Eliz. Stage*, vol. IV, pp. 31–2, but G. C. Moore Smith, 'Misogonus', considers the evidence for its being a Cambridge play, its author Anthony Rudd, *Times Literary Supplement*, 10 July 1930, p. 576.

By lucky lot, yet at the length, his eldest son he knew;
And, that he might his comfort be, sent for him in great haste.
Then, after this, the younger son his life doth lead anew,
Whereat together all the joy and banquet at the last.

The play is called a comedy, and it is divided into five acts with many scenes. The fifth act is missing from the manuscript, however. We can recognize the type characters of ancient comedy as they appear in this Roman comedy, for Misogonus is a prodigal son but also a braggart warrior engaged in mock battles. Orgelus is a servant to Misogonus but also the parasite who flatters the braggart. Cacurgus is the fool but also the intriguing servant of Latin comedy. Eugonus is the counterpart of the dutiful son but also the *filius peregrinus*. And Alison is the *obstetrix* so necessary to the discovery and recognition scene when there is a *filius peregrinus*. This scene of discovery and recognition, which Aristotle advised as the best means of effecting the reversal of fortune and the dénouement of the story, centres about her recognition of the six toes on the right foot of the peregrinating son.

There are other characters that might be found in Roman comedy, but certain additions to the persons of the drama would scarcely find themselves at home in Laurentum. There are Liturgus who keeps the repentant prodigal from despair by urging the teachings of Saint Paul, and contrasted with him Sir John, the dissolute priest given to dicing and whoring. There are the rustics with their traditional rustic speech and long-winded disputes, rustics who still cling to the forms of the old religion though their masters have accepted the new. The fool is sometimes addressed as Will Summer, Misogonus as Robin Hood, the old woman servant as Madge Mumblecrust. There is a reference to the rising in the north, and in fact, the play is strewn with references to places, events, sayings, that mark its English origin. Its two songs are sung to tunes familiar to English ears.[1]

---

[1] 'A song to the tune of Heart's Ease' (pp. 163–4) and 'The Song to the tune of Labondolose Hoto' (pp. 193–5) are discussed by Farmer, pp. 377–81. He would translate *Labondolose* as 'doleful dumps', La bon' (bonne) do'lo'se (douloureuse) hoto (hauteur).

In spite of all the extraneous elements, the play is clearly in the tradition of the prodigal-son drama. Eupelas advises both father and son and is a recognizable successor to Eubulus in *Acolastus*. The prodigality of Misogonus is contrasted with the sober qualities of his brother. The father recognizes his responsibility for his erring son in having neglected to have him properly schooled and, as the tradition requires, he quotes Solomon's wisdom in 'He that spareth the rod hates his child'; sings a song to the tune of 'Labondolose' built on this theme and closing with a prayer that the Lord will forgive him and help him. The prodigal goes his wanton way but is at last repentant and echoes the Biblical account as he cries, 'I have sinned in the sight of God and against you, dear father! most grievously'. He is welcomed and forgiven, but the 'joy and banquet' promised in the prologue as a symbol of the fatted calf is lost to us with the missing fifth act from the manuscript. The play is also in the tradition of such dramas in adorning the story with more grossness than that of the Roman comedy which, according to the theory of the early schoolmasters, it was intended to supplant.

That theory was, however, exhibited in practice in *The Glasse of Governement*,[1] published in 1575, the year in which its author, George Gascoigne, had a large part in the writing and producing of the entertainment offered Queen Elizabeth at Kenilworth by Robert, Earl of Leicester. He might, however, have well figured as a prodigal son himself, one who after a hectic youth turned to writing the most pious of pamphlets. In drama he was an experimenter, first with the classics and now with a Biblical play. In translating Ariosto's *I Suppositi* (adapted from plays by Plautus and Terence) he had given England its first prose comedy, and in translating Dolce's adaptation of Euripides' *Phoenissae* as *Jocasta* he had experimented with blank-verse tragedy. Now, in *The Glasse of Governement*, he tried his hand at a tragi-comedy in prose as well as a Biblical play. The title-page explained the dramatic genre in terms differing from those used by Grimald and Bèze: 'A tragicall Comedie so

---

[1] No. 68. Text from *The Complete Works of George Gascoigne*, ed. J. W. Cunliffe (Cambridge, 1910), vol. II, pp. 1–90.

entituled, bycause therein are handled aswell the rewardes for
Vertues, as also the punishment for Vices.' The Biblical foundation of his story was made certain in the prologue:

> A Comedie, I meane for to present,
> No *Terence* phrase: his tyme and myne are twaine:
> The verse that pleasde a *Romaine* rashe intent,
> Might well offend the godly Preachers vayne.
> Deformed shewes were then esteemed muche
> Reformed speeche doth now become us best,
> Mens wordes muste weye and tryed be by touche
> Of Gods owne worde, wherein the truth doth rest.

In the printed text between prologue and play there is a page
of pious admonition stating that 'This worke is compiled upon
these sentences following, set downe by mee C.B.' (who is,
I take it, the printer C. Baker).

The classical pattern of five acts divided into scenes is adhered to in the play. Though these are in prose, the prologue
and the epilogue as well as the choruses which mark the close
of the first four acts are in verse. Many of the traditional characters of Latin comedy are present: fathers and sons, a schoolmaster, a parasite, a harlot and a pandering 'aunt', an intriguing
servant, and messengers. But there are alien elements: a roisterer, an honest servant, a margrave, and a chorus of four grave
burghers, the chorus probably being one of the adjuncts of
tragedy as Gascoigne conceived it.

The prodigal-son plot[1] is complicated by a doubling of the
main characters, for there are two fathers and two prodigals
and two worthy sons and two servants (one bad and one good).
Though the scene is laid in Antwerp, the characters are given
classical symbolic names except for Dick Drumme the roisterer,
Ambidexter the intriguing servant, and Lamia the harlot.

The two fathers arrange for their four boys to be placed under
Gnomaticus to be prepared for entrance to the university at
Douay, and we have a chance to view Elizabethan education
programmes. The young men of one household explain to their
new master that they have so far been taught the rules of gram-

---

[1] Herford was, I think, the first to recognize this as a prodigal-son play,
pp. 150–2, 158–64.

mar, the colloquies of Erasmus, the offices of Cicero, and the making of verses; those of the other house have, in addition to grammar and versifying, read certain comedies of Terence, certain epistles of Cicero, and part of Vergil; they have even made a beginning in the Greek grammar. Gnomaticus esteems these heathen writers 'yet the true christian must direct his steppes by the infallible rule of Gods woord', and he proposes to teach them on that foundation their duty to God, king, country, and parents. They have no sooner heard their first lecture, however, than by the scheming of the parasite they are introduced to Lamia and her aunt Pandarina. The elder sons fall into the trap, and the fathers hear from Ambidexter of their misdemeanours. The younger sons sample each other's poetry. All four, their fathers decide, must go to the university at once.

Unexplained time has passed before we hear news of them. The elder sons are frequenting bordellos and taverns, while the younger ones have advanced, one to be secretary to the Palsgrave, the other to be a preacher about to go to Geneva.

Remembering Gascoigne's theory of tragi-comedy, we are not surprised that there is nothing of repentance and redemption for the sinners in his play. Instead, one prodigal is executed for robbery, the other is publicly whipped and exiled from Geneva in spite of his brother's pleas. Lamia and her aunt are banished by the Margrave after an experience with the 'cucking stool'. The parasite and the evil servant are also whipped and sent into exile. Thus are the wicked punished and the good rewarded according to the demands of the author's literary theory if not in accordance with Biblical story and Christian teaching.

These prodigal-son plays seem directed to the entertainment of schoolboys in the same spirit with which *The London Merchant or The History of George Barnwell* was presented as an annual treat for the London apprentices in the eighteenth century, though their enjoyment of the constant warnings to parents not to spare the rod would seem doubtful. The plays continued to influence works of literature other than those directed to schoolboys, however, Lyly's *Euphues* being perhaps the most notable.[1]

[1] See John Dover Wilson, 'Euphues and the Prodigal Son', *The Library*, 2nd ser. x (1909), pp. 337-61.

Among the other parables only one seems to have been dramatized in England, and its identification is tentative. The facts are these. In 1566, Thomas Colwell was given licence to print 'a ballet intituled an interlude, The Cruell Detter, by Wager'. Certain fragments published by the Malone Society have been accepted as fragments of this interlude.[1] If the identification is correct, the interlude is based on the parable in the eighteenth chapter of Matthew, in which the king forgives a great sum to a man who owes much, but revokes his action when the man in turn refuses to forgive a debtor who owes only a small sum to him. The fragments reveal a scene between Rigor, Flateri, and Symulatyon, with Ophiletis entering bewailing the spendthrift ways which have made him debtor to King Basileus. The king comes, Pronticus brings Ophiletis before him for judgment. There is no forgiveness in the fragments.

Parables are used in sermons incorporated in a few plays, but no others were made into English dramas as far as our present knowledge goes. Dives appears briefly with Judas in *A Moral and Pitiful Comedie, Intituled, All for Money*,[2] but the parable of the rich man and Lazarus is not dramatized. In fact, the prodigal-son plays are all that we have to represent in England the habit of dramatizing the parables which was current on the continent.[3]

---

[1] No. 43. The fragments are printed in Mal. Soc. *Coll.* I, iv and v, pp. 315–23, and II, ii, pp. 142–4. See Chambers, *Eliz. Stage*, vol. III, p. 505. On the identity of the author, 'Wager', see Greg's account of the confusion concerning Lewis and 'William' Wager, Mal. Soc. *Coll.* I, iv and v, pp. 324–7. See also L. M. Oliver, 'William Wager and the *Trial of Treasure*', *Huntington Library Quarterly* (1946), IX, 419–29.

[2] No. 72.

[3] Extensive accounts of the continental prodigal-son plays can be found in H. Holstein, *Das Drama vom verlornen Sohn* (Halle, 1880) and Franz Spengler, *Der verlorene Sohn im Drama des XVI. Jahrhunderts* (Innsbruck, 1888). See also the prefaces to his editions of *Acolastus* (Berlin, 1891) and *Rebelles* and *Aluta* (Berlin, 1897). Plays on other parables will be found in the comprehensive work of Lebègue so often cited in these pages.

CHAPTER VII

BIBLICAL PLAYS FOR SPECIAL AUDIENCES

T HE sixteenth-century prodigal-son plays are so clearly intended for the admonition of schoolboys and the justification of parental discipline that it seems safe to assume that they were not intended to go far beyond the confines of the schoolroom. There are, however, a number of plays which have come down to us that cannot so easily be presumed to have been performed under any particular set of circumstances, though by reason of form or content they seem fitted for private rather than public performance. We know that plays other than those dealing with the prodigal son were performed in English schools, that plays in English were not unknown in the universities, that they were performed in the royal palaces, in great houses, and in some humbler settings. But where particular plays were produced remains a matter of conjecture. Geoffrey Fenton wished that 'in place of Daunses at mariage, the time were supplied with some comical or historical show of the auncient Mariages of *Abraham* and *Sara*, of *Isaac* and *Rebecca*, and of the two *Tobies*, and theyr Wives, matters honest and tending much to edifye the assistauntes',[1] but the only record of a Bible play so used is one Halliwell accepted on Collier's authority of ' Jube the sane' as a play on Job performed at the wedding of Lord Strange and the daughter of the Earl of Cumberland in the time of Edward VI,[2] and I doubt whether even to Fenton a play on Job would have seemed desirable under those circumstances. It is, in fact, only internal evidence which can be summoned to mark these plays as intended for restricted audiences.

One of the plays that seem directed to the limited audience who might share the current interest in mental games and

---

[1] *A Forme of Christian Pollicie*, pp. 140-1.
[2] James O. Halliwell, *A Dictionary of Old English Plays* (London, 1860), p. 133. See Chambers, *Eliz. Stage*, vol. III, p. 330.

rhetorical prowess was *A newe enterlude drawen oute of the holy scripture of godly queene Hester*, said to have been 'newly made and imprinted this present yere', which was 1561.[1] It is conspicuously lacking in dramatic skill: there is no account of the preceding events which motivate the action, and the characters come successively upon the stage with no interval to mark a change of scene or the passing of time. The bare outline of the Bible story is preserved, to be filled out with quite anachronistic material. King Assuerus chooses Aman as his chancellor. He selects Hester from all the beautiful maidens in 'this region universall' to be his bride, and she is able to save her people from the destruction which Aman devises for them. Aman is hanged on the gallows prepared for her uncle Mardocheus, and the Jews are permitted again to live their lives under their own laws. This framework serves to give opportunity for introducing a *débat* and two orations which have no part in the original story, and new characters seemingly intended as a political mirror.

The prologue is used to pose the question for the *débat*. The king then as the play opens asks his council to discuss the question, 'Which is most worthy honoure to attayne'. Each of the three gentlemen argues the respective claims of high birth, riches, power, wisdom, and virtue. Justice is acclaimed as the chief virtue necessary to a prince, and the king adds truth to this qualification. It is a typical Renaissance *débat* with the question formally proposed and discussed, and the decision rendered.

Assuerus chooses Hester for his wife but sets out his specifications for a queen, demanding that she

> Some what to prove by communication
> Her lernynge and her language eloquent
> And by some problem of hye dubitation,
> To knowe her aunswere and consultation,

whereupon she proceeds to deliver a lengthy oration on the duties of a queen, who must needs have kingly qualities since she may be called upon to advise him and to rule in his stead if he and his council are at war. Kingly qualities will prevent

[1] No. 33. Text from *Materialen*, ed. W. W. Greg, vol. v (Louvain, 1904).

treason, will see that the kingdom is kept rich and strong, that wealth is distributed justly. Aman later delivers another speech full of flattery for the wise rule Assuerus has given his people and of gratitude for his own rise to high estate, but leading up to a bitter denunciation of the Jews and a demand that they all be slain. The king commends his 'oration which is so elegante', and accedes to his demand. The formal *débat* and the two 'elegant' orations are ornaments that would certainly have pleased both in form and content an audience which took delight in books like Castiglione's *Courtier* and the orations which graced special occasions.

New characters as well as exhibitions of rhetorical agility were introduced into the Biblical story. Hardydardy is the court fool with liberty to blow on whom he pleases. Pride, Ambition, and Adulation are not personified abstractions but characters who claim to have given their qualities to Aman, leaving none for themselves. Each makes specific charges against Aman that are not remotely suggested in the Bible, so that critics have recognized in the play a political mirror offering to its own time an image confirming the old saw quoted by Hester, 'The higher they climb the deeper they fall'. Hester in the Bible did not prepare to rule in the king's absence in the wars, Aman was not accused of corrupting the law, of making it possible for the clergy to gain preferment not by preaching but by flattery, of weakening the fabric of the state so that if war should come with Scotland or France, 'Thys geare would not go ryght'; nor did Aman complain to the king that nobles and commons alike spread malicious rumours about him. These and similar departures from Biblical history seem to be accounted for if the writer was describing Wolsey in the person of Aman, for the charges against Aman were those directed against Wolsey. Greg argues, then, that the play must have been written before 1530, before Wolsey's fall and death, 'against abuses actually existent at the time of writing'. To me it seems that the writer must have been remarkably prescient and amazingly careless for his own head if he had presented a play recognizably depicting Wolsey's fall while Wolsey was in power. However, what is important to this study is the fact that the play clearly used Bible history to inculcate Tudor political ideas in the dialogue and orations, and to mirror events of the sixteenth century in ancient story.

At one point in the play Hester calls for a hymn, and the marginal stage direction obliges with 'than the chappell do singe'. Elsewhere Pride, Adulation, and Ambition are called upon to sing, so that the participation of a chapel choir is indicated; but there is no evidence upon which to base further conjecture as to the time and place of the performance of the play.[1]

Another *débat* which must have had its appeal to those who took delight in the formal dialogue and the set speech is included in the play which was described on the title-page as *A Pretie new Enterlude both pithie & pleasaunt of the Story of Kyng Daryus, Beinge taken out of the third and fourth Chapter of the thyrd booke of Esdras*.[2] Entered and printed in 1565, it had a second edition in 1577.

The ancient story in the apocryphal books of Esdras is of the king who made a great feast. After his royal guests had departed, he slept, and his three bodyguards decided each to write a sentence to test his wisdom, arguing whether the greatest strength was to be found in wine, in the king, or in a woman. They sealed their sentences and put them under the king's pillow, and when he awoke each argued his case. Darius gave the award to Zorobabell, who had argued that the power of a woman could conquer a king since the concubine Apame had conquered their king. Darius had promised the winner whatever he asked for, and Zorobabell demanded that Jerusalem be rebuilt and the temple restored.

Though the 'Prolocutor' indicated something of the story which was to follow, actually the first part of the interlude is taken up by long preachments (with a large strewing of Bible texts) by Charity and Equity, interrupted by scoffing comments

---

[1] An account of the various attributions of authorship is given by Farmer, *Early Eng. Dr.* (1906), vol. x, pp. 434–7. Mrs C. C. Stopes repeated her arguments for Hunnis as author in *William Hunnis and the Revels of the Chapel Royal, Materialen*, vol. xxix (1910), p. 265. Chambers discusses the mention of a traverse in the play, *Eliz. Stage*, vol. iii, pp. 25–6.

[2] No. 40. Text from Farmer, *Early Eng. Dr.* (1906), vol. xi, pp. 41–92.

from Iniquity, the vice, and his companions, who also obligingly
sing a few stanzas of warning to those who may without heed
fall into the traps they set.

At last Darius appears ordering his servants Agreeable and
Preparatus to prepare a feast as Curiosity joins them. They
immediately see a great crowd approaching. Four kings greet
Darius, are seated, eat, give thanks, and depart in the space of
some fifty-odd lines. Iniquity returns singing, his former companions rejoin him, and Charity, Constancy, and Equity come
to take up the old bickering with him but leave with a hymn of
praise just as Darius returns to the scene.

The basic Bible story comes at the end of the play, and there
it is complicated by two additional characters who set forth the
terms of the award and the question to be argued. The three
contestants make formal speeches. Zorobabell is judged the
victor and asks for rewards only slightly less overwhelming than
those he claimed in the First Book of Esdras, making another
formal speech. Constancy comes, 'saying as it were a Sublo-
cutio' to point a moral. Charity and Equity join her to pray for
queen and council and to sing a sacred song. The chapter in
Esdras must have seemed a golden opportunity to those who
took their pleasure in wit combats and the rhetorical arts.

After these interludes oriented toward literary 'kinds', the
débat and the oration, it is a welcome change to come upon
a play that is fundamentally dramatic and written with skill and
charm. Entered on the Stationers' Register in 1557 but not
printed so far as is known until 1568 was *A newe mery and wittie
Comedie or Enterlude, newely imprinted, treating upon the Historie of
Jacob and Esau, taken out of the .xxvii. Chap. of the first booke of
Moses entituled Genesis.*[1] The title-page gives the further information that the characters 'are to be consydered to be Hebrews
and so should be apparailed with attire', an unusual direction.
It should be noted too that the play is called both an interlude
and a comedy. As a matter of fact, it represents the fusing of
three traditions: (1) the Bible play to be written without im-
morality and to serve as a proper vehicle for sound doctrine;
(2) Latin comedy, a model for the techniques of structure and

. [1] No. 51. Text from *ibid.* vol. x, pp. 1–90.

staging; (3) the prodigal-son play, a pattern of the good and the naughty sons with the subordinate theme of parental responsibility.

The Bible story is preserved intact, embodying, however, parts of Chapters xxv and xxviii as well as Chapter xxvii of Genesis. The promised mirth and wit are added as is the good instruction on theology and education.

The prologue and epilogue, the five acts subdivided into scenes, the classification as a comedy, all mark the classical influence. The tents are placed about an open space, all the action taking place out of doors. Rebecca summons Jacob to 'come forth' so that she can speak to him secretly. Characters are directed to enter or come out of the tents. What happens indoors, such as Esau's eating of the pottage, is told by a recital. Rebecca conceals herself to overhear the conversation between Isaac and Esau. The main characters are described before they come on the scene, and even the minor characters are identified by name and the classical sort of here-he-comes pointing.

The prologue serves also the purpose of the classical argument, and the five acts are built up as in Latin comedy. The first act introduces the characters and explains the existing situation: in spite of Rebecca's pleas for Jacob, Isaac is determined that Esau shall have his rightful inheritance as the elder son. In the second act Esau, faint from hunger after his unsuccessful hunting expedition, sells his birthright. In the third act Rebecca overhears Isaac promising Esau his blessing when he has fetched and cooked a mess of venison. In 'Actus Quarti' Rebecca plots and executes the device by which Jacob, his neck and arms covered with the skin of the kids which he serves to the blind Isaac for venison, wins his father's blessing. The fifth act finds Esau desiring vengeance but putting on the pretence of being reconciled as Jacob is sent away to find safety and to secure a wife under Laban's protection. It is a well-constructed plot.

It is in the portrayal of the characters of the play, however, that the dramatist shows most skill and gives interest and charm to the play. Isaac and Rebecca, Jacob and Esau play their

Biblical roles, and Isaac and Jacob are respectfully portrayed with only variations upon the historic account. The minor characters added to the story come alive on the stage as real people: Ragau, a typical ingenious servant; Debora, 'the nurse of Isaacs Tente'; Mido, a little boy who leads the blind Isaac about; and a very intriguing little wench, Abra, who serves Rebecca. There are also two gossiping neighbours. Ragau serves his master but mocks him in his absence and outwits him, managing to get a portion of the pottage which Esau has denied him:

> My mother taught me that lesson a good while agone.
> When I came to Jacob, his friendship to require,
> I drew near and near till I came to the fire:
> There hard beside me stood the pottage-pot,
> Even as God would have it, neither cold not hot;
> Good simple Jacob could not turn his back so thick,
> But I at the ladle got a gulp or a lick;
> So that, ere I went, I made a very good meal,
> And din'd better cheap than Esau a good deal. [II. iii.]

The little boy Mido is a talented mimic, whether showing just how the blind man gropes his way along or imitating Esau licking the pot from which he has wolfed all the pottage that purchased his birthright. The little Abra is an obedient child, gathering thyme and parsley and borage and other good English herbs for the Hebrew tribesman's 'broth and farcing' and sweeping 'with a broom' while she sings her song of

> It hath been a proverb, before I was born,
> Youth doth it prick, that will be a thorn. [IV. iv.]

It will be remembered that Abra's song is developed about the same proverb which was used in the poem printed on the title-page of *Nice Wanton* and furnished the theme of that play. There are other indications of the influence of the prodigal-son tradition in this play, however. The two sons of Isaac and Rebecca represent the typical prodigal and the good boy. Esau is wild and rude, cares only for hunting, and takes no heed to the comfort of others. He speaks to his 'three greyhounds, or one, as may be gotten' more kindly than to his servant or his brother. He gets up before dawn and wakes his parents and their neighbours with his horn. Faint from hunger, he sells his birthright for a mess of red pottage and then, 'wiping his mouth' after gorging his meal, he refuses to listen to Ragau who has shared his hardships. The two neighbours discuss the boys and take the place of Eulalia, the neighbour in *Nice Wanton* who advises the mother of the two prodigals in that play. One of the neighbours here is full of complaints and wonders that 'old father Isaac, / Being so godly a man, why he is so slack / To bring his son Esau to a better stay'. The other protests that Isaac must have been a good father, and that he and his wife have set a good example

> As by their younger son Jacob it doth appear.
> He liveth no loose life: he doth God love and fear.
> He keepeth here in the tents, like a quiet man:
> He giveth not himself to wildness any when.
> But Esau evermore from his young childhood
> Hath been like to prove ill, and never to be good.

Then he too quotes the key proverb:

> Young it pricketh (folks do say), that will be a thorn,
> Esau hath been naught, ever since he was born.

With this consolation to the good fathers of bad sons they lament in the fashion of all prodigal-son plays the future of youths that will follow none but their own bridle [I. ii.].

The play demonstrates the workings of predestination and the necessity for faith and obedience to God's will. Rebecca and Isaac have a realistic dispute over their sons, and Rebecca exerts all of woman's wiles in her partisanship for Jacob, but Jacob himself will not connive at the deception his mother proposes until he is convinced that she advises him as God has decreed:

> It shall become me to show mine obedience,
> And to thy promise, O Lord, to give due credence.[1]

Esau's acceptance of his supplanting is not strictly Biblical, for he seems to intend to forgive and forget while he qualifies his 'gentle part' in an aside to his servant:

> It must now be thus; but when I shall Jacob find,
> I shall then do as God shall put into my mind.

[1] In I. iii, IV, i, and IV. vii.

Isaac calls upon all his household to 'with one voice sing unto the Lord', and after the hymn,[1] the Poet enters to justify the ways of God to men in predestining some to be saved and others damned, urging all to be worthy to be among the elect. His speech is a setting-forth of the harsh Calvinistic doctrine.

Isaac and Rebecca and Jacob and Esau in turn pray for the clergy, the queen, her councillors, and the nobility. Since the play was entered in 1557, the only queen for whom this prayer could have been invoked was Queen Mary, and the question therefore arises whether it could have been played or printed during her reign. Changes may have been made in it before its 1568 printing, but the choice of the story for dramatization would seem to indicate a Protestant author. Bang thought the author was Nicholas Udall, Wallace insisted that it was his, and Chambers accepts his authorship as 'plausible'. Other suggestions have been offered that are less plausible, it seems to me, and we can only wish that Udall's play on *Ezechias* had survived its Cambridge performance so that we might observe in it Udall's way of handling scriptural story.[2]

In 1566–7, almost ten years after the entry for *Jacob and Esau*, a play was entered on the Register which evidenced much less skill in the writing. The title-page, however, proclaims the author, Lewis Wager, to be a 'learned clarke' and anticipates the modern blurb in announcing *A new Enterlude, never before this tyme imprinted, entreating of the Life and Repentaunce of Marie Magdalene: not only godlie, learned and fruitefull, but also well furnished with pleasaunt myrth and pastime, very delectable for those which shall heare or reade the same.*[3] Little is known of the 'learned clarke' except that he was made rector of St James, Garlick-hithe, in 1560. In 1566 also, it will be remembered, there was entered 'a ballet intituled an interlude the Cruell Detter by Wager', but since a W. Wager was writing interludes at this time, it can with no certainty be ascribed to either Wager. That Lewis Wager was a university man is suggested by his

---

[1] The three songs in the play are found in II. iv, IV. iv, and v. x.
[2] Chambers, *Eliz. Stage*, vol. IV, p. 22. See above, pp. 189–90.
[3] No. 47. Text from Frederick I. Carpenter, ed. (Chicago, 1902).

being called a learned clerk and by his clerical appointment.[1] The frequent interpolation of Latin quotations from the classics reinforces this suggestion as does the defence of the acting of plays in the prologue:

> I marvell why they should detract our facultie:
> We have ridden and gone many sundry waies;
> Yea, we have used this feate at the universitie;
> Yet neither wise nor learned would it dispraise:
> But it hath ben perceived ever before our dayes
> That foles love nothing worse than foles to be called!
> A horse will kick if you touch where he is galled!
>
> Doth not our facultie learnedly extoll vertue?
> Doth it not teache God to be praised above all things?
> What facultie doth vice more earnestly subdue?
> Doth it not teache true obedience to the kynge?
> What godly sentences to the mynde doth it brynge?
> I saie, there was never thyng invented
> More worthe for man's solace to be frequented.

That the play was, nevertheless, offered on occasion to some sort of paying audience is indicated:

> Truely, I say, whether you geve halfpence or pence,
> Your gayne shalbe double, before you depart hence.

Pleading the worth of wisdom to be gained from this story 'Written in the .vii. of Luke with wordes playne' and rehearsed by 'Doctours of high learnyng' as well as by Mark and Luke, the prologue announces the 'godly mirth' which is to follow.

Like other editors of sixteenth-century Scriptural plays, Frederick Ives Carpenter was bothered about the genre of this play and finally described it as 'essentially a biblical play in a morality setting, or a biblical morality-play' without recognizing the existence of the new divine literature of which the Biblical drama was a part. Its close alliance with the morality is evident in its labelling of Iniquitie as the vice and in the predominance of personified abstractions as 'players'. The leading characters, however, come from Bible story: Marie,

[1] Chambers, *Eliz. Stage*, vol. III, pp. 503–4. Carpenter discusses the sources for the play, pp. xxvii–xxxiii. On the difficulties in identifying the Wagers see above, n. 1, p. 206.

Simon the Pharisee, and Christ. Furthermore, the plot is not an allegory but follows the historical narrative.

There is a deal of theological exegesis, but *Marie Magdalene* is a lively play in spite of it, and the mirth is not always as godly as the prologue would have us expect. Perhaps the author considered the parody of phrases from Catholic services in Infidelitie's opening speech godly mirth, but the amount of quite secular hugging and kissing prescribed in the stage directions is striking and unusual.

The play begins with Infidelitie shouting his mocking scraps of Latin, announcing that 'In Jurie, Moysaicall Justice is my name', and boasting of his plans to thwart the purpose of Christ, who has lately come into the country. Mary enters 'triflyng with her garments' and complaining about her bungling tailor. Infidelitie sympathizes with her and flatters her 'so tender and yong', kisses her, and promises to introduce her to friends who will give her the good time that is her due. The whole crew of tempting sins under the assumed names of virtues surround her with advice as to how to lift up her head, roll her eyes, curl her hair with a hot needle, dye her hair yellow, paint her face, dress elegantly with a showing of her breasts, and establish a small waist. They also advise her to boast of her wealth and her family, choose lovers young and gay, and add to her own wealth. She acknowledges her skill on the virginals, the regals, and the recorder, and Infidelitie leads them in a song of 'Hey dery, dery' which manages to compare her with Lais and Thais and Helen. The tempters take their departure with kisses, and Mary and Infidelitie after more fondling start for Jerusalem.

Simon and Malicious Judgement enter, discussing the Christ whom Simon plots to invite to dinner and to examine curiously. Infidelitie comes to explain the mischief he is creating, and when he is alone, Mary enters pursuing him. Now the Law of God, Knowlege of Sin, and finally Christ enter to perform the work of regeneration. After Christ has cast out Infidelitie and the seven devils that have possessed her, 'Mary falleth flat downe' and the devils 'Cry all thus without the doore, and roare teribly' [l. 1285]. (The stage directions do not adequately explain how all this is effected.) As Mary prays for help, Faith and Repentance come to her aid, instructing her in the way of salvation.

Again Simon and Malicious Judgement enter as Christ is left alone on the stage. They greet Christ, and Simon extends his dinner invitation. Infidelitie joins them as they walk in the garden and manages to talk with Malicious Judgement in apparent secrecy. Without stage directions they are at Simon's table, but Christ will not sit down until he has said grace. Christ speaks good doctrine, and Mary comes, repenting at great length. She creeps under the table and she is directed to abide there 'a certayne space behynd, and doe as it is specified in the Gospell'. The others scoff while Mary anoints Christ's feet with precious ointment and washes them with her tears, but Christ rebukes the scoffers, telling them that 'many sinnes are forgiven hir, bicause she loved muche'. Mary can rejoice that no sinner need despair, but Simon and Malicious Judgement plan the complaints against Christ which will bring him to justice under the law he defies even as they hurry off to the evening service and their sacrificial offering. Mary tells her story to Justification, Justification expounds its significance, and Love enters to complete the exegesis:

> By the word came faith; Faith brought penitence;
> But bothe the gyft of God's magnificence.
> Thus by Faith onely Marie was justified,
> Like as before it is playnly verified:
> From thens came love, as a testification
> Of God's mercy and her justification.

The usual prayer for the sovereign is not added, the audience being dismissed with Mary's hope for a happy reunion at the last day.

In connection with the next play to be considered the question again arises as to what was the relation between a 'ballet' and a play. It will be remembered that in 1566 Thomas Colwell was given a licence to print 'a ballet intituled an interlude, the Cruell Detter, by Wager', and the play of *The Cruel Debtor* was apparently published. In 1563 Colwell was paying for his licence to print certain 'balletts', one of which was 'the godly & constante Susanna', and in 1568–9 he was paying for his licence to print the 'playe of Susanna'. Whether the permits were for the same work, therefore, remains a conjecture. Apparently he did not himself print the play, for Hugh Jackson, who had married Colwell's widow and succeeded him in his printing-house, was seemingly telling the truth when in 1578 the title-page of the play announced *The Commody of the moste vertuous and Godlye Sussanna, never before this tyme Printed*.[1] The title-page said it was compiled by Thomas Garter, who seems to have no recorded history, though a Bernard Garter was writing about this time. Whoever or whatever he was, Thomas Garter writes like an academic fledgling, youthfully awkward about indecencies and proud of his undigested learning.

Susanna is printed as a comedy rather than an interlude, probably because the term *interlude* was less popular by 1578. Like *Marie Magdalene* it is not divided into acts and scenes, and with its numerous personified characters introduced into the Bible story it resembles that play, though it is less skilfully written. The dramatis personae in *Susanna* are sometimes confusingly identified, presumably because, as was a common practice, the writer gave several parts to one actor. This is his arrangement:

1. The Prologue and the Gaylour for one.
2. Joachim and Judex for another,
3. Sathan and Voluptas another,
4. Sensualitas alone.
5. Susanna alone.
6. Helchia, True Report, Ancilla, another,
7. Ill Reporte the Vyce, and Cryer, another.
8. Helchias wyfe, Danyell, Servus, Serva, for another.

The would-be dramatist does all the usual things in his prologue: he starts with a Latin quotation, refers familiarly to 'Bullus Tully', notes that the story is true as well as good, rehearses the argument, urges it be used as a mirror, gives God praise, and finally asks for silence as he points to the entering

---

[1] No. 76.5. Since a copy of the play was not discovered until 1936, the description was added on p. xxii of the Greg *Bibliography*. Text from Mal. Soc. *Reprints*, vol. LXXVI (Oxford, 1936 [1937]), eds. B. Ifor Evans and W. W. Greg.

Sathan. He is self-conscious about the bits of obscenity in his play:

And though perchaunce some wanton worde, doe passe which may
    not seeme
Or gestures light not meete for this, your wisedomes may it deeme
Accoumpt that nought delights the hart of men on earth,
So much as matters grave and sad, if they be mixt with myrth,
Of both which here I trust you shall, as in a myrrour see,
And that in such a decent sort as hurtfull shall not be.

The plot, as is apparent from the list of characters, is more complicated than in the Bible account. Devill, as he is called after the prologue, summons Ill Reporte to effect the destruction of Susanna, the fair wife of Joachim, for she has refused the lure of pride, gluttony, envy, sloth, and covetousness. Ill Reporte suggests that they try lust, and when she yields, he will be able to blow the trumpet of slander and please his Satanic 'Dad'. Voluptas joins him and calls in a downcast Sensualitas, whose secret sorrow Ill Reporte diagnoses at once, quoting *Amor vincit omnia*. He speaks words that show the author fresh from reading a book of moral philosophy—any book of the time:

Love hath a pleasure in it selfe, yet love is full of feare,
Love helpes and it doth harme a man, love is not this good geare,
Love from the Sences of a man, can steale away the might,
Love can make mad the mynde of man, and love can blynde the
    sighte,
But is not he a jolly man that love can so subdue,
As he can lose it when he list, and it agayne renue.

After Ill Reporte receives an advance payment from the rascals, the Bible characters begin to appear.

First comes Joachim, a man of God, always praying. Then the judges appear (identified in the margin as Voluptas and Sensualitas), then Susanna with whom they become enamoured. Susanna goes to the orchard 'her to wash, which is a wholesome thing'. Voluptas and Sensualitas come from their hiding places to ravish her but are repelled. The servants who answer her cries for help are met by the 'judges', who carry her off, accusing her of being a 'secrete whore'. The servant prays for

her, and True Report somehow is there to speak in her defence
and prophesy the doom that will befall the judges. Susanna's
parents appear to mourn her fate. Court is convened with
'Gaylour' (*née* Prologue) and Ill Reporte to shout the 'O yes'
which summons attendance. Susanna stands forth as the
accused, and the judges, duly sworn on the book, recite their
evidence. Susanna prays, Judex condemns her to death, she is
led forth to her execution, 'and God rayseth the spirite of
Danyell'. Judex convenes the court again, and Danyell refutes
the testimony of the liars by questioning them separately and
showing that their stories are in conflict. Judex sentences them
to be stoned to death. They are allowed to pray for mercy
rather than justice but are stoned after being bound to a stake.
Ill Reporte lets a stone fall on Bayly's (or Gaylour's) foot, and
they fight for a bit.

Ill Reporte, in the gown of one of the dead judges, meets
Servus and True Report, and the cousins engage in an academic
battle over what the altering of a letter in a word can do, over
'*aphaeresis*' and '*appocope*', and over similar matters. True
Report has evidently been at Oxford, and his cousin Ill has
been there a year himself 'fast tyed by the legge'. Gaylour
comes on to lead Ill off to be hanged, the rope already about his
neck. The Devill bemoans the outcome, thinks that God still
does him wrong and takes off for his 'infernal lake'. All the
righteous characters unite in thanking God for his mercy. The
prologue apologizes for the lack of music in the play, but hopes
the author will be encouraged to write another. As in *Marie
Magdalene*, the usual prayer for the queen is noticeably absent,
but the prologue expresses a final desire to give God the praise
for whatever is good in this play and a hope that all will be
granted eternal life.

It is a crudely written drama, and the confused identity of
the speakers, the careless shifting of speakers, with the stoning
to death of the judges on the stage would suggest that it may
never have been played. Yet the author has made some attempts
at giving his characters reality. The judges invoke the help of
Venus and Cupid and the heathen gods in their wicked designs.
There is a semblance of life in the dialogue when Joachim is

late for dinner, when Susanna's maids talk about life at court in contrast with what in their country homes they had imagined it to be, and when the Report cousins engage in their pseudo-linguistic and rhetorical quibbling. But Thomas Garter does not seem to have met with the hoped-for demand that he continue his career.[1]

[1] Chambers, *Eliz. Stage*, vol. IV, pp. 398–404, lists among the lost plays three Bible plays in addition to the play on Job ascribed to Greene and *Susanna*, since recovered: '*Joseph's Afflictions*, An interlude in the lists of Archer and Kirkman'; '*Nineveh's Repentance*. An interlude in Rogers and Ley's and Archer's lists'; and '*The Two Sins of King David*. S.R. 1561–2. "An new enterlude of the ii synnes of Kynge Davyd".'

CHAPTER VIII

BIBLICAL PLAYS FOR THE COMMONS

T HE common people as well as the more privileged classes were to have a new scriptural drama in the sixteenth century, but the new drama was not the first based on Bible stories which they had known. In England and on the continent, there had been a traditional Christian drama originating in the liturgy of the church itself. It had been a drama which in spite of 'the reverent intention of the clerics who composed and performed the plays',[1] in the words of Karl Young, yet included plays which appear to have been composed 'in a spirit of literary and dramatic independence, and to have been attached to the liturgy as appendages, rather than as intimate accompaniments of central acts of worship'.[2] The Council of Trent had finally to decide to do away with the modifications and additions to the older rites of the church, and thereafter the liturgical plays were not to be found in the service books of the church, though there were a few lingering local survivals.[3]

In England the religious drama moved out of the church service, out of the church, out of the churchyard, and away from ecclesiastical control. It became a vernacular drama. Nevertheless, it continued to declare its essential purpose of strengthening the faith of the devout and educating others in Christian story and Christian doctrine. But the secular control of the plays introduced another element well shown in the old record of Chester:

of old tyme not only for the Augmentacion & increase of the holy and catholyk ffaith of our savyor cryst Jehsu and to exhort the myndes of the comen peple to gud devocion and holsom doctryne therof but Also for the comen welth and prosperitie of this Citie A play and declaration of many and dyvers stories of the bible begynnyng

---

[1] *The Drama of the Medieval Church* (Oxford, 1933), vol. II, p. 410.
[2] *Ibid.* p. 399.   [3] *Ibid.* p. 421 and n. 2.

with the creation and fall of lucifer & endyng with the gen'rall Judgement of the world to be declared & playde now in this whison weke....[1]

This desire to make the miracles serve also for the common wealth and prosperity of the city required that they be adapted to the taste and talents of the fellow-townsmen who served as actors and audience. Comedy and other extraneous elements were added, so that they became entertainment and furnished grounds for criticism as being irreverent.

Opposition had, however, been of long standing on other grounds. Perhaps the nature of the opposition can best be illustrated by what Young calls 'the most careful and energetic challenge to the religious drama uttered during the Middle Ages',[2] the Wycliffite *Tretise of Miraclis Pleyinge*, which pro-phetically introduced most of the arguments elaborated and endlessly repeated in later centuries. Those who favour such representations, the treatise says, contend that they are part of man's worship of God; that they often convert men to good living; that by the sight of the sufferings of Christ and the saints men are moved to tears; that some men can be reached only by 'gamen and pley'; that human nature requires recreation; and that, since the miracles of Christ and the saints may be delineated in painting, they may appropriately be imitated also in action.

To such defenders of the playing of miracle plays the author answers that the actors are concerned rather to please men than God; that the miracles by making play out of earnest take the name of God in vain; that those who are not converted by the sacraments of the church will not be converted by plays; that the recreation of Christians should be found in doing works of mercy and in Christian fellowship; that plays delight rather than teach and are not like religious pictures and religious books, which are concerned only with telling the plain truth plainly.

The miracles had not, of course, been the only type of play known in the earlier periods in England. The morality had held

[1] W. W. Greg, 'The Lists and Banns of the Plays', *Chester Play Studies*, Malone Society (1935), p. 132.
[2] Young, p. 415. Chambers, *Med. Stage*, vol. II, pp. 102–3.

a second place, but an important one. With its allegorical plot and personified abstractions or generalized characters such as Everyman it continued to exercise an influence on all dramatic writing. It was performed before both private and public audiences.

In spite of opposition the playing of miracles and moralities continued even in Shakespeare's day, but a new drama which arose under the impetus of the revived knowledge of the ancient classical drama gradually displaced the older dramatic types. This new humanistic drama aroused a reaction against its inherent secularism and paganism, and I have tried to show the course of the movement to create a new scriptural drama to oppose to it as that movement spread from the continent to English schools and universities and select circles. The masses naturally desired to enjoy what the more privileged were enjoying, and their enthusiasm for all dramatic entertainment reached such excess that in 1542 Bishop Bonner felt called upon to send his clergy restrictive injunctions:

That no parsons, vicars, ne curates, permit or suffer any manner of common plays, games, or interludes, to be played, set forth, or declared within their churches, or chapels, where the blessed sacrament of the altar is, or any other sacrament ministered, or divine service said or sung; because they be places constitute and ordained to well disposed people for godly prayer, or wholesome consolation.[1]

It must be noted that interludes are specifically mentioned, for as I have recorded in an earlier chapter, the new plays were regularly identified as interludes, the term being loosely used without regard to dramatic genre.

The sixteenth century was a time of strife between religions; Christians fought each other even as Christians were fighting Turks. Quite inevitably the interpretation of Biblical stories was made by dramatists for whom truth took on different hues in the minds it passed through. The morality often merged into theological polemic as the conflict between the Roman church

---

[1] Gilbert Burnet, *The History of the Reformation* (Oxford, 1865), vol. IV, p. 515. See also Greg, 'Dramatic Records of the City of London', Mal. Soc. *Coll.* II, iii (1931), 287–9, for licences granted 1527–9 for churches to raise money by stage plays.

and the gradually developing Protestant sects became violent and passionate. The strictly polemical plays are out of the range of this study, but the Biblical plays are apt to be coloured by the theological preoccupations of their authors.

The converting of Biblical plays to polemic is most fully demonstrated in the plays of John Bale, who was not without reason known as 'bilious Bale'.[1] Five out of the twenty-two that he said he wrote 'in idiomate materna'[2] constitute the largest group of survivals from the first half of the sixteenth century. *King Johan* is a history play oriented toward the politics of church and state; the other four are religious plays, three of them drawn from the Bible. Chambers wrote in his *Mediaeval Stage* of these three: 'In *God's Promises, John Baptist,* and *The Temptation,* Bale was simply adapting and Protestantizing the miracle-play.'[3] They may be parts of a cycle of such plays, he thought. Bale's latest biographer, Honor McCusker, writes of them:

They are not great plays, often not even interesting plays so far as their content is concerned. Their chief value lies in the fact that they are a late survival of a form which even in 1538 was very nearly outmoded, and (which is still more important) are the earliest instances of a completely new use of that form.[4]

My contention is that they are not survivors of the miracle play at all but pioneers of the new Bible play and present not 'a completely new use of that form' but an attempt to use a new form, the interlude, then growing into acceptance in the secular drama. Most of Bale's lost plays were, as their titles indicate, either theological or Biblical, and his dramatic efforts seem to me to indicate that he was trying to do what others on the continent were doing: offer religious rather than secular fare in the drama. My reasons for saying so can only be given in a review of his life and work, however.

Bale, it will be remembered, was reared by the Carmelite

[1] W. T. Davies, 'A Bibliography of John Bale', Oxford Bibliographical Society, *Proceedings and Papers*, v, iv (1939), 203–79. Jesse W. Harris, *John Bale, Illinois Studies in Language and Literature,* XXV (Urbana, 1940). Honor McCusker, *John Bale* (Bryn Mawr, Pennsylvania, 1942).

[2] The list is also given by Chambers, *Med. Stage*, vol. II, p. 447.

[3] *Ibid.* pp. 224 and 131.   [4] McCusker, p. 78.

monks. After studying at Cambridge and on the continent, he took a degree in divinity in 1529 at Cambridge and became himself a monk, afterward being in turn prior of the Carmelites at Maldon, Ipswich, and Doncaster. Though apparently zealous in his early faith, he was certainly in difficulties with the church authorities while he was still a Catholic cleric, and he finally became a passionate Protestant. We do not know when he began to write plays, but when he was called before Archbishop Lee in 1534, he was protected by Cromwell 'ob editas comedias'. He seems to have held the curacy of Thornton in Suffolk well into 1536, but in that year he was called to answer a charge of heresy to Bishop Stokesley in London and, in his defence, he said he had advised his hearers to accept circumspectly Christ's descent into hell, 'And not to beleve yt as yei se yt sett forth in peynted clothes, or in glasse wyndowes, or lyke as my self had befor time sett yt forth in ye cuntre yer in a serten playe'.[1] Some evidence has been adduced to suggest that his *Three Laws* was written before he left the cloister in 1531.[2] At any rate, McCusker concludes that he must have been in charge of a travelling company of players before 1536 and have written a good number of his plays before that time. It is recorded that 'Bale and his ffelowes' played before Cromwell in 1538 and 1539, and that 'Lord Cromwell's players', with whom Bale's players have usually been identified, were playing in various towns during the late thirties.[3] It is supposed that they had to eke out a living playing where they could.

When Cromwell fell in 1540, Bale escaped to the continent, but from this distance he entered into a dispute over an act passed in 1543 and under the name of Henry Stalbridge wrote in an *Epistel Exhortatorye of an Inglyshe Christian*:

None leave ye unvexed and untrobled—no, not so much as the poore minstrels, and players of enterludes, but ye are doing with them. So long as they played lyes and sange baudy songes, blasphemed God, and corrupted men's consciences, ye never blamed them, but were verye well contented. But sens they persuaded the

---

[1] *Ibid*. pp. 5–7.
[2] Harris, pp. 68–9. Bale listed fourteen of the plays in *Anglorum Heliades* as written for the Earl of Oxford. See also McCusker, p. 74.
[3] McCusker, pp. 75–6.

15-2

people to worship theyr Lorde God aryght, accordyng to hys holie lawes and not yours, and to acknoledge Jesus Chryst for their onely redeemer and saviour, without your lowsie legerdemains, ye never were pleased with them.[1]

The epistle seems to display his rancorous opposition to secular plays on the usual grounds that they were based upon lies as distinguished from the truth of the Bible and that they included bawdry, but he obviously opposed also the Catholic plays, presumably including the old miracles and moralities written when England was a Catholic country.

Bale returned to England at the accession of Edward VI, and the offending law was soon repealed.[2] In 1552 Edward made Bale Bishop of Ossory. During his troubled stay in Ireland he continued to use his dramas, and he recorded the events at Kilkenny on 20 August 1553, the day of Mary's accession:

The yonge men in the forenone played a Tragedye of Gods promises in the olde lawe at the market crosse, with organe, plainges and songes very aptely. In the afternone agayne they played a Comedie of sanct Johan Baptistes preachinges, of Christes baptisynge and of his temptacion in the wildernesse.[3]

With Mary on the throne, Bale had again to escape to the continent, and he ultimately reached Basel, where in 1555–6 he matriculated at the university, probably living in the Clarakloster, the common home of English refugees. John Foxe was there too,[4] and Bale wrote of him in 1556: 'For nearly ten years he had been my Achates; in England we dwelt together in the house of the illustrious Duchess of Richmond, and now once more we are dwelling together in Germany.'[5] Both were friends of the printer Oporinus, who had published the works of Stoa and the great collection of Biblical plays, *Dramata Sacra*. In 1556 he was publishing Foxe's *Christus Triumphans*. He was to print other works of both men, but he is known today chiefly for

---

[1] Chambers, *Med. Stage*, vol. II, pp. 446–7.
[2] *Ibid.* p. 222.   [3] McCusker, p. 22.
[4] Christina H. Garrett, *The Marian Exiles* (Cambridge, 1938), pp. 78 and 156.
[5] Herford, p. 138.

having printed Bale's Latin catalogue of British writers and Foxe's first Latin edition of what became in English the *Actes and Monuments*, the latter published jointly by Oporinus and Brylinger. It is important to note that Bale had a long association with these men who were the promoters of the new Biblical drama. At some time Bale translated the *Pammachius* of Kirchmeyer included in the Brylinger volume. He was certainly in intimate contact with the men interested in the movement. But when he was able to return to England after Elizabeth was on the throne, he was an aged and ailing man, and his days as a dramatist were over. When he died in 1563 he was a canon of Canterbury Cathedral.[1]

The four of Bale's printed plays that have come down to us—*The Chief Promises of God*, *John the Baptist's Preaching*, *The Temptation of Christ*, and *The Three Laws*—were probably first printed by Dirik van der Straten in 1547–8 at Wesel, but they all according to their title-pages were 'compiled' in 1538.[2] They may have been revised before they were printed. *The Three Laws* certainly must have been revised, for the concluding prayer mentions Queen Katherine and the Lord Protector, and when it was printed in England in 1562, the prayer was for Queen Elizabeth, a fact not noted by Greg. The only other play of Bale's to be printed in England was *The Chief Promises of God*, and it was not printed until 1577. It may be of some significance that three of the plays which have survived in print out of his twenty-two written were those which were performed on that fatal day at Kilkenny.

In conformity with the current usage in secular drama, all four of the plays were printed as interludes, but the *Promises of God* was also called a tragedy and the other three comedies. There has been a good deal of discussion concerning the reason for this double ascription of dramatic genre without recognition of the fact that Bale's plays were not unique in this practice. *Jacob and Esau*, for instance, was published as a comedy or interlude, and the prologue of *Ralph Roister Doister* (the title-

---

[1] McCusker, pp. 27–8.
[2] Chambers, *Med. Stage*, vol. II, pp. 448–50. Concerning the original printer see Greg, *Bibliography*, under each play.

page of which is missing) refers to 'our comedy or interlude'.[1]
Like the interludes written by the Sir Thomas More circle,
Bale's plays had little action, consisting mostly of dialogue.

That Bale was writing in the tradition of those who were
trying to present their religious plays as rivals to secular offerings
seems indicated by the address of the Prolocutor in the *Promises
of God*:

> If profyght may growe, most Christen audyence
> By knowledge of thynges, whych are but transytorye,
> And here for a tyme. Of moch more congruence
> Advantauge myght sprynge, by the serche of causes heavenlye
> As those matters are, that the Gospell specyfye.
>
> .   .   .   .
>
> Yow therefor (good fryndes) I lovyngely exhort
> To waye soche matters, as wyll be uttered heere,
> Of whome ye maye loke, to have no tryfeling sport
> In fantasyes fayned, nor soche lyke gaudysh geere
> But the thynges that shall, your inwarde stomack streere.
> To reioyce in God, for your justyfycacyon,
> And alone in Christ, to hope for your salvacyon.[2]

The plays differ somewhat in construction, probably because
of the differences in the material which they present. All,
however, have prologues spoken by a prolocutor (Bale), all
have their stage directions written in Latin, and all, as I have
said, depend on dialogue rather than action for their story.

*A Tragedye or enterlude manyfestyng the chefe promyses of God unto
man by all ages in the olde lawe, from the fall of Adam to the incar-
nacyon of the lorde Jesus Christ*[3] is divided into seven acts, presumably because there are seven promises recorded as made by
God to Adam, Noah, Abraham, Moses, David, Esaias, and
Joannes Baptista after the sins of mankind and the punishment
that ensued have been described. Each act closes with one of
the seven O's of the Christmas antiphons, the 'chorus cum

---

[1] Note also no. 10, Rastell's play on women [Calisto and Melebea] referred
to earlier and no. 57, W. Wager's *A Comedy or Enterlude Intituled Inough is as good
as a feast*.

[2] The edge of the text as reproduced by John S. Farmer, *The Tudor Facsimile
Texts*, vol. XVII (1908), is marred, and I have supplied the missing words from
the 1577 edition in the Huntington Library.

[3] No. 22.

organis' which accompanied them suggesting the classical use of the chorus. Why God's promises should constitute a tragedy remains a mystery, for the salvation promised ultimately through Christ when sought by faith would seem to mark a happy ending. Perhaps the sins of men which made such redemption necessary seemed to Bale tragedy.

A brefe Comedy or enterlude of Johan Baptystes preachynge in the wylderness, openynge the craftye assaultes of the hypocrytes, with the gloryouse Baptyme of the Lorde Jesus Christ is available now only in the reprint of 1744 in *The Harleian Miscellany*.[1] There is no division into acts and scenes. The 'interlocutores' are listed in Latin, but with their English equivalents. 'Pater coelestis, i.e. the heavenly Father' appears only as a voice from heaven. Pharisee, Sadducee, and Soldier speak as generalized characters rather than individuals, and 'Turba vulgaris, The Common People' are apparently represented by one character. John and Christ speak somewhat elaborated versions of their Biblical speeches. There is no action save the baptizing of the Common People and the baptism of Christ. The stage directions call for Pharisee and Sadducee to enter from different places, and the Holy Spirit in the likeness of a dove descends from above as the voice of the Heavenly Father is heard. How these things were managed at Kilkenny is not indicated. A *gloria* is directed to be sung in English and is followed by Bale as prolocutor speaking an epilogue anti-Catholic in its appeal.

A brefe Comedy or enterlude concernynge the temptacyon of our lorde and saver Jesus Christ, by Sathan in the desart[2] was clearly intended to follow immediately the account of Johan's preaching and Christ's baptism as it did at Kilkenny, for Bale as prolocutor says:

> After hys baptyme. Christ was Gods soone declared,
> By the fathers voyce, as ye before have hearde.

and the foliation of the printed edition indicates that the two plays were published together. It is referred to as 'thys acte', and there are, as in the preceding play, no act and scene divi-

---

[1] See account in n. 1 to no. 23 in Greg, *Bibliography*. Text from *Harleian Miscellany*, vol. 1, pp. [97]–110.
[2] No. 23. Text from *Tudor Fac. Texts*, CXL (1919).

sions. The play shows, however, a more sustained effort to make real the characters of Christ and Satan than appears in the characterization of the principals in his other plays. Christ enters explaining that he has been fasting for forty days, but that he does not want the audience to think he has done so because he wants them to fast, and in like manner throughout the dialogue Bale attributes to Christ his own doctrinal beliefs. The dialogue between Satan and Christ makes up the whole of the interlude until the two angels appear at its close, and it is more interesting than usual. Satan presents himself as a simple hermit who has heard the strange voice from heaven proclaiming Jesus as the Son of God and he has come to find him. The stage direction supports Bale's theology: 'Hic simulata religione Christum aggreditur.' He speaks flattering words to Christ and proposes to walk with him, solicitously asking how long he has been in the desert. Christ acknowledges that his stomach is declaring the weakness of his body after his long fast, but he repels all the temptations Satan offers. In accord with Bible story Satan finally leads him to a mountain top and there offers him all the delights of Araby, Affryk, Europe, and Asye, which seem to have represented all the kingdoms of the world to Bale, but there is no indication how the mountain and the panoramic view were offered to the audience. Satan, having failed in his purpose, departs as two angels come to comfort Christ. They bring him food, saying, 'And now these vytales, we have for you prepared', but Christ will not eat until he has said a proper grace. (It will be remembered that in *Marie Magdalene* Christ will likewise not sit at Simon's table until after he has said grace.) The play ends with each angel contributing to the explanation of the story, but Bale adds the final preachments.

A Comedy Concernynge thre lawes, of nature Moses, & Christ, corrupted by the Sodomytes. Pharysees and Papystes,[1] when it was printed in England in 1562, was made to conform to the other plays by becoming *A NEWE Comedy or Enterlude*. It is a bitter polemical drama, its characters personified abstractions, and it need concern us here, being outside our particular study, only in

[1] No. 24.

so far as it can throw some light on Bale's dramatic method in the other plays. I have said that the nature of the material determined the organization of his plays rather than any dramatic theory. There were seven acts in *The Chief Promises of God* because it recorded seven promises and each act could close with one of the seven O's of the Christmas antiphons, and there are five acts in this play for a similar reason as shown in his outline of their content:

> De Legibus divinis Comoedia. Actus primus.
> Naturae lex corrupta. Actus secundus.
> Moseh lex corrupta. Actus tertius.
> Christi lex corrupta. Actus quartus.
> Restauratio legum divinarum. Actus quintus.

There are songs introduced, some secular like the 'Brom, brom' of Infidelitas, but the closing *Benedictus* is composed in the spirit of an anathema.

The three Biblical plays of Bale are clearly not built around miracles but about simple stories that can be used as a background for religious and theological instruction. They seem like extensions of the sermon. Nevertheless, Bale used the interlude form, as I have tried to show, and by listing each as comedy or tragedy he at least bowed to the habits of his friends on the continent who were organizing their plays in conformity to classical models. All of his surviving plays reveal Bale, as do his other works, in the vanguard of the religious struggle which was being waged, but that he was also a participant in the move among Christian humanists to create a Christian drama seems likewise evident.

There were certainly others than Bale who were writing Biblical plays for the public in his generation, and others than Bale were looking to Cromwell for support in their dramatic ventures. Thomas Wylley, the Vicar of Yoxford in Suffolk, was petitioning him for help in order that he might have 'fre lyberty to preche the trewthe' in spite of the opposition of the priests of Suffolk, but the plays which he describes are plainly anti-Catholic plays directed to polemic rather than to the creation of a new Biblical dramatic literature. Nicholas Udall in 1538 was paid five pounds 'for playing before' Cromwell while he was the schoolmaster of Eton. It is unlikely that Udall, the author of *Ezechias* as we hear it described and of *Ralph Roister Doister* as we know it, would have offered an old-fashioned play. Whether he was the author of a play which had been presented in Braintree while he was vicar there in 1533 we just do not know.[1]

Since this generation is not much inclined to find entertainment in the asperities of dramatized conflicts over theological dogma, we can be reconciled to the fact that most of the polemical plays like those of John Bale and Thomas Wylley did not achieve the permanence of print, but all students of drama must be grateful that we do have enough of the early interludes, both secular and religious, to mark the course by which English drama developed in the sixteenth century.

A copy of one of the more curious of these early interludes, dated tentatively by Greg as about 1550 but with the suggestion that there may have been an earlier edition, is *Saynt Johan the Evangelyst*.[2] An interlude on Saint John the evangelist was sold in 1520 by an Oxford bookseller, but there is no way of identifying this play which we have with that which we do not have. This is a crude play though strewed with Latin, and it is in fact a morality with Saint Johan preaching Christ's parable of the Pharisee and the Publican introduced in an incongruous setting. What makes it interesting is that it is set in England with English place-names and English customs identified. Throwing eggs at unwelcome speakers and the courteous English habit of greeting all women with a kiss (which pleased Erasmus, it will be remembered) are especially to be noted. Prologue and epilogue are absent, though Saint Johan makes opening and closing speeches. There are no act or scene divisions and no stage directions, only a record of dialogue, but it is not without interest. Iridision's discourse to Eugenio on the *via recta* which

[1] Chambers, *Med. Stage*, vol. II, pp. 220–1 and 451. The nature of the play is unknown. Chambers suggests a play on Placidas.

[2] No. 26. The title-page reads: *Here begynneth the enterlude of Johan the Evangelyst*, the head title reads merely, *Saynt Johan the Evangelyst*. Text from ed. W. W. Greg, Mal. Soc. *Reprints* (1907). The introduction gives an account of the earlier drama.

leads to the new Jerusalem and the *via obliqua et via circularis* is marked by a Dantesque description of hell:

> There is froste / there is fyre
> Hope is loste and her desyre
> There care hath no recover
> Without pytie there is payne
> To crye for mercy it is in vayne
> For grace is gone for ever [ll. 172–7].

Johan's words are sometimes moving:

> Moche can I shewe you of Christes incarnacyon
> And of his passyon / for verely I was there
> I sawe hym hange on the crosse on hye on hye
> His mother and I stode there under
> And I herde whan he cryed Hely Hely
> And sawe Longes smyte his herte a sonder [ll. 241–6].

But the dialogue in which Idlenesse and Ivell Counsayle and Actio engage is lusty and trivial and bawdy. Johan's final hearers are converted summarily at the end of the play. As I said earlier, the most interesting fact about the play is that it transports Saint John to England to do his preaching.

Extensive fragments of a much more important play survive only in a manuscript which is without title, date, or indication of authorship. The editors for the Malone Society edition, who give it the title of *The Resurrection of Our Lord*,[1] are inclined to date it between 1550 and 1560, but Greg as general editor adds a note to their comments suggesting rather that the date is between 1580 and 1630. The editors are tempted to father the play on John Bale, which may account for their inclination to the earlier date, but I must confess that I have no such temptation, for it is wholly unlike Bale's plays in tone and is the work of a far better craftsman. It is, however, like Bale's, clearly addressed to a public audience.

This resurrection drama is written for production on two days. No acts and scenes are indicated, but five times during the two days of playing Appendix comes on to speak as a chorus might speak, and within the sections thus set off there

---

[1] Eds. J. Dover Wilson and Bertram Dobell, Mal. Soc. *Reprints* (1912). The general editor's note is, however, dated 1913.

are episodes so treated that they might well be marked as scenes. The term *Appendix* is literary rather than theatrical, and some of the speeches are so long that it seems likely that any audience would grow restive hearing them. Yet there are evidences of a somewhat developed dramatic sense in the way in which the episodes are used to build up the plot, and technical devices used in classical drama are used here. The lacunae in the manuscript make analysis difficult, of course.

Though the first eight leaves of the manuscript are missing, they cannot have been necessary to the understanding of the story, for the first fragment begins with the Centurion recalling the antecedent action, giving to Pilate an account of events when Christ was crucified, even using the ancient device of telling him what he already knew:

> Yea, your honour doth remember, how yester night last
> a worshipfull Senatour here was not agast
> bouldye to request his corps, to be buried [ll. 42–4].

He uses another ancient device with his 'yonder come the high Priests' to identify Caiphas and Annas as they appear. The high priests demand that, because his disciples have spread the rumour that Christ will rise on the third day, the tomb be guarded; Pilate gives the order to the Centurion; and the Centurion relays it to the soldiers. The soldiers guard the tomb, but they 'fall downe as deade in hearing the gonnes shott of & thunder', and 'Jesus riseth throwynge of Death [&] the Angell'.[1] Frightened, the soldiers flee. Appendix, in explaining events, manages to insert a diatribe against those who would prohibit the reading of the Bible by the people. Then come the episodes showing the four Maries lamenting as they view the empty tomb, the angels comforting them, and Christ appearing to them like a gardener. The manuscript resumes after a lost section with the high priests bribing the soldiers to say that the disciples of Christ have stolen his body. Appendix is speaking as another lapse in the manuscript occurs, a lapse which covers the beginning of the second day's playing.

---

[1] The stage direction is at the bottom of the page, marked to be inserted after l. 241.

When the manuscript resumes the story, Christ is comforting Peter and the others, recalling to Peter events which the audience needs to know. Appendix offers Biblical authority for the story the play is telling but is frank to explain: 'Then where we have in scripture, but two words of the matter/the rest you must attribute, unto our invention' [ll. 611–12]. Christ preaches a sermon to Luke and Cleophas of some 250 lines on the fulfilment of prophecy and the foreshadowing of events. He quite literally breaks bread with his disciples and then vanishes mysteriously. After Appendix has spoken, the two disciples walk aside but join the others to discuss Christ's vanishing at Emmaus. Another gap in the manuscript, and Appendix is again speaking. Eight days have passed with the disciples in hiding before we hear the others trying to convince the doubting Thomas of what has happened, and there the manuscript breaks off.

I have tried to show that even the broken story reveals a writer consciously building his episodes to a well-rounded plot. The author has also shown some skill in introducing realistic touches in characterization. Marie Magdalene is tempestuous in her anger, she is careful with her box of ointment and asks someone to hold it when she dashes off to get Peter and John, and twice the stage directions call upon her to lament. The disciples are sceptical of the tale about seeing Christ as told by the women, for they cannot believe that Christ would have first appeared to women. The author's 'invention' adds to the interest of the story, but the chief interest of the play for the historians of the drama must lie in his careful building of a plot, in his adopting old theatrical devices, and in his use of the play to reveal the death and resurrection of Christ as a fulfilment of a divine plan long prefigured.

CHAPTER IX

BIBLICAL PLAYS IN THE PUBLIC THEATRES

AFTER 1576 the English drama was given a home of its own, for in that year the Theatre was built. In the same year rooms in the old Blackfriars monastery were made into a 'private' theatre. More theatres followed, the Curtain in 1577. The Theatre and the Curtain were frankly commercial houses; Blackfriars, where the children's companies were supposedly readying plays for presentation at court, was less frankly so. Plays had previously been performed in churches and churchyards, in schools and universities, in inn-yards and on the village greens, as well as in places provided for their presentation before the rich, the noble, and the royal. The inn-yards, it is said, actually had an increased patronage immediately after the erection of the Theatre and the Curtain,[1] but as theatres multiplied and the writing and producing of plays became the work of professionals, the patrons of the village green and the inn-yard seem to have congregated more and more at the playhouse. The commercialization of the theatres made necessary a regular production of plays and, as everyone knows, the writers of the period became in innumerable cases playwrights. Yet the record of the plays produced by them is neither clear nor complete.

Aside from incidental references our knowledge of the dramas of the last quarter of the sixteenth century in England is largely derived from three sources: (1) the Stationers' Register, (2) the documents preserved in the Office of the Revels, and (3) the diary of Philip Henslowe. After 1557 plays to be printed should have been entered on the Stationers' Register, but not all plays were printed, and not all that were printed were entered on the Register. Plays were being presented at court, and the Office of the Revels made provision for them, but the

William Ringler, 'The First Phase of the Elizabethan Attack on the Stage, 1558–1579', *Huntington Library Quarterly*, vol. v (1942), pp. 391–418.

Revels accounts[1] were perforce more concerned with the expenses for 'bote hier & horshier' and 'viserdes' than with the titles of plays, and the name of a tailor is more apt to be recorded than the name of an author. The public playhouses had only one contemporary chronicler, but for him we are grateful. Philip Henslowe is called by Chambers a capitalist, and that term may be broad enough to describe this man of many ventures in finance who is known today chiefly because he left a record of his manifold dealings as builder, landlord, and banker in connection with theatrical enterprises. His famous *Diary*[2] is, as Chambers says, 'not in fact a diary at all, but a folio memorandum book, which Henslowe used principally during 1592–1603, and in which he entered in picturesque confusion particulars of accounts between himself and the companies occupying his theatres, together with jottings on many personal and business matters'.[3] Here he recorded advances made to individuals and to companies for theatrical properties and apparel. Here, too, he listed the receipts or his share of the receipts for each individual play produced by these companies and the payments advanced or finally paid to dramatists for the writing or altering of plays. Occasionally he entered a note of sociological interest as when in 1601 he recorded money 'Layd out for the company to geatte the boye into the ospetalle wᶜʰ was hurt at the fortewne [Fortune]'.[4] I may add that his highly personal orthography sometimes demands the imaginative reconstruction which Greg, who edited the diary, has offered. It is, of course, to Chambers and Greg in large measure that we owe the amassing of such facts as we have to work with when we try to interpret the Tudor drama. It is evident, however, that our knowledge is still limited, for the Stationers' Register does not furnish a complete list of printed plays, the Revels accounts give little heed to the literary side of dramatic

[1] Ed. Albert Feuillerat, *Documents Relating to the Office of the Revels in the Time of Queen Elizabeth, Materialien* XXI (Louvain, 1908); and *Documents Relating to the Revels at Court in the Time of King Edward VI and Queen Mary (The Loseley Manuscripts), Materialien* XLIV (Louvain, 1914).

[2] *Henslowe's Diary*, ed. W. W. Greg, part I, Text (London, 1904), part II, Commentary (London, 1908).

[3] Chambers, *Eliz. Stage*, vol. I, p. 360.　　　　[4] *Diary*, vol. I, p. 136.

production, and Henslowe's diary, beginning in 1592, can give no information concerning plays produced before that time or by companies other than those with which he was associated.

If we look to the Stationers' Register for entries of Scriptural plays printed between the opening of the Theatre in 1576 and the end of Elizabeth's reign, we find just four: Golding's translation of Bèze's *Abraham Sacrifiant*, which does not seem to have been performed in England; *The most Virtuous and Godly Susanna*, which I have already discussed as probably intended for production before limited audiences; and finally *A Looking-Glass for London and England* and *The Love of King David and Fair Bethsabe*, the only two prepared for the public theatre, it would seem. Since the Revels accounts give little help in this search, it is therefore Henslowe's *Diary* which proves our most important if still limited source of information. The *Diary* gives information, indeed, about a considerable number of these plays, and perhaps I can best indicate what it is by summarizing the facts gleaned by Greg concerning them:

A Looking-Glass for London and England was performed as an old play by Strange's men four times between 8 March and 7 June 1591/2.[1]

Jerusalem was also performed as an old play by Strange's men on 22 March and 25 April 1591/2, but it may not have been a Bible play.[2]

Abraham and Lot was performed as an old play by Sussex's men three times in January 1593/4.[3]

Hester and Assuerus was performed as an old play by the Admiral's and Chamberlain's men twice in June 1594.[4]

The Seven Days of the Week, possibly a Bible play as the title may suggest, but doubtfully so classified, was played as a new play by the Admiral's men twenty-two times between 3 June 1595, and 31 December 1596. *The Second Week* was played twice in January 1595/6.[5]

---

[1] No. 14. The plays are given numbers in ch. III of the Commentary (vol. II). I am indicating the number he assigns to each play there.

[2] No. 18. [3] No. 34. [4] No. 41.

[5] Nos. 73 and 86. It may possibly be of significance that parts of Du Bartas's *Divine Weeks and Works* were receiving attention at this time. *The First Day of the Worldes Creation*, translated by an unidentified author, was published in 1595, as

Nabuchodonozor was performed as a new play by the Admiral's men eight times between 19 December 1596, and 21 March 1597.[1]

Judas was noted four times in the *Diary*. On 27 May 1600, William Haughton was given an advance on it for the Admiral's men. For probably the same play, William Birde (alias Borne) was given twenty shillings 'in earnest of a Boocke called Judas wch samewell Rowly & he is a writtinge some of' and, on 24 December 1601, the two were paid in full by the further sum of five pounds. Then in January of the following year, a payment was made for properties for the play.[2]

Pontius Pilate (Henslowe writes 'ponesciones pillet') was furnished with a prologue and epilogue for the play for the Admiral's men by Thomas Dekker in January 1601/2.[3]

Jephthah ('Jeffa' to Henslowe) necessitated several entries. On 5 May 1602, Anthony Munday and Thomas Dekker were paid five pounds in advance on the book for the Admiral's men. Later in the month two shillings was spent 'when they Read the playe of Jeffa for wine at the tavern'. Five entries in May and June record rather lavish expenditures for costumes and properties.[4]

Tobyas was secured for the Admiral's men by payments to Henry Chettle in May and June 1602.[5]

Samson was paid for in full on 25 July 1602 by men of the Admiral's company, but to whom the payment was made is not indicated. That a play on Samson was being performed a few years later is inferred from a reference in Middleton's *Family of Love*.[6]

Joshua was secured for the Admiral's men by a payment in full to Samuel Rowley on 27 September 1602.[7]

was W. L'isle's translation of part of the *Seconde Weeke*. From this time on translations of Du Bartas's *Divine Weekes and Workes* were coming regularly from the presses. See chs. IX and X of part I of this study.

[1] No. 97.
[2] No. 207. For details see *Diary*, vol. I, pp. 122, 151 and 152.
[3] No. 230.
[4] No. 234. For details see *Diary*, vol. I, pp. 166 and 168.
[5] No. 235. See also Harold Jenkins, *The Life and Work of Henry Chettle* (London, 1934), p. 240.
[6] No. 241.   [7] No. 247.

Absalom is known only by a payment in October 1602, made on behalf of Worcester's men for pulleys and workmanship 'for to hange absolome'. The reference may be to *David and Bethsabe*.[1]

Of these fourteen plays, eleven were certainly based on the Bible, three are in doubt, and only the *Looking-Glass* is extant unless the reference to *Absalom* is indeed to *David and Bethsabe*. Yet it is clear that during the decade beginning in 1592, and for those companies with which Henslowe had dealings, Bible plays were being produced in the public theatres which were written by an impressive roster of Elizabethan authors: Robert Greene, Thomas Lodge, Samuel Rowley, Thomas Dekker, Anthony Munday, and Henry Chettle, as well as by the less familiar William Haughton and William Birde.

Whether the Biblical plays of these ten years for which Henslowe bore some responsibility are to be regarded as the product of exceptional circumstances as R. B. Sharpe seems to think or no,[2] they did not escape the wrath of the unco guid which was poured down on plays generally after the public theatres were built. William Ringler has argued persuasively that 'The attack on the stage, which was unheralded and unprecedented, began quite suddenly in the latter part of 1577, and continued in the succeeding years with increasing vigor and acrimony'.[3] Certainly two sermons preached at Paul's Cross suggest a spirit of envious rivalry in the divines. 'T.W.' preaching there in 1577 cried out in his distress: 'Look but uppon the common playes in London, and see the multitude that flocketh to them and followeth them: beholde the sumptuous Theatre houses, a continuall monument of Londons prodigalitie and folly.'[4] John Stockwood at Paul's Cross in 1578 was more explicit:

Wyll not a fylthye playe, wyth the blast of a Trumpette, sooner call thyther a thousande, than an houres tolling of a Bell, bring to the Sermon a hundred? nay even heere in the Citie, without it be at this place, and some other certaine ordinarie audience, where shall you find a reasonable company? whereas, if you resorte to the

---

[1] No. 269a.
[2] *The Real War of the Theatres* (Boston and London, 1935), pp. 28–31.
[3] See note 1 on p. 238 above [4] Chambers, *Eliz. Stage*, vol. IV, p. 199.

Theatre, the Curtayne, and other places of Playes in the Citie, you shall on the Lords day have these places, with many other that I can not recken, so full, as possible they can throng.[1]

In 1579 the most famous of the attacks on the stage[2] appeared under the all-embracing title of *The Schoole of Abuse. Conteining a pleasaunt invective against Poets, Pipers, Plaiers, Jesters and such Catterpillers of a Commonwelth.* It was written by 'Stephan Gosson, Stud. Oxon.' and dedicated to Sir Philip Sidney. Apparently the dedication was made without due regard to the 'inclination and qualitie' of the recipient of the honour, and the work played at least a part in eliciting Sidney's great defence of poetry.[3] Later in 1579 Gosson published in the volume of his *Ephemerides of Phialo*, another work dedicated to Sidney, *A Short Apologie of the Schoole of Abuse, against Poets, Pipers, Players, and their Excusers.* In this work he wrote:

It is tolde mee that they have got one in London to write certaine *Honest excuses,* for so they terme it, to their dishonest abuses which I revealed....How he frames his excuses, I know not yet, because it is done in hudder mudder.[4]

Thomas Lodge has been identified as the one in London who had thus come to the defence of plays and players, instancing the poetry of the Bible and the approval of certain of the church fathers along with that of ancient classical writers.[5] He noted Buchanan's works and Erasmus's translations of Euripides and added:

The Germans, when the use of preaching was forbidden them, what helpe had they I pray you? Forsoth the learned were fayne covertly in comedies to declare abuses, and by playing to incite the

[1] *Ibid.* pp. 199–200.
[2] A full account is given by William Ringler, *Stephen Gosson* (Princeton, 1942), pp. 53–82. A table of the documents is given by G. Gregory Smith, *Elizabethan Critical Essays* (London, 1937, reprinted from 1904 edition), vol. I, pp. 61–3. Chambers prints important selections, *Eliz. Stage*, vol. IV, pp. 197–258. See also N. Burton Paradise, *Thomas Lodge* (New Haven, 1931), pp. 66–74.
[3] Spenser wrote to Gabriel Harvey, 'Newe Bookes I heare of none, but only of one, that writing a certaine Booke, called THE SCHOOLE OF ABUSE, and dedicating it to Maister SIDNEY, was for hys labor scorned, if at leaste it be in the goodnesse of that nature to scorne. Such follie is it not to regard aforehande the inclination and qualitie of him to whome we dedicate our Bookes' (Smith, vol. I, p. 89).
[4] *Ibid.* vol. I, p. 62.   [5] *Ibid.* vol. I, pp. 68–71.

people to vertues, when they might heare no preaching. Those were lamentable dayes you will say, and so thinke I; but was not this, I pray you, a good help in reforming the decaying Gospel?[1]

Lodge's work exists without title-page or dedication. In *An Alarum against Userers*, published in 1584 and also dedicated to Sidney, Lodge addressed a letter to his fellows in the Inns of Court, in which he explained that his reply to Gosson '(because it was in defence of plaies & play makers) the godly & reverent that had to deale in the cause, misliking it, forbad the publishing'.[2]

In 1582 Gosson replied to Lodge's arguments concerning Christian precedents in his *Playes confuted in five Actions* with the honey and gall comparison, 'So the Devill, at Playes, wil bring the comfortable worde of God, which, because it norisheth of nature is very convenient to carry the poysen into our vaines'.[3] To explain away the writings of plays by Christian writers cited by Lodge he added:

So Naciancen and Bucchanan perceiving the corruption of the Gentiles, to avoyde that which is evill, and yet keepe that which is good, according to the true use of Poetrie, penned these bookes in numbers with interloqutions dialogue wise, as Plato and Tullie did their Philosophy, to be reade, not be played.... Therefore whatsoever such Playes as conteine good matter, are so out of print, may be read with profite, but cannot be playd, without a manifest breach of Gods commaundement.

As to the play about John the Baptist, Buchanan had written it for the King of Scots to read and to profit thereby.[4] Gosson's facts are all askew, but the attack indicates that there were Biblical plays being acted, else he would have been shadowboxing. The *Plays Confuted* ended the Gosson–Lodge controversy, but Lodge was to change sides later.

Meanwhile in 1580, *A second and third blast of retrait from plaies and Theaters* was published by 'Anglo-phile Eutheo', generally identified as Anthony Munday. If the author was Munday, it was also the work of a man who changed sides.

[1] Smith, vol. 1, p. 84.
[2] *The Complete Works of Thomas Lodge* (Printed for the Hunterian Club, 1883), vol. 1, *Alarum*, p. 6. (Each work is given separate page numbers.)
[3] London [1582], D 5ᵛ–6ʳ. [4] *Ibid.* E 5–7.

Early apprenticed to Allde the printer, he did not finish his apprenticeship but took to his pen. After a trip to Rome, he wrote against the Jesuits. Appearing as an actor, he was hissed off the stage and wrote against the stage but again took up acting.[1] From Henslowe's diary we know him as a writer of plays after 1594, but Anglo-phile Eutheo claimed in 1580 to have been 'a greater affecter of that vaine art of Plaie-making' and able to speak with authority against the Theatre, which he termed 'the chappel of Satan'. He specifically attacks the Bible plays being then presented:

The reverend word of God & histories of the Bible, set forth on the stage by these blasphemous plaiers, are so corrupted with their gestures of scurrilitie, and so interlaced with uncleane, and whorish speeches, that it is not possible to drawe anie profite out of the doctrine of their spiritual moralities.[2]

In *The Antomie of Abuses* Phillip Stubbes was renewing the attack in editions from 1583 to 1595. A section 'Of Stage-playes and Enterluds, with their wickednes' made an interesting division of plays into two kinds:

All Stage-playes, Enterluds, and Commedies are either of divyne or prophane matter: If they be of divine matter, then are they most intollerable, or rather Sacrilegious; for that the blessed word of God is to be handled reverently, gravely and sagely, with veneration to the glorious Majestie of God, which shineth therin, and not scoffingly, flowtingly, and jybingly, as it is upon stages in Playes and Enterluds, without any reverence, worship, or veneration to the same. The word of our Salvation, the price of Christ his bloud, & the merits of his passion were not given to be derided and jested at, as they be in these filthie playes and entreluds on stages & scaffolds, or to be mixt and interlaced with bawdry, wanton shewes, & uncomely gestures, as is used (every Man knoweth) in these plays and enterludes...beware, therfore, you masking Players, you painted sepulchres, you doble dealing ambodexters, be warned betymes, and, lik good computistes, cast your accompts before, what wil be the reward therof in the end, least God destroy you in his wrath: abuse God no more, corrupt his people no longer with your dregges, and intermingle not his blessed word with such prophane vanities. For at no hand it is not lawfull to mix scurrilitie with divinitie, not divinitie with scurrilitie.

---

[1] Chambers, *Eliz. Stage*, vol. III, pp. 444–6.   [2] *Ibid.* vol. IV, pp. 209–11.

That he is referring to plays performed in the public theatres is made clear by his added warning to Christians to keep away from theatres, 'For so often as they go to those howses where Players frequent, thei go to *Venus* pallace & sathans synagogue to worship devils, & betray Christ Jesus', with the note in the margin 'Theaters and curtaines Venus pallaces'.[1]

Thomas Lodge, as I have said, changed sides in the matter when he in 1596 wrote in *Wits Miserie* that 'in stage plaies to make use of Hystoricall Scripture, I hold it with the Legists odious, and as the Council of Trent did, *Sess 4. Fin.* I comdemne it'.[2] It was a curious comment when the Bible play which he had written with Robert Greene was even then enjoying a new popularity in print after its day in the theatre.

In 1603 the attack on plays in general was being continued in Henry Crosse's *Vertues Commonwealth* which did not neglect scriptural plays that

many times (which is most sinfull) intermixe the sacred worde of God, that never ought to be handled without feare and trembling, with their filthy and scurrillous Paganisme: is not this abhominable prophanation? is not that humble reverence of the oracles of God, hereby blasphemed, and basely scorned? is this fit to be suffered where Christ is professed? must the holy Prophets and Patriarcks be set upon a Stage to be derided, hist and laught at? or is it fit that the infirmities of holy men should be acted on a Stage, where by others may be inharted to rush carelessly forward into unbrideled libertie?[3]

Since an attack presupposes an offending subject, it seems evident that Bible plays were continuously being offered at the public theatres during the last quarter-century of Elizabeth's reign; yet only two which can with some confidence be assigned to the public theatres have been preserved. The first of these was described on its title-page, when it was first printed in 1594, as *A Looking Glasse for London and England. Made by Thomas Lodge Gentleman, and Robert Greene. In Artibus Magister.*[4]

[1] Chambers, *Eliz. Stage*, vol. IV, pp. 222–3.
[2] *Works*, vol. IV, *Wits Miserie*, p. 46.   [3] Sig. 3ᵛ.
[4] No. 14 in *Diary*, no. 118 in *Bibliography*. Bibliographical facts are given also in W. W. Greg (ed.), Mal. Soc. *Reprints* (1932). See too C. R. Baskervill, 'A Prompt Copy of *A Looking Glass for London and England*', *Modern Philology*, vol. XXX (1932), pp. 29–51.

The fifth edition was published in 1617, and five passages were quoted from it in England's *Parnassus* in 1600, so that Greg concludes with some assurance that there must have been a good many Englishmen who liked to read it even if it had lost its popularity as a stage production after its 1592 revival. Just how long before this revival the play had been composed is uncertain, and the problem has brought a flock of contradictory opinions based on sound reasoning from inadequate facts. It is generally agreed that it bears some relation to Marlowe's *Doctor Faustus*, but which owed what to the other can be argued indefinitely as long as the dates of both remain in dispute. There are resemblances to *Tamburlaine* also, but resemblance does not always indicate direct indebtedness. Fortunately such matters need not concern us. The title-page bears witness to the authorship of the play, Henslowe attests its having been played four times in 1592 as an old play, and after 1594 it had a history as printed literature.

Both Greene and Lodge were university men and are generally classed in histories of English literature as among the 'university wits', men who came up to London from the universities and made something of a profession of letters. That they combined to write a Bible play testifies to its having been the thing to do. Greene took his B.A. and M.A. degrees at Cambridge, and a later degree at Oxford enabled him, as Chambers says, to describe himself as *Academiae Utriusque Magister in Artibus*.[1] He has left for the romancers adequate records of his own dissolute life and later repentance. Lodge[2] took his degree at Oxford and apparently supplicated for his degree while a member of Lincoln's Inn, but he was not admitted to the bar. He became a Catholic, perhaps while he was at the university, but the time of his conversion is not clear. At various times he suffered for his recusancy. In his dedication to the work by which he is generally known today, his *Rosalynde*, he said he had written it while on a voyage 'to the Islands of Terceras & the Canaries', the date of which has, however, been

---

[1] Chambers, *Eliz. Stage*, vol. III, pp. 323, 327.
[2] *Ibid.* pp. 409–10. This biography by Paradise (see n. 2 on p. 243 above) supersedes earlier accounts. A list of Lodge's works is given, pp. 231–43.

in dispute. He was also with the ill-fated voyage of Thomas Cavendish which sailed for America in 1591. His sea-going experiences are reflected in the *Looking-Glass*. Another experience influencing the play is that which is reflected in his *Alarum against Usurers*, published in 1584. Quite evidently there are links between his voyaging, his pamphlet on usury, and the play. Lodge's translations are many, but it must be noted that they included a translation of Goulart's summary of the great work of the Protestant Du Bartas among the many Catholic works of devotion. Since the *Looking-Glass* shows that Josephus was consulted to supplement the Bible story, the fact that Lodge's translation of his works was entered on the Stationers' Register in 1591 though it was not printed until 1602 is also of some importance. Of Lodge's other works and of his later life as a physician there is no need to speak here.

Robert Greene is said to have written a play on Job which was lost in the famous conflagration set by Warburton's servant,[1] but nothing is known of it. The story of the sin and the repentance of the prophet Jonah must have been an even more congenial one to him, however. The *Looking-Glass* is, of course, firmly based upon the Biblical story of Jonah (or Jonas), and R. A. Law has proved, I think, his contention that it was the Bishops' Bible that furnished the play's authority.[2] He concludes, indeed, that 'Careful comparison of the play with the Bible text shows hardly a single verse in the entire four chapters of the *Book of Jonas* that has not been worked into the play, most of the verses in the same succession as in the original'. But the play is not simply a dramatization of the book in the Bible. The history of the Jews as told by Josephus was also used,[3] and Lodge may well have been working on his translation when the play was written, as I have said. There is also much material added with an idea of admonishing London and

[1] W. W. Greg, 'The Bakings of Betsy', *The Library*, 3rd ser. vol. II, pp. 225–59, esp. pp. 231–2.

[2] R. A. Law, 'A Looking Glasse and the Scriptures', *Studies in English* (University of Texas, Austin, 1939, no. 1939), pp. 31–47. It should be noted, however, that Cicilia is mentioned in Lodge's translation of Josephus (London, 1602), p. 238, and that Law's argument so far as it concerns that name is not convincing.

[3] Paradise, p. 154.

England rather than enlightening them in regard to Jewish history.

The first part of the play, more than a third, is devoted to the sins attributed to Ninivie, sins which in this looking-glass reflect the current sins of London and England as the authors saw them. It closes with Jonas's final appeal which it would seem impossible for Lodge to permit if he was already a Catholic:

> O London, mayden of the mistresse Ile,
> Wrapt in the foldes and swathing cloutes of shame;
> In thee more sinnes than *Ninivie* containes....
> London awake, for feare the Lord do frowne,
> I set a looking Glasse before thine eyes.
> And thinke the praiers and vertues of thy Queene,
> Defers the plague, which otherwise would fall.
> O turne, O turne, with weeping to the Lord,
> Repent O London, least for thine offence,
> Thy shepheard faile, whom mightie God preserve,
> That she may bide the pillar of his Church,
> Against the stormes of Romish Antichrist:
> The hand of mercy overshead her head,
> And let all faithful subjects say, *Amen.*[1]

The *Looking-Glass* is not constructed on classical lines; it has no formal prologue and epilogue, no act and scene divisions. Instead, it consists of a series of scenes introducing in succession three sets of characters who need to repent; then, after depicting Jonas's own sin and repentance, a series showing the repentance of each of the three groups in turn as a result of Jonas's preaching. The spectacle is ingeniously devised and as memorable as that to be expected in the decade of the *Spanish Tragedy* and *Doctor Faustus*. Like all the Bible plays it followed in its structure a current fashion in secular plays.

The first set of characters is introduced with Rasni, king of Ninivie, celebrating with the kings of Cecilia, Creete, and

---

[1] Quoted from the Mal. Soc. edition. The lesson of the play is that of *Newes from Ninive to Englande brought by the prophete Jonas*, trans. by T. Tymme from J. Brentius and published in 1570. It admonished:

> Repent England in time,
> as Nineve that Citie did
> For that thy sinnes before the Lorde,
> are not in secret hid.

Paphlagonia, the overthrow of Jereboam, king of Jerusalem. Rasni boasts in the Tamburlaine vein and announces his marriage to his sister Remilia, though Cecilia's king calls such a marriage incestuous. Then the prophet Oseas is brought by an angel and 'set over the stage in a throne'. And there he sits in his throne over the stage to denounce the sins of the people as they obligingly come before him to commit their sins. Twelve times he speaks to decry their sins and to act as a chorus between the unmarked scenes.

The second group of characters, in contrast to the first group, is made up of characters of the lower class usually reserved for comedy, 'the Clowne and his crew of Ruffians' including a smith. They speak prose in contrast to the royal group of the first scene, but they also are clearly sinners, fighting and going off to drink and wenches.

The third group offers opportunity to exploit Lodge's alarum against usurers, for the usurer is shown dealing meanly and unjustly with a young gentleman and then with a poor man who is made to forfeit his cow. They too speak in prose.

As Rasni commands a shrine for his love, his magi beat the ground with their rods, and a great arbour arises. There are thunder and lightning, a curtain is drawn, and Remilia is seen 'strooken with Thunder, blacke', but Rasni is promised consolation with the wife of the Paphlagonian king. A lawyer betrays his clients, and a judge and the usurer go off to feast together. A drunken brawl among the clown-and-ruffian set results in murder, but Rasni coming on the scene shows unconcern and proceeds to his adulterous wooing. The willing queen of Paphlagonia ingeniously gets rid of her husband by luring him to a poisoned drink.

At last the Bible story commences as Jonas appears bemoaning the sins of Israel, and an angel comes to command him to go to Ninivie. Instead he decides to flee to Joppa and sail to Tharsus with merchants and seamen who appear opportunely bound for that city. [Here Lodge begins to show his knowledge of the seafaring man's life.]

Other characters intrude on the Scriptural story briefly, and we are back in Ninivie for more sins. Rasni's parasitic adviser refuses to honour his parents, and when his mother curses him, 'a flame of fire appeareth from beneath' and swallows him. The clown makes love to the smith's wife and gets a beating.

As we return to the Bible and Joppa, the very wet sailors and merchants come dripping from the sea to tell the governor of Joppa of the great storm (certainly a Lodge contribution), of their casting Jonas into the sea at his demand to appease the fury of his God, and of their own conversion from paganism by these events. Then comes the scene which has made the story famous, for Jonas is 'cast out of Whales belly uppon the Stage', and an angel again appears to send him on his way to Ninivie.

Still more sins are enacted for Oseas to denounce, and there is more spectacle. Rasni's wooing of the murderous queen is interrupted by the priests of the sun, 'With the miters on their heads, carrying fire in their hands' and rehearsing the terrible omens that have appeared when 'A hand from out a cloud, threateneth a burning sword'. After the clown has fought with and killed one dressed as a devil, and the parasite's family has tried to pawn stolen goods to the usurer, Jonas arrives calling them to repentance, and an angel removes the prophet Oseas, leaving Jonas to effect the conversion of Ninivie.

As Jonas preaches, it is first the members of the court who repent and take to sackcloth and ashes. Then the usurer comes 'with a halter in one hand, a dagger in the other', and is further tempted to the final sin of despair, self-slaughter, by an evil angel 'offering the knife and rope'. But he seems to hear a voice bidding him stay, for the Lord is merciful to those who repent, and he too in sackcloth turns to prayer. It is a scene reminiscent of Spenser's Cave of Despair, of a scene in *Doctor Faustus*, and indeed of the many accounts of cases of conscience which the age produced.[1] The king and his nobles join the usurer to go to the temple.

Jonas himself now has to learn the lesson of God's mercy. Sitting in the shade of a great vine, he sees a serpent devour the vine, and is moved to disgust and anger. The angel comes

---

[1] I have discussed the pattern established in these cases of despair in '*Doctor Faustus*: A Case of Conscience', *P.M.L.A.* (1952), vol. LXVII, pp. 219–39.

to tell him that even as he sorrows for the good vine, so God sorrows over the people of Ninivie and is moved to pity by their repentance. All the Ninivites do indeed repent except the clown, who refuses to fast for five days as the king has decreed even on pain of death. As all turn to God, Jonas recites his final admonitions to London which must serve as an epilogue to the drama.

Greg has called this a morality, Law calls it a miracle, but no one seems to have related it, not to these medieval genres but to the 'divine' or Biblical drama recognized in England as well as in Europe. But again I must stress the fact that it was following a current method of writing plays for the public stage as a series of events without the classical observance of act and scene division. Furthermore, when spectacle was valued for its variety and ingenuity, the popular taste was appealed to by a prophet sitting over the stage in a great throne, a bower rising magically through a trap-door, thunder and lightning with a lady 'strucken Blacke' by the thunder, a flame springing up to devour a man, a whale belching forth a man on the stage, a procession of priests carrying fire in their hands, a hand out of a cloud threatening with a burning sword, a vine that appears and is eaten up by a serpent, not to speak of angels. Surely the offering could compete with any presented in the contemporary theatre. Besides, there are incest and murder and low-comedy horseplay and sound moral and religious teaching. The recipe has had long success in the commercial theatre and the moving-picture industry.

It remained for George Peele to write a divine play in the tradition of divine poetry. *THE LOVE OF KING DAVID AND FAIR BETHSABE. With the Tragedie of Absalon*[1] is clearly the work of a poet experimenting with a Biblical play, but as a drama it cannot be judged fairly since it has come down to us in what is clearly a mutilated form. Its history is uncertain. It was entered on the Stationers' Register in 1594 but

[1] No. 160 in *Bibliography*. Text from W. W. Greg, Mal. Soc. *Reprints* (1912). Greg divides the play into seventeen scenes. J. M. Manly, *Specimens of the Pre-Shakespearean Drama* (Boston and London, 1900), vol. II, pp. 419–86, divided it into three acts and numbered scenes. Spellings of Bethsabe and Rabath vary in the text.

apparently was not published until 1599. The title-page says that 'it hath ben divers times plaied on the stage', but unless the 1602 entry in Henslowe's diary for the poles and workmanship 'for to hange absolome' refers to its production then, there is no record known of its performance.

That Peele should have experimented with a divine drama is not surprising, for as early as 1589 Thomas Nashe called him 'the chiefe supporter of pleasance now living, the *Atlas* of Poetrie and *primus verborum Artifex,* whose first encrease, the Arraignement of Paris, might plead to your opinions his pregnant dexteritie of wit and manifold varietie of invention, wherein (*me judice*) hee goeth a step beyond all that write'.[1] Like Greene and Lodge he is classed as one of the university wits in histories of English literature. He had his Oxford B.A. in 1577–8, his M.A. in 1579, but he stayed on in Oxford until 1581. He translated a play of Euripides, perhaps during his Oxford years, and in 1583 he went back to supervise the production of two of William Gager's plays.[2] His original dramas show that he was always experimenting with new types. His *Arraignment of Paris* is the only play that has survived to give us an echo of the old satyr play, *Edward I* is an early chronicle play, *The Old Wive's Tale* uses an induction to introduce the romantic folk-tale plot which is echoed in Milton's *Comus.*

Peele wrote his play as a poet fully conscious of the traditions of divine poetry, and certain passages were derived from the great work of Du Bartas.[3] He does not use Bible story as just another narrative to make into drama, however, but as a plot on which to build a divine drama. He uses the Bible as a frame of reference in his figures of speech, in the lyric forms he introduces, in the very words his characters speak. He chose a divine hero, 'Joves musition', and invokes a divine muse in his prologue as the divine poets were doing. That Peele was also aware of the classical literature and the secular poetry of

[1] Smith, vol. 1, p. 319.
[2] D. H. Horne, *The Life and Minor Works of George Peel* (New Haven, 1952), the first volume of an edition of Peele's works proposed with C. T. Prouty as general editor. See also Chambers, *Eliz. Stage,* vol. III, pp. 458–9.
[3] See H. Dugdale Sykes, 'Peele's Borrowings from Du Bartas', *Notes and Queries,* ser. 13, vol. CXLVII, pp. 348–51; and Horne, pp. 93–4.

his own time is evident in his prologue in the epic tradition, in the epithalamium and in the elegy introduced into the narrative, but he composes them in the tradition of divine poetry.

The original form of the play or plays is uncertain, as I have already noted. The title indicates that two stories are to be told, the love of David and Bethsabe and the tragedy of Absalon, which might well have been made into separate dramas, but Peele has linked them with a third which is indeed a part of the Biblical account. The events covered in the play begin with the eleventh chapter of the Second Book of Samuel where David, having remained in Jerusalem while his armies are besieging Rabath, falls in love with Bath-Sheba. The twelfth chapter continues the story of their love and records the final crowning of David in Rabath. The story which Peele uses in his drama as a connecting link is complete in the thirteenth chapter, the story of Absalon's vengeance for the rape of Thamar by Ammon. The third story, of Absalon's treachery, his rebellion against David, and his defeat begins in the fourteenth chapter. What Peele tried to do was to weave the three stories into a continuous whole, changing the sequence of events as he found necessary. Then he introduced Solomon at the end of the play as a fore-taste of things to come. The play as it exists is divided into three parts (perhaps called discourses originally) by a chorus.

It is as a divine epic that the play begins, with the prologue first announcing the theme:

> Of Israels sweetest singer now I sing,
> His holy stile and happie victories,
>
> .   .   .   .
>
> Of this sweet Poet Joves Musition,
> And of his beauteous sonne I prease to sing.

Then comes the invocation to his divine muse:

> Then helpe devine Adonay to conduct,
> Upon the wings of my well tempered verse,
> The hearers minds above the towers of Heaven
> And guide them so in this thrice haughty flight,
> Their mounting feathers scorch not with the fire,
> That none can temper but thy holy hand:
> To thee for succour flies my feeble muse,
> And at thy feet her yron Pen doth use.

If there is a suggestion of Icarus in the prologue, the opening scene of the play likewise shows Peele's David as having an experience strikingly like that of Chapman's Ovid in *Ovids Banquet of Sence*.[1] The Bible says simply that David from the roof of the king's house 'saw a woman; and she was very beautiful'. Chapman's Ovid found a way into the emperor's court, and there

> in an Arbor whereof, Corynna was bathing, playing upon her Lute, and singing; which Ovid over-hearing, was exceeding pleasde with the sweetnes of her voyce, & to himselfe uttered the comfort he conceived in his sence of Hearing.

So the odours used in her bath make their appeal to his sense of smell, her beauty to the sense of sight, a kiss to the sense of taste. (Chapman chastely omitted any appeal to the fifth sense.) In Peele's play, the Prologue

> drawes a curtaine, and discovers Bethsabe with her maid bathing over a spring: she sings, and David sits above vewing her.

Her song is one of conscious modesty, concluding,

> Let not my beauties fire,
> Enflame unstaied desire,
> Nor pierce any bright eye,
> That wandreth lightly.

The apostrophe which follows carries the suggestion of the appeal to the sense of touch as well as to the sense of smell, though the reference is Biblical:

> Come gentle Zephire trickt with those perfumes
> That erst in Eden sweetned Adams love,
> And stroke my bosom with the silken fan:
>
> . . . .
>
> Then decke thee with thy loose delightsome robes,
> And on thy wings bring delicate perfumes,
> To play the wantons with us through the leaves.

David's response is like that of Ovid:

> What tunes, what words, what looks, what wonders pierce
> My soule, incensed with a suddain fire,

[1] Printed London, 1585. The *S.T.C.* does not record an entry in the Stationers' Register.

but Peele keeps still the Bible as the frame of reference:

> Faire Eva plac'd in perfect happinesse,
> Lending her praise-notes to the liberall heavens,
> Strooke with the accents of Arch-angels tunes,
> Wrought not more pleasure to her husbands thoughts,
> Then this faire womans words and notes to mine.

As David summons Cusay to fetch the woman, she is

> Fairer then Isacs lover at the well,
> Brighter then inside barke of new hewen Caedar,
> Sweeter then flames of fine perfumed myrrhe.

His epithalamium as she is brought in to him has too a Biblical ring:

> Now comes my lover tripping like the Roe,
> And brings my longings tangled in her haire
>
> .   .   .   .
>
> Open the dores, and enterteine my love,
> Open I say, and as you open sing,
> Welcome faire Bethsabe King Davids darling.

To leave Peele's methods of writing divine poetry and continue the consideration of his dramatic plot, we find David quieting Bethsabe's scruples by ordering Cusay to fetch her husband, who is fighting under Joab at Rabath. Then a spectacle of war is presented. The tower which provides the inhabitants of Rabath with water is taken just as the message reaches Joab to send Urias home.

At this point the love story is interrupted to introduce Thamar going at the king's command to minister to her brother Ammon in his supposed illness. The rape of Thamar takes place off-stage while the pandering conspirator Jonadab soliloquizes concerning it. Rudely thrust from Ammon's tent, Thamar somewhat incongruously compares herself to Eva expelled from the Garden of Eden, but Absalon comes to comfort her and to promise that he will avenge her wrongs. He then goes to David and invites him to his sheep feast. The king refuses but grants his request that Ammon shall go with the other lords to the feast.

We return to the story of David and Bethsabe to hear Urias giving an account of the Rabath battle. Twice David urges him to rest and to go home to his wife, and twice Urias refuses to accept the lure. He drinks to the king's health but skilfully avoids drinking the health of the king's children proposed by Absalon. Defeated in craft, David orders Urias back to Rabath carrying a letter to Moab which sends him to the forefront of danger. The first part of the drama is here ended with the chorus sorrowing over the sin of the king but also giving an account of the events which must be understood to have happened before the next part begins:

> Urias in the forefront of the wars,
> Is murthered by the hateful Heathens sword,
> And David joies his too deere Bethsabe,
> Suppose this past, and that the child is borne,
> Whose death the Prophet solemnly doth mourne.[1]

The second section of the drama reveals Bethsabe and David mourning for the child of their love who is sick unto death, and sorrowing for the sin that is so punished. Nathan the prophet comes to rebuke David, telling the parable of the rich man who seizes the poor man's one ewe lamb, and pronouncing the curse upon him which we are to see fulfilled. Evil in his own house will rise against him, and his wives will be taken by another. Yet as David repents, Nathan prophesies that he shall live, though his child must die. When news is brought that the child is indeed dead, David feels that his shame is blotted out and turns to comforting Bethsabe and praising the Lord of hosts. A banquet is set before those assembled with the king and to the accompaniment of many instruments 'They use all solemnities together, and sing, &c.' Then David becomes the man of war and prepares to set off for Rabath lest Joab claim the glory of victory.

The *Tragedie of Absalon* announced on the title-page now becomes the business of the stage. Though David's sons have supposedly set out for Absalon's sheep feast, we find Ammon welcoming them as his guests at the celebration. A mood of gaiety prevails while a 'company of sheepeheards' dance and sing. The gathering is soon dispersed, however, for Absalon,

---

[1] The chorus closing the first section comprises ll. 572–95.

bent on avenging Thamar's wrongs, murders his brother host with poison in his drink and escapes, uttering defiant words.

Peele put forward the final battle for Rabath at this point, and it is fought on the stage with alarums and excursions and the noise of drum and trumpet. The triumph of victory is soon overshadowed for David, however, for even as he is about to ascend the conquered throne, word comes of the events at Ammon's sheep feast. As he sits alone sorrowing for his dead son, a widow sent by Joab comes to plead for her son whose death is sought by their kindred because he has killed his brother. The death of now her only son will leave her desolate. Her story moves the king, and her plea that he forgive his own son Absalon is answered. Joab is ready with the repentant Absalon, who then remains on the stage as the others depart. His soliloquy marks the beginning of his rebellion against his father with his purpose to win the tribes of Israel announced.

Swiftly events crowd the stage: David's grief over Absalon's treachery, compounded by his acceptance of it as a divine punishment for his own sins; the strategy for Absalon's forces as planned by Achitophel brought to failure through its discovery by Cusay; David's urging that Absalon's life be spared; Achitophel 'solus with a halter' uttering the words of despair that lead to self-slaughter.[1] Finally the scene is enacted the story of which is almost as famous as that of Jonah and the whale, for as Absalon goes forth to conquer, his long hair is caught in the branches of a tree, and helpless, he is dispatched by Joab's men, his body thrown into a ditch and covered with stones as the Bible decrees. The Chorus ends this part of the play, moralizing the story and announcing

> a third discourse of Davids life
> Adding thereto his most renowmed death,
> And all their deaths, that his death he judgd,...[2]

The third 'discourse' does not fulfil the promise of the Chorus, but it offers some surprises. First we find Absalon's

---

[1] Note a similar picture of despair in *A Looking-Glass*, and see n. 1 on p. 251 above.

[2] The chorus closing the second section comprises ll. 1647–58. The misplaced fragment follows, ll. 1659–63.

forces surrendering to Joab, who makes a great speech. Then a group enters which includes one whose advent into the world or into the play has not been previously suspected, for Salomon comes with David and Bethsabe and the prophet Nathan and their train, making his parents' hearts glad with the precocious wisdom which may have seemed authorized by his Biblical reputation. The news of Absalon's death, however, throws David into such uncontrolled mourning that Nathan is forced to chide:

> These violent passions come not from above,
> David and Bethsabe offend the highest,
> To mourne in this immeasurable sort.

In spite of this reproof David greets the victorious Joab bringing 'conquest pierced on his speare',[1] with such a torrent of reproach that he threatens to lead his armies to serve another king. Bethsabe speaks calming words, and suddenly David without any transition between moods speaks a formal elegy that shows Peele once more as the divine poet, the forerunner of Milton. In David's elegy Platonic Ideas seem to mingle with saints and angels, and 'the drinke of Seraphims' and 'archangels food' substitute for the nectar and ambrosia of the pagan gods. There is a familiar ring to

> Thy eyes now no more eyes but shining stars,
> Shall decke the flaming heavens with novell lampes.[2]

And it would seem that Saint Paul is in the poet's mind rather than David as the elegy closes:

> Thy day of rest, thy holy Sabboth day
> Shall be eternall, and the curtaine drawne,
> Thou shalt behold thy soveraigne face to face,
> With wonder knit in triple unitie,
> Unitie infinite and innumerable.

---

[1] The line must be compared with the line in the chorus preceding Act v in Shakespeare's *Henry V* which has been the subject of dispute, 'Bringing rebellion broached on his sword'.

[2] Compare: Two of the fairest stars in all the heaven,
> Having some business, do entreat her eyes.
> To twinkle in their spheres till they return.
> > *Romeo and Juliet*, II. ii. 15–17

See also III. ii. 21–5, and *Lycidas*, ll. 168–71.

David is at peace with himself and with Joab as the play closes, the 'third discourse' having failed to complete the promised story.

Peele seems to me to stand as the lone poet of the age to undertake a divine play conscious of its place in divine literature and aware of traditions and practices of the poets who were writing divine poems. The Bible stories which he linked together to make his play were not embellished with additional characters or comic scenes, but with poetic ornaments in phrase and forms. He used an epic prologue, invoked a divine muse for the telling of a divine story. The comparisons are drawn from Biblical story,—Adam and Eve, Isaac and Rebecca, Pharaoh and the Red Sea, the cedars of Lebanon. The epithalamium and the elegy are treated as ornaments of divine poetry. Joab's great speeches are kept in the mood as they echo the language of the Bible. If the plot seems cluttered with episodes sufficient for three 'discourses', Peele's play can, nevertheless, be recognized as a part of the divine literature of the sixteenth century.

INDEX